Bob Hoskins

AN UNLIKELY HERO
KAREN MOLINE

SIDGWICK & JACKSON
LONDON

First published in Great Britain in 1988 by Sidgwick & Jackson Limited

ISBN 0-283-99508-4

Typeset by Hewer Text Composition Services, Edinburgh
Printed by Adlard & Son Ltd
Letchworth, Herts SG6 1JS
for Sidgwick & Jackson Limited
1 Tavistock Chambers, Bloomsbury Way
London WC1A 2SG

CONTENTS

FOR THE GUY WITH THE SMILE

PREFACE

Some people will sit through anything in a cinema, but I've always believed in the Popcorn Rule. If, after munching your way down to the last unpopped kernels, the film has not yet grabbed you by the butter-slick thumbs, then it's quite all right to step on a few toes and make a quick getaway.

Yet sometimes you can't leave, because the people you're with believe in sticking it out till the bitter end. One winter's evening, when the popcorn box had long been discarded in a draughty cinema only a few miles north of the original Cotton Club and I was amusing myself with calculating how many pairs of tap shoes would add up to $47 million, I found myself riveted by a short, squat fireplug of a man with an indeterminate accent, who, in this movie, was called Owney Madden. 'Who's that actor?' I asked. No one knew. *The Cotton Club* was suddenly far more interesting. We waited as the credits unfurled for his name. 'Bob Hoskins,' someone said. 'Never heard of him.'

When I began working on this book, I had little idea of the size and range of Bob's talent. He'd won raves and a mantelpiece of awards in America and England for his tender-hearted George in *Mona Lisa*, although the Oscar eluded him. I also had little idea what I was getting myself into: the amazing life and career of a multitalented, highly intelligent tearaway showoff with a big mouth from Finsbury Park. I only knew that Finsbury Park was where many Londoners said you lived if you preferred burglars at teatime instead of crumpets.

Bob was asked by his agent if he would consent to an interview, but politely declined. In order to make this book as comprehensive as possible without the subject's participation – I lost count of the people who wondered why I was writing a biography of a person who 'wasn't dead yet' – and since it's obviously not intended as a critical treatise, I approached a great many people who have known and worked with Bob over the years. To my good fortune the response was overwhelming. Wherever possible, I have tried to tell the tale and shape this book through their still-vivid recollections – Bob seems to inspire them! No third-party commentary can replace the immediacy of shared experiences. These stories are crazy, thoughtful, hilarious, as close to Bob as if he were still hoisting up his trousers to tell off Vanessa Redgrave or holding court in a mud hut in Zululand. And since enough copy to sink the *Queen Mary* has been printed, often repeating the same stories so much that Bob must wish he'd never started telling them, I have concentrated on earlier projects that are equally, if not more, interesting than Oscar trivia or glowing descriptions of private jets used for those special occasions.

Some people that I asked refused to speak to me out of respect for Bob and because the book is unauthorized, which is understandable; some declined on the justifiable grounds of ongoing professional commitments with him. While this is regrettable, an unauthorized biography does have the important advantage of allowing for complete candour on the part of those who did agree to be interviewed. Bob does have his darker side and his darker moments – as do we all – and many of these have been lived out in front of witnesses who have been deeply hurt and disappointed, and who can still choose to talk about them without fear of censure from the man himself.

For those who took the time and energy to contribute to this book I am grateful more than any words can express. A thousand thanks to: Dickie Arnold, Pat Ashton, Spencer Bankes, Colin Bennett, Perry Benson, Sue Blane, Edward Bond, Joan Brown, Roy Clarke, Nicholas Clay, Kenneth Colley, Oliver Cotton, Richard Eyre, Ronald Eyre, Pat Fox, Mike Gibbon, Julian Glover, Wilfred Grove, Barry Hanson, Dave Hill, Gordon Jackson, Estelle Kohler, Ben Lewin, Alec McCowen, Charles MacDonald, T. P. McKenna, Julia McKenzie, Philip Madoc, Jonathan Miller, Adrian Noble, Thaddeus O'Sullivan, Edward Petherbridge, Peter Postlethwaite, Norman Rossington, John Schlesinger, Margaret Soames, Norman Tyrrell, Andrew Wadsworth, Kevin Williams, Snoo Wilson, Penelope Wilton; and to everyone else who responded to my queries, whether we were able to talk or not.

Special thanks to Sally Hope, Ann Hope, Jane Hope-Kavanagh, and Kerry Hope-Kavanagh for the facts, laughs, hospitality, and more suggestions than they can possibly imagine; to Jane Hoskins for taking the time to discuss the past with courage and humour; to Don McCullin for a marvellous excursion to Finsbury Park; to Ken Campbell for laughs; to John Mackenzie for a great chat; to

John Byrum, because he's not only scathingly funny, but a genius as well; to Lynne Robinson and Chris Voisey, two great fans, for memories and memorabilia; to all those who provided mayhem, meals, and moral support in London when I needed it most: Lanny Aldrich, Maggie Alderson, Jon Astrop (who doesn't deserve it), Adele Cherrison, Vanessa Cole, Caris Davis, Josephine Fairley, Jill Furmanovsky and Ron Berglas, Fenella Greenfield, Elise Hageman, Gill Hudson, Rebecca Hunter, Kim Lonsdale, Versa Manos, Ian Martin, Eddi Reader, Hugh St Clair, Ann Sullivan, Ruby Wax, Andreas Wisniewski, Mary Lee Wolf, John Wood (you deserve all the Oreos in the world), and Donald and Wendy Woods.

And to those Stateside: all the Molines, parents, sisters, and Adam for laughs; Vanessa Briscoe, Stephanie Chernikowski, Deborah Feingold, Linda Fiorentino, Judy Green, Terry Hyland, Sara Lee, Madeleine Morel, Michael and Caroline Perkins, Jill Selsman, Ethlie Ann Vare, Dan Yakir, and Charlyn Zlotnick.

Special thanks to Steve Grant of *Time Out* and John Powers of *L.A. Weekly* for permission to quote from their absolutely wonderful articles; to Jane Woods for such comprehensive photo research; to Jane Gregory, my agent and friend, for everything; and to Susan Hill, my editor, who is not only the best any writer could be fortunate to have, but a wonderful woman, too.

INTRODUCTION

'I am ready to be tested, I want to put myself in the arena, you know what I mean. I shudder, but I go forth.'

Joe Veriato in Charles Woods's
Has 'Washington' Legs?

Bob Hoskins is a most unlikely hero.

He's shaped like a rocket in a 'Flash Gordon' serial with a face as round as a snooker ball and eyes that veer from malevolent to merry in the time it takes takes to wink, and a mouth both feral and facetious. His neck and waistline can politely be described as disappearing, his hair an ancient memory, his ears as sticky-out, as he's fond of saying, as those of Fungus the Bogeyman. He finally found his true calling one enchanted evening at the Unity Theatre, or so the myth goes, and he has since become one of Britain's most recognizable and marketable resources, blessed with a great energy and charisma and that intangible yet obvious aura that is usually called 'star quality'.

If he had been born a generation earlier, the thought of acting probably would never have entered his man-in-the-moon-shaped head. Or if it did, he'd be more likely to have thought of himself as an Edward Everett Horton to a Fred Astaire instead of the Cagney or Edward G. he more closely resembles. It took television, the great leveller, John Osborne's 1956 play *Look Back in Anger*, and then a crop of extremely talented, working-class young actors like Alan Bates, Tom Courtenay, Albert Finney, and Michael Caine, for whom RADA was just a four-letter word, to enliven, open up, and invigorate the acting profession in England so that the effetely stiff mannerisms of a Leslie Howard or the polished vowels of a Ronald Colman were soon seen as old-fashioned as a horse-drawn milk cart.

As Albert Finney remarked, it was films like *Saturday Night and Sunday Morning*, *Billy Liar*, and *Alfie* which enabled young people

1

from working-class backgrounds to think of acting as a career. 'They no longer had to be prim, proper and stuffy to qualify for a life in the theatre,' Finney said. 'They no longer had to lead their lives on certain, predestined, doled-out tracks. Acting became a wide-open profession.'

And Bob Hoskins fell into acting as easily as most people fall into debt. He has perfected his craft and operates under his own wisdom, too. He disguises his enormous talent; he doesn't make a great deal of it, or – don't forget – he doesn't seem to. His characterizations appear effortless so that he's practically as approachable as the bloke next door. But, in a sense, by assuming a mantle of humility he demeans his own talent and that of his colleagues. (Acting only looks easy.) In another it accounts for his popularity across the board, because he touches some common chord in everyone, and retains a huge contact with the man in the street. Without saying a word he makes you want to be his friend. Mums and dads dote on him; cabbies adore him; the younger generation wants to emulate his bravado; men are his mates, quaffing a pint down the pub; women want to mother him and then seduce (or be seduced by) him: one actor called Bob 'every middle-class woman's ideal of a bit of rough trade'. Yet his love for the ladies is certainly hard for a woman who loves him, for how can a wife stand by her man when her man's definition of loyalty is not found in the dictionary?

Bob *looks* as if life has a meaning. He embodies it. And this look combines innocence and ruthlessness, sensitivity and power, affability and cruelty. When he grins, he even more closely resembles a 'smiley' face; when he cries, the tears are for real. When he is annoyed, his lips pull back in an involuntary snarl, and when he is really angry, you would not want to be in a dark alley with him. And if he is betrayed, then prepare your speech for St Peter.

Yet Bob's great strength is that he's very warm-hearted and not villainous by intent; his acting always plays to that emotional edge. 'You look at Bob and you can really project your fantasies on him,' says Ken Campbell. And there is always some memorable twist to Bob's characters that makes them more real, more human: the *Cotton Club* gangster/owner Owney Madden caressing his pigeons, and limp with relief when his friend Frenchy is released after a kidnapping (arguably the best scene in the film); every possible emotion flickering wordlessly across his face as he is driven off to his doom in *The Long Good Friday*; Arthur Parker confessing his need for over-the-rainbow in *Pennies from Heaven*; Nathan Detroit sheepishly trying to worm out of marrying Miss Adelaide, a point

2

with which Bob could sympathize; the yearning vulnerability of George in *Mona Lisa*.

'Bob has the most extraordinary imagination,' said Sally Hope, his friend, confidante, and agent for fourteen years. 'For some roles he has researched; for others, not at all. He goes away and reads and quite quickly, intuitively, gets into character. There's a lot of knowledge in him – either that or he tells extraordinary stories!'

Bob's generosity to other actors is legendary. Every person interviewed, who had worked with Bob in any capacity, had nothing but praise for Bob's remarkable talent to charm anyone, defuse backstage problems, and keep the juices flowing. He was often compared to an energy source, like a magnet towards which one was inextricably pulled – towards which one *wanted* to be pulled. It's hard to stay away from a man who lives life with gusto, and you'd have to be pretty boring or else blind to resist the twinkle in Bob's eye.

Naturally, he responds immediately to an audience. The theatre director Howard Davies once said that he thought Bob became an actor because it was 'the most social way to earn a living'. If anyone is listening, Bob will perform. He's *into* acting. He can sing well in an idiosyncratic jazzy sort of way – 'melodic foghorn', he calls it – and he dances as well as you'd expect a five-foot-six barrel with legs to dance. His laugh is infectious, and he has a mischievous sense of humour; he's always been a great comic. He'll try anything.

Don't be fooled when Bob says he's not ambitious. He loves and needs his roles as much as he loves and needs the adulation and applause.

This desire for attention is not always, however, an asset. 'He wants to be wanted,' explained Sally Hope, who knows Bob better than most ever will. 'If you meet him in a pub and offer him a script, chances are he'll say yes. They'd usually have some novelty value, like coming on stage with a beached whale.'

And oh, how Bob loves a good story.

'Bob is a PR person's dream,' Sally continued, 'especially if a story goes down well. That's one of the qualities that makes him the actor he is – he does make it his own.' Even if it never happened to him. 'We once took a bet,' said a colleague who worked with Bob early in his career, 'on how long it would take Bob, when we were swapping stories, to change the "he" or "she" to an "I", so it looked like Bob had that adventure. The quickest he ever did it was about ten minutes.'

3

As George Bernard Shaw once said, 'I often quote myself; it adds spice to my conversation.'

'Bob always talks about the project he just worked on or else the same old stories,' said another friend. 'Of course, people keep asking for them, too.' But Bob *likes* to tell stories. And if a little imagination creeps in to make a tale more entertaining, well, why not? Who's to know? There's no intended maliciousness, just fanciful embroidery.

'Bob has taken years off his age because it's convenient,' said ex-wife Jane. 'For him life is just a game, but it isn't – not when you've got people who need you.'

The dilemma for my purposes has been to sort out the fact from the fables, and often the two are so blurred in Bob's life that there is nothing to distinguish one from the other. When this has happened, for example with Bob's involvement with the Finsbury Park criminal element, or his discovery at the Unity, or his breakdown, or his penurious post-divorce financial state that had him 'living in a Jeep', I have tried to present as many (often conflicting) views of the incidents as I was told in order to keep this account as balanced as possible and so that readers can draw their own conclusions. At least some of these tall tales provide amusement. And laughter and capers have always been part of who Bob is and what Bob does.

However, one of the far-from-amusing and only-hinted-at traits of who Bob is and what Bob does is his temper. Although Bob's lurking tenderness is only a tear away – and he truly is a sentimental softie – his barely suppressed rage is equally evident. 'Part of Bob's power as an actor is that you feel that he could easily break your legs and neck but never goes quite that far,' *Long Good Friday* producer Barry Hanson once told a *Newsweek* reporter. 'Even in real life I wouldn't like to get on the wrong side of him.'

'He is pretending to be nice and mellow,' said a long-time colleague, 'and usually he is. But he operates on a very short fuse.' While Bob has said of himself, 'I make a lot of noise now and then, shouting and all that. But I'm not an aggressive type.'

Bob's view of himself is also at odds with the view of his ex-wife Jane. 'Bob has the power of a performer, but he has always been violent,' said Jane. 'I hate violence,' Bob has said. 'I wouldn't call myself a violent person. I don't like it.'

Bob has always had a tendency to become the character he's playing, which is fine if he's a blustering, good-hearted sergeant in *Zulu Dawn* or a devoted father and copper in *Lassiter*, or an eager-to-please scriptwriter in *Sweet Liberty* (parts that have not made him famous); but not so fine if you're the philandering

4

dreamer in *Pennies*, or a merciless gang boss in *The Long Good Friday*, or Iago or Bosola or Ronnie Kray (parts that have).

'I haven't seen anything that isn't him,' said Jane Hoskins. 'Our daughter Sarah saw him on television, and she said – about his expressions – "That's just Daddy being Daddy."'

'Bob does live certain roles,' said Sally. 'He went through a more radical change after *The Long Good Friday*; he would quote lines from it and you would look at him askance, and he'd say something like, "I've made you". It *is* difficult if you live the role you're playing – people do want to be touched by some part of it.

'Bob is very ambitious and very talented,' she explained. 'He can write and draw and he has great enthusiasm and confidence and a very positive attitude; he always had. And this was responsible for a huge part of his success. Within Bob is actually a very simple guy, and he's doing the things he wants to do. But he has no comprehension of failure and could be quite ruthless. People can become part of the "past" very quickly. This is *now* . . . therefore what's gone on before *now* is of no relevance. If he wanted to get a part, he'd go for it, no doubts. And if he upset someone it's yesterday, it's gone. I have never known him to apologize, ever to say, "Oh, sorry".

'When actors aren't working they *don't* exist, and when they are it's a hundred per cent. It's a psychology, a drive to do it,' she said with a logic that Bob has doubtless used many times in the past to justify some of his rougher tactics. 'Because of Bob's positive attitude to life, it becomes difficult to deal with things, introspectively, and you can have terrible times when you sort it out.'

Bob *has* had his share of terrible times, some of them of his own making: poverty, bouncing from one lousy job to another, slogging through rep to unappreciative or nonexistent audiences, a nervous breakdown, acrimonious divorce, failed relationships, and a few unsuccessful roles. Yet his share of wonderful times has undeniably outweighed the bad.

'I like the way I am. I think I'm all right,' he told the *New York Times* humbly. 'I'm happy with me. I'd be happy to meet me. It's a matter of integrity, you see, and of necessity. Whoever I become, I must have a starting-off point. I must be sure of who I am, so sure it doesn't worry me, before I become someone else.'

He has also almost never gone without work, a reality elusive to most in his chosen profession, and is now a certifiably bankable star. He is happily remarried with two young children, a semi-detached Victorian house not far from where he grew up, and his children from his first marriage are now charming and charismatic

5

teenagers. He is directing and starring in a film he has written himself, and his millions of fans will still love him even if it flops, because he hasn't lost the common touch.

Nothing will tear him from his North London roots: 'I'm happiest among costermongers and all that,' he claimed. 'Nobody's impressed by me in Islington. I don't want to lose the street, because that's where I act from.'

This is his story.

1

The Mean Streets of Finsbury Park

Late one night, the legend goes, King Sven Forkbeard of Denmark, invader of Anglia, had a dream. And in this dream, in the year 1010, he saw the handsome young ruler of East Anglia, who had been tortured and brutally murdered – shot in fact with so many arrows that he resembled a porcupine before he was beheaded – 141 years before, rise up in anger, a lance clenched in his fist. In his terror the monstrous King Sven cried out and woke from his nightmare, but even as his son Knut rushed to his side, he lay dying, the name 'Edmund' on his lips.

Knut had heard the whispered tales of the miracles wrought by the martyred Edmund Ironside, and he quickly left for home before returning, heavily reinforced, six years later, to conquer the land that had killed his father. But he was no fool. He offered restitution to the Church and appointed twenty Benedictine monks to protect the holiness of Edmund's shrine.

And so St Edmundsbury prospered. It was there, 200 years later, that Cardinal Langton and the barons swore at St Edmund's altar that they would obtain the ratification of the Magna Carta. And it was there, on 26 October 1942, when the British forces launched their third counteroffensive against the Germans in the deserts of North Africa and the bombs dropped like so many whistling dark monsters on the cities of the Fatherland, that Robert William Hoskins came into this world.

Young Bobby Hoskins would soon exchange what Daniel Defoe called the 'wholesome aire' of Bury St Edmunds for the unwholesome, grimy streets of Finsbury Park in North London. His parents, Robert and Elsie, like so many others, moved to the capital after the war in search of better opportunities. When their only child was registered at Stroud Green Primary School in Woodstock Road, three days after his fifth birthday, Robert was employed by the transport firm of Pickford's. The family was living in a small, two-bedroomed flat at 46 Upper Tollington Park, near the railway tracks where naughty boys would scamper up to drop bricks on the fog signals.

Bob Hoskins was marked as indelibly by his upbringing in Finsbury Park as were the children with cuts and bruises who would be swabbed in the school treatment clinic with a vivid stain of gentian violet, leaving huge purple splotches all over their bodies.

In the postwar days, after the rubble from the bombing had been cleared away, homes rebuilt, and rationing gone from bad to worse, the neighbourhood resumed its prewar demarcations: split into two by Stroud Green Road. To the east and north, working-class families struggled for some kind of decent life; to the west, in the notorious Campbell Bunk, people simply gave up. The rows of squalid dosshouses provided 'accommodations' for the desperately poor, the desperately drunk, and the desperately criminal. Bonfires often raged in the street, fuelled by stolen coal. Fire engines would not waste their time in that place. Nor would the coppers.

'The children from the Bunk were very poor and grubby, and not well cared for,' explained Margaret Soames, who grew up in Finsbury Park and is currently Headmistress of Stroud Green Primary. 'They were all flea-ridden and had head lice.'

'The worst of the riff-raff came from the Bunk,' said photographer Don McCullin, who grew up a block away, in Fonthill Road. 'The most horrendous people lived there. It was beyond dereliction.'

It was a neighbourhood lived on the streets and with good reason – most accommodation was overcrowded and barely habitable with few 'luxuries' like bathrooms, proper heating or ventilation. Bob was lucky and highly unusual as an only child not have to share a room with squabbling siblings.

Of course there was Finsbury Park itself, the wonderful green space with the Italian ice-cream seller at its gates, where young lads would disregard the 'Do Not Walk on the Grass' signs, and more well-behaved families would walk sedately on their Sunday expeditions up to Kite Field. Finsbury Park had been named by the mourning daughters of Sir John Fines, who'd died in the Holy Land fighting the Saracens. In a patch of green they buried his heart. Unfortunately there were no known miracles from this sacred mound – the locals could certainly have used them.

A favourite sport was fighting. One group of lads from a particular street would muster twenty or thirty 'soldiers' for combat with another street. It was simple territorial gang warfare, as popular today as it's always been.

The local characters were people like Dizzy Lizzie, who used to get pissed on ruby wine and scream obscenities at the hooligans who broke her windows for the fun of it; or Mad Hannah, a doddering Victorian lady with great masses of white hair, who used to appear at the door of her imposing and decaying house, clad only in a negligée, if anything. Naughty boys, hoping to see her nude, would tie long lengths of dark cotton to her door knocker and pull interminably until she was driven mad, not being able to see the dark thread at night.

There were the usual crazy drunks who'd sit in the sanctuary of their pubs like the Earl of Essex or the Duke of Edinburgh, with their young sons waiting outside for a penny to buy an arrowroot biscuit. There were the Flanagans, the local crime lords, who, while not on a par with the Kray twins, had their own way of policing the area. They were far more respected than the corrupt police, who if they weren't on the take or brutish, abused the 'sus' laws by arresting people 'loitering with suspicious intent'.

Petty crime was a way of life, whether by smashing shop windows to grab a jar of sweets – this could land a youngster three years in prison – or pinching boxes of Cape grapes from Covent Garden and selling them at school, or nicking coal from the repository near the filling station.

'Growing up in Finsbury Park was so very competitive; there was always some deal to be made, as if you had to do it,' explained McCullin. 'If you couldn't fight or play football or do something else or get a really good conviction at the age of fifteen, in reform school or borstal, you were nothing. And the other guys used to kick ass all the time. We'd all get terrific hidings – the bravado we had to put on in front of each other, the pressure of the criminal or semi-criminal activities . . . the only true admiration you got was when you could fight.

'The way out for our generation in terms of creativity or money was to win the football pools. Or our dreams were to pull off a huge robbery. People used to say, "I'm going to get lucky" or, "Be lucky." *Luck* had nothing to do with using the grey matter. It was all to do with whether you would suddenly get showered with gold sovereigns from up above. If you grew up in Finsbury Park, it would never enter your head to be a millionaire. A high point would be to be invited to dinner with the Flanagans or the Kray twins.'

By all accounts, Bob had as normal a childhood as anyone could have in Finsbury Park, although it seems he enjoyed his neighbourhood lessons more than his school lessons. For one thing, he was a lucky, spoiled only child, living with parents who worked; his father was an accounts clerk and his mother a nursery-school cook (although some sources say she worked as a nursery-school teacher). They lived on the better side of Stroud Green Road and Bob would have started school just as things were settling back to normal after the war. There a new breed of teacher with slightly more liberal attitudes was gradually replacing the dreaded sadistic, cane-in-hand old guard. Corporal punishment was still used unstintingly to maintain discipline, but it began to be administered with less severity.

Bob would trot off to school in his bottle green tie and jumper and grey shorts, and he would try not to be naughty as he pored over his Beacon readers or attempted not to fidget in morning assemblies, where it always seemed that how you behaved was more important than what you learned. Hopefully he would not be caught running in the corridors by Miss McCormack, who would painfully pull up shameful little students by the ears while she scolded. The children who were lucky enough to be able to go home at lunchtime did so, while the rest were doomed to lukewarm sludge cooked in a central kitchen and sent over in heated containers.

By July 1950 Bob had moved on to the junior school, proving that he knew at least a hundred words, but he did not like to study. It's not hard to imagine him full of humour, boisterous high spirits, and undeniable intelligence, and not the type to accept discipline from domineering teachers or blindly to follow rules about where he should sit or how he should play or what hymn to hum. And because he was streetwise and funny he was far more popular with the other children than with the harsh disciplinarians.

He had, he's often said, a 'very happy childhood. My family were never that poor. . . . My mum and dad were going to have a big family till they had me. Put them right off, when they saw my face. Sod that! they thought.' (Ever the joker.) 'I was the first one. And I was the *only* one. That's the sort of little boy I was . . . but I did stick my neck out. I was always one of the fellas that if someone dared me I would always do it. I always had a lot of mouth and not a lot to back it up with. I was very merry, into everything, thought everything was hilarious. My parents were always very humorous too, full of gags and stories.'

One milestone of his young life was on 24 April 1949, the day sweets were no longer rationed. Another was the time he went missing, a story he's often told to great effect. Reportedly, his panic-stricken mother was told to stay calm by his pragmatic auntie. Don't worry, she reassured Elsie, just think of your darling son's face. 'If he's been stolen,' his aunt said, 'I can tell you they'll soon bring him back.' He had not been kidnapped, and returned home safe and sound.

As Bob grew older, he appreciated school less and acted out his frustrations more. 'Everybody thought I was a bit crazy,' he has said. 'But I wasn't a delinquent. I was simply ill-disciplined and over-enthusiastic.'

'You went to school to defy the system,' McCullin explained, 'and in doing so we succeeded. But instead of cheating the headmasters and the system we wound up cheating ourselves. We were not only bigoted, ignorant, and ghetto'd, but created so many unnecessary problems for ourselves.'

'I really hated school,' Hoskins also said. 'It didn't like me much either. Except one teacher, a big rugby-playing Welshman who gave me Camus and Hemingway to read.'

Because education and anything smacking of authoritarianism was so highly disregarded by Bob and his fellow students, those who passed their 11 plus and moved on to grammar schools were as unusual in this neighbourhood as a fleet of gleaming Silver Shadows. Having a mentor was a bit of Finsbury Park luck. And in addition to having Mr Jones instil in him a love of reading, Bob was fortunate to have been influenced by a local landmark that was to have a lasting impact on his life: the Finsbury Park Empire.

One of the most stunning theatres in London, it opened on 5 September 1910 and was shamefully torn down in 1960 to make way for a block of flats, ironically known as Vaudeville Court. Designed by the famed Frank Matcham, known for his more-is-never-enough style of marble, plush-red velvet, glittering chandeliers, and beaming cherubs, the 2000-seat Empire was an immediate success. Even the local Little Caesars respected such ostentatious opulence. If they were too lazy to sneak in, it only cost a few pence for a seat in the gallery, and even the most hard-core hooligans would sit enthralled, mesmerized by the pantomime.

All the best English and American music-hall and theatrical acts played the Empire; despite the wartime blackout, wildly popular performances continued, even through air raids. As soon as their young son was old enough to appreciate the mayhem, Robert and Elsie took him along for an evening's entertainment.

'Max Miller, Jewel and Warriss, Mrs Shufflewick, Norman Evans – all of 'em were my heroes,' claimed Bob. 'The Cheeky

Chappie', Max Miller, has been described as 'exquisitely vulgar, loud, earthy, and blue.' Tastelessly clad in garish suits, a diamond ring flashing, he brashly let rip with jokes as blue as his trademark trilby was white. Many claim he was the role model for John Osborne's Archie Rice in *The Entertainer*. ('I consider it a compliment to be insulted by Sir Laurence Olivier,' Miller supposedly retorted.)

For Bob, the greatest of all was Jimmy James, whose use of body English in his acclaimed drunk routine, his Chipster (as in chipped potatoes), and Shoebox routines had audiences in stitches.

'Once he came on and sat on the corner of the stage, talking to the band,' Bob said. 'It was the funniest number I've ever seen in my life. Just brilliant. Seeing that you think, *that's* talent, sunshine, real talent. And you think – bang! I can have a go.'

Yet Bob was not to 'have a go' for many years, although he did play Ali Baba in panto at the age of six and Humpty Dumpty at a later date.

He always had a highly developed dream-life, seeing himself as a detective, Tom Mix, a knight in shining armour, or, of course, as a gangster. 'Fantasy has always been important to me,' he once said. 'I love science fiction and I love cartoons. But as I got older I spent more and more time with the gang, with the boys and, naturally, with the girls.'

One thing he did want to be was out of school. He soon got his wish. At the age of fifteen and with one O level to his name, Robert William Hoskins became just another school-leaver with nowhere to go.

One of Bob's first endeavours at the wonderful world of employment was as a white singer in an all-black blues band. Unfortunately two of the band members were hauled off to prison for armed robbery. So much for showbiz.

At sixteen, Bob began working as a porter in the old Covent Garden Market. Covent Garden used to be just that – the garden of the Abbot of Westminster, tended by its monks, and it was here that young porter Bob Hoskins had a surprising encounter with a ghost one night when he was shifting some crates.

'I saw a shadowy figure,' he said. 'It was a ghost . . . the ghost of a nun from the convent that the market was built on. I told this old porter about it, but he didn't laugh. He said, "You're privileged, son. You've seen the lady – you're going to have a lucky life."'

Bob's 'luck' at this stage was a matter of debate. With no skills, perfunctorily educated, a true son of Finsbury Park and at odds with the system, he was not exactly employable at any job that would excite his interest. But he was still young, and like most teenagers had no idea what he wanted to do with his life. There were two real options: to work at some menial, yet honest job until you found what it was you thought you were looking for, or to join forces with society's dropouts and become a villain. Bob has claimed – or rather implied – at various points in his career that he was actually a part of the nearly inescapable criminal activity in Finsbury Park. It may simply be an example of Hoskins hyperbole, for through the years Bob has constantly contradicted himself when talking about this period of his life: 'I think I was destined to be a major criminal. . . .' 'I wasn't deprived. All the myths about me are *totally wrong*. I wasn't this tough guy criminal who suddenly became an actor. It's not true at all. . . .' 'I've come a long way from my tearaway days. I was a sort of lunatic then. But I was never a violent person . . . even though I had a rough street background and knew and drank with gangsters, I never got mixed up in any crime. . . .' 'There were a lot of villains around but I couldn't say they were particular friends of mine. . . .' 'I was a bit of a worry . . . I was an anarchic hedonist looking for the good life. . . .' 'Fortunately for me, I never got in any trouble with the police; a lot of my friends learned the criminal trade in borstal. . . .' 'Everyone said I was going to end up on the gallows. . . .'

'No one ever said Bob was going to end up on the gallows,' a close friend laughed. 'That's absurd. He's far too middle-class. If he weren't an actor, well, he still needs to perform. He could be a busker, but not a thief.'

A rare piece of testimony may exist to Bob's involvement with local gangland. 'I've got a picture of a boy,' said Don McCullin, 'a famous picture – the one that got me started in photography. I took it one afternoon just in front of the Rainbow Theatre, and it's of a group of hooligans who hung around Fonthill Road. The photograph is called "The Guv'nors" and the one on the end is called Bobby.' Bob has said that he thinks he was that Bobby. Maybe he was. Maybe he just wanted to be.

Bob's problem of course is that the 'myth' is one of his own making, and as his fame grows and he embellishes his life for the press, he becomes trapped by his own words. And since he has always had a flair for the dramatic – long before he channelled it into a profession – it is not unfair to assume that while he may have flirted with petty crime at some point, the down side of Finsbury Park did not truly appeal to him. After all, he'd been raised in a conventional home by loving, stable, working parents. When he was faced with a choice in life between dead-end jobs or dead-end crime, he chose the jobs. If he claimed to be an 'anarchic hedonist' it was more likely because his father raised him to be a 'total socialist and total atheist'. And what young man, seemingly trapped on the treadmill of failure, does not lose himself in the pursuit of hedonistic pleasures?

Bob Hoskins was not cut out to be a crook, although he wouldn't be a bad con man.

After his stint hauling crates of swedes and cucumbers around, he moved on to jobs that were often even more demanding physically, but as unstimulating as ever. He worked as a building labourer. He dug roads. He drove a lorry. He was a steeplejack. He was a filing clerk. He trained as a commercial artist for some time, because he's always been interested in art, especially painting and sculpture. He hung out. On his days off he rode a scooter down to the Mod riots at Brighton, a bird perched on the back. 'He also trained as a stage manager of a little theatre,' says Jane Hoskins. 'His parents got the job for him. They kept him going.'

At one point Bob signed on in the Norwegian Merchant Navy, and gave a typical reason: 'I fancied being a Viking – big hats with horns and swords. But I was just picking up fuckin' synthetic manure.' Reason enough to jump ship in Amsterdam after a long haul of two weeks. 'If you've ever been there you'll know why,' Bob confessed. 'Great city. The girls are gorgeous.'

Back home it was time to find a real job. No doubt encouraged and aided by his father, the accounts clerk, Bob got a job in his father's office and began a three-year training course as an accountant. It was the worst possible choice for this rambunctious character, and when a certificate came tumbling through the letter box and Bob realised he was 'halfway to being everything I hated, some-body most people loathe,' he panicked. 'All I wanted to do was disappear.

'Can you imagine me let loose in an office – flicking elastic bands at people's necks and chasing the secretaries? I never went back to accounting school.'

He went from being driven nuts by columns of figures to being driven nuts by hordes of flies. He disappeared all right – to a Bedouin tribe in Syria. They thought he was a 'holy fool' and adopted him as one of their own. 'They said to one another that there was a mad Englishman wandering around and that if someone didn't look after him he'd be dead.'

Enjoying the decidedly un-English phenomena of sand and

sunshine, he stayed for quite some time, supposedly a 'couple of years', although it is hard to know how he survived with non-English-speaking foreigners in the desert for this amount of time.

Eventually, saturated with camels and sandstorms, Bob crossed the border and ended up on an Israeli kibbutz in Gaza, where the land of milk and honey began to resemble the land of mangoes and bananas, which he spent all day planting, picking, and packing. The collective ideal of kibbutz life must have appealed to his socialist tendencies and anarchic vision, but when the Israeli army demanded of him what his own country did not – National Service was abolished before Bob reached call-up age – it was time to go home.

Bob's travels in the Middle East taught him some valuable lessons. 'I learned in Israel that the community – the whole thing – is worth more than just one person,' he has said.

Upon his return to leaden skies and dismal opportunities, Bob started up a window-cleaning business. It was not what he wanted any more than the other jobs had been. He was, in fact, quite lost.

'I had wild fantasies about my life, but I wasn't going anywhere,' he said. He was 'more of a tramp, really, at the time.' This tramp's luck would, finally, begin to turn. It may have been Finsbury Park luck; it may have been the Covent Garden ghost; or it could have been sheer coincidence, but after a sozzled experience in the Unity Theatre bar, Robert William Hoskins's life would never be the same again.

2

To Be or Not to Be

It was a momentous year, 1968. Saigon bombed to shreds in the Tet Offensive, Czechoslovakia overrun by Soviet tanks, Martin Luther King and Robert Kennedy assassinated, French students rioting, Chicago students rioting, and 'Hey Jude' on the radio.

Yet even as *Oliver!* scooped the Oscars, an event with far more significance to those in showbiz took place in 1968 as the Swinging Sixties wound down: the relaxing of theatrical censorship. Even Princess Anne joined the free-for-all dancing in the youth-orientated *Hair*, although her clothing remained firmly in place. Fringe theatre began to thrive as never before. There was the Open Space, the Arts Lab in Drury Lane, the Portable Theatre, the Ambiance Lunch Hour Theatre Club, the Wherehouse Company, Incubus, the Pip Simmons Group, and the Theatre Upstairs at the Royal Court.

But before all of them was the Unity Theatre, London's first working-class cultural centre, that 'agitational playhouse for Labour', that amateur space responsible for introducing Odets, Brecht, Soviet playwrights, the Living Newspaper, and other political revues. It had first opened in February 1936 and remained immensely popular until the war. Nearly thirty years later it was lurching from one financial crisis to another, yet when Bob Hoskins wandered into the converted mission hall in Goldington Street, the life he'd been searching for truly began.

Bob's 'discovery' is the stuff that dreams are made of. It has become such a gold-plated 'myth' – just like Lana Turner's 'discovery' while sipping a soda at Schwab's drugstore – that it is no longer possible to know what exactly did happen. For Hoskins's fans, believing the Brothers Grimm version of the tap on the shoulder is, in the end, far more satisfying than wondering if a slight bit of invention has crept into the story over the years.

For one thing, Bob had been quite a regular at the Unity, because that's where he met the woman who was to become his first wife, Jane Livesey, in 1967.

Also, in a June 1971 interview with John Ford that appeared in *Plays and Players*, Bob gave this answer to how he became involved in the theatre: 'A friend of mine adapted his book into a play and they asked me to be in it – not because I was an actor or anything. I hadn't done anything before then. . . . My friend's literary agent came along to the Unity and said, "Why don't you take it up seriously?" So I did.'

Lucky break? Certainly. Fabulous fairy tale? Hardly. Does it matter? Well, it got him started, didn't it? The Hoskins theme and variations (as it's been told over the years) is much more fun.

This storyline goes, in the words of the *Sun* headline, 'Pint Turns Bob Into Instant Actor'. While knocking back a few at the Unity bar, Bob had no idea auditions were being held upstairs for an amateur production of *The Feather Pluckers*, a play about yobs and drifters. A man handed him a script, said, 'You're next', and pointed to the stairs. Up went our hero, where he saw some serious-looking people sitting around a table, He was asked to read from the script he'd been handed. He read; he was hired. It was talent; he was a perfect physical embodiment of the leading yob. Inexperience was evidently not a drawback.

'Bob was there as a painter,' said director Jonathan Miller. 'His story get more garbled as the myth grows.'

Roger Frost told Linda Hawkins of *TV Times* in 1985, 'I belonged to an amateur drama club in Stoke Newington. One night, Bob said, "What's it like, this club of yours?" I told him it was all right and he came along with me to see what went on. Not long afterwards, I was going for an audition at the Unity Theatre, St Pancras, and Bob came with me. We had a few beers in the bar. I did my audition for the lead role, then they asked Bob to do a reading, and the next thing I knew, he'd got the part and I was his understudy! . . . Bob looked just right, whereas I'm tall and thin. What's more, Bob was a natural. He just got up on stage and was brilliant.'

Not only that, Bob discovered he liked acting, even if he claimed his performance 'wrecked' the show. His raw presence and energy brought him to the attention of an agent, who advised him to turn pro. He cheekily asked the agent to get him a job, and *voilà*, was recommended to Peter Cheeseman, director of the repertory company at the Victoria Theatre, Stoke-on-Trent.

Under Cheeseman, Stoke was a tightly knit, highly professional organization. Three years after production began in 1962, Cheeseman claimed that his aim was for a 'community-based repertory theatre', with a 'creative life closely linked to the area it serves', a goal that most would say has been remarkably fulfilled. There was an obvious difference between the inexperienced, extrovert, know-it-all Hoskins and his taskmaster, who had stated, 'We must all work together sympathetically and sensitively as a group of artists, ready to respond in a positive way, but as artists, to the needs and demands of the community.'

'I was a very bad actor to start with,' Bob has admitted. 'There was a lot of energy but no actual craft.'

Cheeseman evidently agreed. 'He was a very promising young actor,' he told *TV Times* in 1985, 'but rather undisciplined because he hadn't been to drama school. I had to read the riot act to him on one occasion for not learning his lines properly and not remembering his moves. It's a common fault with inexperienced actors. They have to learn to organize their lives and work out a personal system for learning the play, their moves, and other people's cues.'

Bob made a memorable impression in a play not normally thought of as humorous: *Romeo and Juliet*. 'I turned it into one of the great comedies of all time,' he said. 'The audience was falling about.' Because the company was small, there was some doubling of roles. Bob played Peter, the nurse's servant, as well as a guard in the crypt. He was, as he put it, 'the wrong shape'. More like an 'Elizabethan black pillarbox'. 'The audience heard this little fellow scurrying round backstage and reappearing, panting, in time for the next scene. . . . My two fellow soldiers were six inches taller and wardrobe made all the clothes the same size,' Bob explained. 'Towards the end of the run I'm sure people were coming in to see *me*.'

Cheeseman had every right to be angry, and according to Bob, he told him he was the worst actor in world. Bob has a faulty memory at this stage. He was either given the sack, or, far more unlikely, told his boss to tear up the contract and 'hand over a fiver' and he'd be only too happy to bugger off.

Neither story was quite true. Cheeseman said, 'By the end of his six months' contract, Bob was playing the lead role. He did very well with us, but I think he was uncomfortable in a formal set up. He needed to develop where there was more freedom.'

At any rate it had been a very worthwhile experience. 'It was like *Alice in Wonderland*,' Bob remembered of those times. 'It was like I'd actually stepped through the mirror. Suddenly, there it was. . . . When I finally got to the stage, it was like entering kindergarten for the first time. It was like I'd been locked up in a cupboard and suddenly – bang! There's all these people, all working towards an aim. . . . There was such a sense of creation. It was extraordinary.'

He also met a kindred spirit at Stoke who was to prove instrumental in unleashing Bob's comic talents on the unsuspecting world. Ken Campbell had been playing Tony Lumpkin in *She Stoops to Conquer* as well as putting on a show he'd written himself, called *Jack Sheppard*, at Stoke. He'd had the audience eating out of his hand.

'I'd been at Stoke and I was meant to come back and in the intermediate time Peter had hired Bob,' Ken explained. 'Peter is very good at finding people, but I don't think he was very good for Bob. He found it difficult to make Bob fit the house style.

'I wrote and directed a play for Bob at Stoke called *Christopher Pig*. He was a brilliant Christopher, who was a sort of halfwit who helped work at a rubbish dump, and fell in love with an usherette. He'd heard that, if you *believed*, when it was a "magical evening", you could throw your ice-cream cornet into the beam of light that hits the cinema screen and it would ride down the beam until it hit the screen. He didn't know he was in love with the usherette, actually, so when he had a funny feeling, he assumed it was this "magical evening" and threw his cornet up. The ice-cream splattered all over the audience.'

Though their paths would not cross for more than a year after that, it was a fortuitous encounter, and one Campbell would remember when he put into action his thoughts about popular theatre and took a small group of comics out on the road.

In the meantime, life on the home front veered from ecstasy to agony. Bob had married Jane Livesey in 1967. She had grown up in India, the daughter of an army colonel, and had been working in the East End as a drama teacher. Jane describes their meeting in the Unity bar: 'I just walked in one Sunday afternoon, and this man said, "Woman, come here!" No one had ever treated me with such disrespect in my life. It was obsession at first sight.' The two were soon inseparable and in love.

Bob had been thrilled with the birth of his son Alexander on 8 August 1968. As Jane explains: 'I had Alex because Bob said, "Let's have a child."' They were not yet married. 'I believe it was right, and I will never believe it was wrong . . . and it was Bob's idea. If it hadn't been, I might have done something quite different.

'My parents were not happy with my relationship with Bob –

and it was good at the start – but I was certainly the class enemy in those circumstances. I thought I had broken free, and everything was going to be different. It was the sixties, and we were going to create a new generation. But being free is all very well when you could afford to be free, and when you had things like money and a home. We lived in a transit van. Bob was kept by me or social security or his parents.'

To compound their problems, Alex had been born handicapped, with a degenerative muscle disease, and the tiny infant was put in plaster when he was only thirteen days old to immobilize his legs (it will never be known whether this compounded the problem and created a plaster paralysis). Jane was no longer able to teach because Alex needed constant attention.

Now that he had a family, Bob decided he wanted to get married, and so they did. 'I have never been more involved with anyone and he must have loved me,' Jane told the *Sun*. 'At first Bob was a devoted father. But I always did the work with Alex, hours of exercise every day.' The physical therapy was exhausting and inescapable; if Alex's muscles weren't strengthened, he might never be able to walk. 'I can see that it made life difficult for Bob. He doesn't like to face reality and, unfortunately, there's a lot of reality around when you have a handicapped child.'

At least Bob was able to escape from reality – from poverty, from the worries about his child – and into a *métier* that gave him the applause he craved. He was hooked. 'I think I always wanted to do it,' Bob said. 'I was always telling jokes in pubs. . . . Anyway, I found that saying you were an actor was a brilliant excuse for being out of work. No one got aggressive, no one called you a layabout. They were very sympathetic when you couldn't find the right part.' Unless of course you were the wife stuck at home with a needy child and no money.

What Bob lacked in experience he made up for in enthusiasm. In one case his exuberance led to an impromptu scene on a busy North London street.

Not one to sit around and wait to be discovered, Bob enrolled in a drama workshop, but, as he explained, he had a 'bit of a set-to' with his drama coach. At one point this hapless instructor was so infuriated with Bob that he chased him up Haverstock Hill with a fire axe. 'I was being lazy,' Bob confessed. 'I suddenly let out a yell with a particular expression, and he said, "That's it, you've got it", and we went back to rehearse, the best of friends.'

Eventually this tough instruction paid off, because Bob landed a part in *Virgo and Sagittarius* at the newly opened theatre at the ICA.

20

Even more important, he was hired to work with the Century Theatre, where he began to prove himself.

'He was brilliant in his early days,' said Jane. 'He can project himself very well – and it is an art in itself to work spatially. With Century, we went up to the Lake District, and he really acted . . . roles like Menelaus in *The Trojan Women*. It was *theatre*. And those vans were an engineering feat.'

The Century Theatre billed itself as 'Britain's Only Mobile Playhouse', and, from its base in Keswick, the huge caravans, linked together to make an auditorium, provided not only drama but late-night music hall and a polka puppet theatre. And a bar, of course. By 1971 they found a permanent base at the Duke's Playhouse in Lancaster, but in the 1969 Northwest Tour the ambitious rep included, among others, Sartre's adaptation of *The Trojan Women*, *The Country Wife* by Wycherley, *The Anniversary* by Pinter, and *A View from the Bridge* by Arthur Miller, in all of which Bob had a role. Their tours went to Lancaster, Rochdale, Newcastle-upon-Tyne, Richmond, Bowness, and Preston.

If Bob learned the power of drama from Arthur Miller and the power of what is left unspoken from Pinter, he found in Pinchwife, the former whoremonger turned possessive husband in Wycherley's satirical Restoration drama, a marvellous comic leading role. And he would discover an even better vehicle for his talents with his off-the-wall performance in *The Trojan Women*. As he told John Ford in *Plays and Players*: 'If you go to drama school, they're going to teach you a load of methods – established techniques – but these can destroy the man himself, not the character. They're training them to be mimics; they're not training them to use their own experience. I played Menelaus in *The Trojan Women* at the Century. I picked up the script, and there was all this boring "Woe!" going on. But really it was the funniest thing I'd ever read. The sarcasm was hysterical. Taking the piss out of everybody – you know what I mean? I went out and I thought what would I be if I were in this situation? The missus has pissed off, I've just had a ten years' fuckin' war, everyone's been butchered, the town's been blown up – and really it's all for plunder, plain greed. You'd feel a right prat. I went out and brought the house down. Everyone thought it was great. Let's face it, if you're sitting there through an hour and a half of "Woe!", like, you want a laugh now and then.

'If you look at yourself and say what would I do in this situation if you're really honest with yourself and the play's good enough, it follows through. You don't need technique, you don't need the right walk. Because if you are a person in a situation, you *will* walk that way without thinking about it. You're in that situation.' Such logic is impressive.

Bob has rarely mentioned his work with Century, although, as Ken Campbell said, 'He certainly talked about it then! It was a mighty enterprise, an incredible theatre. It rests now at Keswick, but they can't move it out because the mechanisms have worn out.'

Bob's six months at Stoke and season with Century had given him invaluable experience in leading roles. They did not provide much income, however, and life was tough. 'We came back to London and thought we had a flat, but we had nowhere, actually,' Jane said. 'Bob's mother said there was only room for Bob – she wanted the man, not me; he is their only focal point.'

Clearly there was tension between the young wife and the doting parents. 'His mum came and fought from real slums, and she had that determination that her son would succeed.' Even if it meant creating an undercurrent of antagonism that would set the stage for the problems to come.

Eventually Jane found a flat in Hackney, and borrowed her rent money. The family stayed there until her daughter Sarah was born in 1972.

'It was the only time Bob has been out of work. We were very, very poor. And when an actor's out of work, he needs every bit of money that comes in to get the next job.'

Bob's next appearances would not provide the pot of gold, and they would be as far removed from the Restoration dandies as the inner sanctums of a convent would be from the *boudoir* of Lola Montez. For him, the money didn't matter. He would be joining a troupe that would at least pay him *something* to play everything from Queen Victoria to the Man Who Disappeared Up His Own Arsehole. As a member of the Ken Campbell Road Show, Bob Hoskins was about to get the theatrical education of a lifetime.

3

Wee on My Socks

'I can remember discussing with Bob that if we ever wrote the book of the Road Show experiences, it would be called *Wee on My Socks*,' said Ken Campbell, 'because we were forever changing in toilets. We were performing in places that weren't really designed to have artists in them, so to speak, so we were in the gents. In those days the gents were quite horrific. There was always piss on the floor, and with the tighter cut of trousers you always had to take your shoes off to change, so you were standing in wee. We all had disgusting shoes; they were all stained with foreign wee.

'There was one time in Liverpool, in a toilet, when Bob got attacked by a guy. This bloke came up and said, "Nothing to do wiv me, bruvver, I think the show's fantastic; you were great, but I'm afraid it's offended the missus." And he popped Bob in the face. Bob went sprawling in the wee. We could have called that bit *Wee on My Jacket.*'

Bob gave an account of it to Steve Grant of *Time Out*: 'This big bloke says, "I think the show's fucking great like, really great, I personally like the cunt – but the fucking missus doesn't like the cunting bad language, so I have to make this fucking complaint." And he hits me! 'So here I am lying in the piss trough in me crinoline dressed up as Queen Victoria and Ken's locked himself in the sit-down loo shouting, "Just ignore him, Bob!" And the bloke who's clobbered me says, "Don't worry I'll be back tomorrow with me mates, whack." '

Ken Campbell is one of the funniest men in theatre. This irreverent, eccentric, uninhibited theatrical genius has provided many merry moments of zany comedy for anyone lucky enough to have seen him and his troupes in action. He started to write and direct his own shows during his early days in rep. The Road Show had its genesis in Bolton. 'There was a notion of a bunch of people who'd spread the good name of the Octagon Theatre in Bolton – they'd go around pubs and stuff, and it sounded like something I'd like to do. I quarrelled with the bloke who ran the theatre at the time so he booted us out. We were so enjoying it that we continued doing it under our own steam. Bob was in it, too. The Octagon Road Show became the Ken Campbell Road Show. There were no auditions,' he said with a laugh. 'I just rang up some people I knew. I knew Bob would be a good idea since I'd worked with him at Stoke. We came from the same sort of not-working-class background – the poor end of the middle class really, the eastish end of London. Our accents are somewhat similar, although Bob adopts the East End a bit like Ian Dury does, which is perhaps a wee bit artificial now.

'At first I wrote all the material myself. On the right day you can write anything when it's easy. And for Bob, there were plays written purely for his talent. He's such a very, very good actor, and tough, because he's *above* text. He's at his best when the text serves his vision. It wasn't a question of teaching him anything, it was a question of serving him properly. He was a *great* actor who required scripts, basically, yet in such an original mould. I encouraged him and wrote for his original mould, as opposed to people who would squeeze him into casts or parts that already existed, or in a manner of playing that was the house style, which is not necessarily the best way of displaying an individual's talent.'

The Road Show was something quite out of the ordinary, inspired by what is not normally thought of as 'theatrical' material. Campbell explained, 'I've always been a collector of oddity and weird stuff. Cranks are always more interesting to me than proper teachers and learned folk. When I did the first Road Show that was one of the ideas of it – that we had the excuse to go and meet a lot of cranks and get people's extraordinary stories off them.

'We were skilled performers and we played to great success in pubs, theatres, dance halls, club rooms, tents, you name it. The clubs were desperately difficult to play in. In fact the show with Bob didn't work in huge working-men's clubs because you can't really do any entertainment that pretends it's somewhere else, which sketches do – you have to have a one-to-one vaudeville attack. But we were very successful in pubs, theatres and art centres.'

'I joined because I thought it might be a bit of a laugh,' Bob said, echoing Campbell's comments. 'Sometimes it was, and sometimes it wasn't. The worst moments were playing working-men's clubs where they were more intent on getting their supper or chattering among themselves than listening to us. When we played the pubs it was a totally different scene. . . . But really, you go into a pub – you can't muck about. You can't give them a load of technique. You haven't got the protection of a theatre, you haven't got the holiness of the theatre, no one's in a church. . . . If you're doing it in a pub, a bloke comes out for a drink, sees a show going on and says, "Ah, fuck me, that's a surprise for a start-off." So what do you do? You've got to do it ten times better than you would do on a stage.'

The sketches Campbell wrote for Bob and later *with* Bob were usually short – a few minutes at most – graphic, often lewd, physically descriptive, leading into a memorable punchline. In *The Man Who Disappeared Up His Own Arsehole*, for example, Bob played Arthur, who starts to feel unwell when he finds he can't stop listening to his own voice, a result of having gone to voice and movement classes. It is one of Campbell's satirical judgments on class distinction. Arthur can't stop thinking about thinking, and it's driving him crazy. As he tries to hurt himself – to take his mind off his mind – his astonished wife moans, 'On Arthur, I've got a lovely stew in the oven' (a comment not unreminiscent of the jabbering Meg in Pinter's *The Birthday Party*). But the harassed Sandra can't pull Arthur's head out of his bum in time.

Another of Bob's famous roles was in *The Vanishing Grandmother* where he played a husband and Jane Wood a wife. Unfortunately the husband's mother has dropped dead of a heart attack while the family is on a camping holiday in Middle-of-Nowhere, Italy. Husband tries to explain in misinterpreted body language to an Italian policeman (played by Sylvester McCoy, who was hired eventually to replace Bob) who speaks no *Inglese* that hapless granny is wrapped up in a tent on top of the car. The policeman finally understands and motions for husband to bring the body into the police station, really so that he can grope the wife. The husband returns sooner than the policeman expects. 'Don't hit him!' the wife cries. 'I'm not going to hit him!' retorts the husband. 'Somebody's stolen our car!'

And Bob was 'a damn fine Queen Victoria', related Campbell. 'Whatever he dressed up as he fit the part and you wouldn't believe it was the same person. He was of course very good at playing tough men – it was an obvious use of him, but he is also an incredibly graphic actor in the sort of variety/music-hall sense. When he played in *The Patient and the Earwig* you could see where the earwig had got to in his brain, by the way he looked. There was an incredible concentration in the journey this earwig made.'

Fortunately for the patient the doctor is able to pull it out. Unfortunately, the punchline has it, it's already laid its eggs.

One of the most successful skits, reminiscent of the Theatre of Cruelty, was *The Man Who Tossed Himself Off*. In it Bob played one of two tramps on top of a monument, who are interrupted by a gent who wants to commit suicide. The tramps don't mean to interfere, but it does make sense for the gent to divest himself of wallet and clothing before his departure. Then the gent changes his mind: 'I seem to have lost the urgency,' he says. 'I can't do it.'

'Don't be a cunt,' says the tramp, and pushes him off.

'There were plenty of laughs, but it was a lifestyle with plenty of drawbacks. The eight of us – Andy Andrews, Dave Hill, Jane Wood, Susan Littler, Christopher Martin, P. K. Smith, Bob, and me – travelled in our own two cars. Bob didn't have his own,' said Campbell. 'We lived off what we earned by passing the hat round after the show – survival money. Not nearly enough to support a wife and kid. But we had our fun.

'One night Bob got drunk with McCoy. They were staying with our road manager and his missus, who were home in bed when Bob and McCoy arrived. They went into their bedroom at three o'clock in the morning, with two road cones they'd found perched on their heads, singing "Wee Willie Winkie". It wrecked the marriage – the missus couldn't take it any more.

'Another time he was stranded somewhere one night and this girl said as long as he didn't make any noise at all he could stay at her parents' house. So she stuck him in the front room, and locked the door, and he needed to pee but there wasn't anywhere to do it. So he peed in all the knickknacks, and filled up all the vases.

'He was always a shining example for the youth of Britain.'

Once, Bob was acting obnoxious, so a sign was stuck on him "My name is Bob Hoskins. Please look after me. I like cornflakes for breakfast."' A box-office lady took pity on the poor lad and took him home for the night.

From 21 October to 9 November 1970 the Road Show played in the Come Together Festival at the Royal Court with their cabaret of 'pub humour, dirty jokes, and songs' along with such groups as Stuart Brisley's *A Celebration for Due Process, AC/DC* (not the rock band but a stunning play by Heathcote Williams), the *1861 Whitby Lifeboat Disaster* from Stoke-on-Trent, Leopoldo Mahler's TV in the Theatre, The People Show, and Theatre Machine, among many others. It was a motley collection of new/fringe groups and the mayhem of the Road Show's wacky skits stood out like a sore thumb, although theatregoers sitting in the front row usually ended up splattered with chocolate cake or eggs. (They were lucky – Brisley barfed on the crowd from twelve feet up.)

'Their credo always was that the only way to act is over-the-top,' said actor Nicholas Clay, who saw them perform. 'They weren't taken seriously; it was all a great wink in the eye.'

Around this time Bob met up with Barry Hanson, who, in 1969, was running the Hull Arts Centre, with Alan Plater, and who was to figure prominently in Bob's future. 'We were great fans of the Ken Campbell Road Show,' Hanson said, who invited them to play in Hull in 1970, and engineered their first tryout in a television studio when he moved to the BBC Pebble Mill Studios in Birmingham in 1971.

'It was the first time Bob – or any of them for that matter – had been on a screen, and he had a terrible fit when he saw himself. He went mad! "Is that me?" he shouted. "Is that little blob there me?" I don't know if they ever showed it – they never actually intended to.'

In April 1971, the Road Show appeared again at the Royal Court in the Theatre Upstairs in *Stone Age Capers*, written by Ken and Bob. Reviewer Irving Wardle had a few points of praise for the troupe as well as prescient and perceptive comments to make about Bob's stage presence: 'The company's style is a product of reinventing theatre from scratch in a particular environment . . . what saves even the most artless phallic joke is in the telling. . . . This laugh is one of the many Mr Hoskins wins by making his spectators wait. He is most remarkable . . . a squat, pugnacious figure throbbing with suppressed energy. Sometimes it is released murderously against other people; more often it sets different parts of Mr Hoskins at war with themselves, so that his hands, eyes, nose are all pursuing violently competitive lives of their own to the distress of the owner.'

For those who read that review in the *Times* or heard the buzz about the bullet-shaped bundle of dynamite in the Road Show and hurried to see him, however, they would be disappointed. Bob had already decided to push off and had given in his notice, so he could act for a bit more money in the hand and no wee on his socks. He had, in fact, as will be explained later, already become a familiar face at the Royal Court Theatre.

'Ken taught me a hell of a lot,' Bob said to Steve Grant, years later, 'how to survive on stage. In fact, if I hadn't worked with him, I might have bottled it when it came to the big parts. A lot of natural modern actors get the chance to do Shakespeare and they start prancing around doing "performances". Ken taught me irreverence. He taught me that it's all just a show for the punters. We used to go into boozers and we had to put on a show for total strangers who weren't even interested. I mean, everyone's doing pub theatre now, but Ken was the first.'

Campbell is equally complimentary about Bob.

'With Bob I saw a great talent. I nurtured it and I was very sorry to see it go. I wasn't surprised – it just made my life more difficult that he left. It was like we were married and you've got to stay because of the kids. He was unquestionably the most interesting and most talented person that I was working with; we built the Road Show around him and we were all going to get famous. It was as if we were all on a ride, and the driver pulled out. When he left, there was an enormous hole – he's got such great energy, great gusto, and great love of life. We never went back to that show, really, although we had to fulfil some gigs.

'Bob did have star quality, and I thought he was the kind of person who ought to go far. Had he remained he would have been huge but in a different way. History would be different and he could have been an out-and-out entertainer/comedian. There was something in him that didn't want to go that way, actually, and so he turned his back on it. I don't know what the reason was – it certainly wasn't ability – but I do think one of the reasons he left was to avoid being stamped in a purely comic/clown role. Looking back, yes, his starry future was guaranteed, but I didn't realize there was any guarantee of it if he went. I only knew it was guaranteed if he stayed.

'Sometimes you get somebody who does stand out like that, but they are complete arseholes. I've known others who've had similar singularity to Bob's, but essentially they were not as likeable as Bob is. There was a period when there was a sense in which I fell out with Bob, and that was only due to his going. We were really friendly but if he got drunk the old affray would return. *What the hell did you fuck up for, Bob?*'

The Road Show continued for a few years, putting on *The Great Caper* in 1974, and adding Warren Mitchell to the cast, before mutating into the Science Fiction Theatre of Liverpool. A splinter group also went off to the States calling themselves the Madhouse Company of London.

One of the best decisions Bob had made was to join the Road Show. Not only had he learned to perform in the worst of circumstances, how to control and manipulate even the most hostile and unappreciative crowds, but he learned timing and spontaneity and how to control his body on stage as well as the discipline needed to work with an ensemble. The Road Show was not sophisticated theatre, certainly, but the intense demands it made on its members (and the fun they had, too) gave Bob not only self-confidence about his comic talents, but the realization that he had much hard work ahead of him as an actor. Campbell also gave him invaluable lessons in writing, and this influence – seeing the absurd and surreal in everyday life – would reappear in many of Bob's own scripts.

The best thing he'd learned, though, was to know when to leave.

4

Beyond the Fringe

Yes, the timing was right, but Bob had not been idle during the stretches when the Road Show was temporarily off the motorway.

'Bob had contacted me at the Hull Arts Centre,' said producer Barry Hanson, 'and said he wanted to work with me. I asked why and he said, "Because you're a nutcase. This place is fucking crazy and I want to work with you." I said, "Well, come along," which he did. Bob actually has a very American attitude, demanding to be hired. That's just not done in this country!

'I thought, what am I going to do with him, because here is this extraordinary guy. . . . Well, the first production I was doing was Pinter's *The Homecoming* and he played Lenny in it like you've never seen in your life. Not only that – we took it around to the top-security prison in Hull and a lot of Bob's friends were there – he knew them from Finsbury Park.' (His crime lordship Ronnie Kray was there, too.) Considering the anarchic nature of the play itself, performing Pinter in prison was not such a ridiculous idea.

The Royal Shakespeare Company had first performed Pinter's play at the Aldwych Theatre on 3 June 1965. The subject of the play is the 'homecoming' not of the educated Teddy, but of his beautiful young wife Ruth to his old home in North London, where his brutish father and brothers, Joey and Lenny, and Uncle Sam live. What have they come home to? Lenny, for one, is a pimp.

'It was an extraordinary performance in the prison,' said Hanson. 'At that point, the play was like a great sort of bourgeois hoot, but in the prison environment it was absolutely like a straightforward play. The audience there was totally electric; they understood *everything*, and it was funny. A lot of that was due to Bob's interpretation of the character.'

Pinter once said, early in his career, 'A character on the stage who can present no convincing argument or information as to his past experience, his present behaviour, or his aspirations, nor give a comprehensive analysis of his motives is as legitimate and as worthy of attention as one who, alarmingly, can do all these things. The more acute the experience the less articulate the expression.'

Though he certainly wasn't a pimp, a lot of Bob – the Finsbury Park part – was Lenny. In an amazing monologue, after telling of how he 'clumped' a prostitute because he 'decided' she had the pox, he goes on: 'I am very sensitive to atmosphere, but I tend to get desensitized, if you know what I mean, when people make unreasonable demands on me.' Any prison inmate could understand that.

Although not quite as dramatic in its setting, Bob's next adventure with the Hull Arts Centre would provide him with a tale that has enlivened many a rehearsal, dressing room, and bleary evening. In this case the story is undeniably true.

'We were set to do *Richard III*,' explained Hanson. 'Bob had never done Shakespeare before, never seen an iambic pentameter or anything like that, so the read-through took about five hours. All the other actors were Shakespearian-trained, and they all thought I was mad, actually. Bob sat looking at the words of the Bard and then turned to me and said, "Fuckin' laundry list. Listen, we gotta get rid of some of this." Of course, because he couldn't bloody well learn it!'

Because Hanson had problems casting the Duke of Buckingham, Bob helped out and recommended an actor he knew from Stoke, who came up and probably regretted it. 'He was a proper, trained actor,' Hanson said, 'and he and myself worked with Bob on the iambic pentameter because there wasn't any. . . . What happened was that Bob nearly strangled the Duke because he was actually too patient.

'Bob quite liked the play, the fact that it was so violent and everybody got killed.'

It was not, however, a success with the audience who didn't take to a radical reinterpretation which cut the play to half its original length.

One exceedingly memorable afternoon, a resounding total of three people showed for the performance. Bob launched into his opening 'Now is the winter of our discontent' lines, then gazed out at the enraptured trio. 'A horse! A horse! My kingdom for a horse!' he cried out a few acts early. 'Sod this,' said His Majesty the King. 'See you all down the pub.' With that he limped off, hump and all, to buy the intrepid theatregoers a round of drinks.

'Bob always had these ideas. Basically Bob is an anarchist. He was also into Syndicalism – I don't know what he meant exactly, but it's a form of communism based on something in Bob's head . . . organized labour for the general good,' said Hanson. 'And he wanted to tour *Richard III* in Cuba. Well, we didn't. We all disappeared – did, as they say, a fast run.'

And Bob disappeared, as they say, on a fast run that would eventually take him to Sloane Square.

The Royal Court is the showcase of the avant-garde in all things theatrical. The English Stage Company was founded there in 1956 to present the works of new writers; its Theatre Upstairs was created by director William Gaskill to take low-budget risks and boldly go where no other venue had gone before, exploring experimental and new forms of theatre in an audience-friendly and inexpensive atmosphere. Although the Royal Court had been home to the best and brightest playwrights, directors, and actors, it was not without its management woes. According to director Ronald Eyre, it was a bit like 'the Borgia Court. You couldn't walk straight down a corridor – you had to keep your back to the wall for fear of being stabbed.'

And into this heady drama in 1971 strode Bob Hoskins.

'While he continued work with Ken Campbell after Stoke,' explained Barry Hanson, who was, with Campbell, one of the prescient few who noticed Bob's talent early on and featured it whenever he could, 'he came to the Royal Court in odd productions. He'd sort of just be around the place. He was the type of actor who'd go on saying, "I think I can play this part", and they'd say, "Well, you're really not fit for that, sorry, we just don't see you." And he'd come back a second and third time and say, "Look, I'm sure I could play this part, I just wanna be in it", and they'd give him a part. Bob was always like that – a fantastic mixer.'

Bob had made an impression with the Road Show when performing with other acts during the Come Together Festival. The powers-that-be organizing the festival, however, had decidedly mixed feelings about the whole thing. Its publicity stated: 'The Royal Court is committed to new work and has a long history of discovering and defending new writers, but this is the first time that we have presented new music and performances that have their basis in sculpture and the visual arts, rather than theatre as we know it.' Perhaps one of the reasons for discontent was that the festival lost money. Despite criticism, resident director Gaskill claimed that he was 'pleased'. He was, however, ready to move on to his next production, Brecht's *Man Is Man*, opened by the companion piece *The Baby Elephant*, directed by Bill Bryden, which premièred in the Theatre Upstairs on 7 February 1971.

It didn't matter much to Bob what internal battles were fought on Royal Court turf as long as he got work out of it. Rehearsals for the Brecht plays began on 9 January 1971 and continued for five weeks. Translator Steve Gooch remarked that the two 'joke-dropping extroverts' – Henry Woolf and Bob Hoskins – were a bit surprised at Gaskill's laid-back directorial style. Certainly Bob was used to getting away with murder with the Road Show. 'Gaskill lets them clown around,' said Gooch at the time, 'but is obviously not overimpressed. He wants to tone down the flamboyant clowning and is content to bide his time until the cast falls into line with his thinking.'

Man Is Man has always been a problematic play, 'a tangle of threads', according to the notes in the Methuen edition, 'each starting at a different point in the playwright's own evolution and each leading in a different direction.' Yet Hoskins made sense of the play about a man and his place in society, and the essential point that no man's ego is so important that it cannot be replaced with another.

The Baby Elephant was originally the penultimate scene of the play itself; reworked and separated as an appendix that also stands on its own, its players also, obviously, appearing in the longer *Man Is Man*. The cast included Anthony Milner, Dave Hill (from the Road Show), Mark McManus, Tim Curry (later famous for *The Rocky Horror Picture Show*), Derek Newark, Barrie Rutter, Oliver Cotton, Trevor Peacock, and Georgia Brown. The English-language première – forty-five years after *Man Is Man* was originally written – on 1 March 1971 was a major event, for it had taken Gaskill and the Royal Court many years of wrangling before the rights could be obtained from the Brecht estate.

Man Is Man ran for thirty-eight performances, only playing to half-capacity audiences. Gaskill has said that it is not considered to be among his best work.

'Bill Gaskill,' went one review, 'a sensible Brechtian . . . staged the thing as a fairly genial knockabout with no terror and little pathos. . . .'

'I'd read the play in drama school,' said Oliver Cotton, who played one of the soldiers, Polly Baker, alongside Bob's Uriah Shelley, 'and I found it hard. . . . I don't think it's a very good play; it's more like a sketch. In this production nothing worked. It was a great cast and we all got along wonderfully, but we got lost. We used to twiddle each other's toes, me and Bob and Derek, playing soldiers in India, eating porridge as the lights came up. We found our places in the dark and were always spitting porridge at each other. That at least was hysterically funny.'

For the actors, that is.

'It was very disturbing that we didn't get it right,' he continued. 'And it's almost impossible to say why. It was like watching through gauze. We kept asking each other what the hell was going on. It was most peculiar. If it's *you*, then you have to keep working and you stand a good chance of getting better. But if it's the production, no one can function and there's nothing much you can do, except to keep trying. If the bricks of your house are made of paper, once it starts raining you're going to get wet.'

That year Bob was also introduced to the works of the acclaimed Edward Bond, who, like Brecht, has demonstrated with his plays that what is theatrical is inextricably intertwined with what is political. He was also treated to a taste of overwhelming public approval from a gigantic crowd. On 11 April 1971, an open-air set-piece production of Bond's *Passion* was presented by the Royal Court Theatre as part of CND's Festival of Life.

'I have written very committed plays,' Bond said, 'but I couldn't work by asking, what's the audience going to think about this, or what must I tell the audience this week? Of course, if one's going to write a play for the Campaign for Nuclear Disarmament, one assumes that it's going to relate somehow to politicians and bombs – but that's just part of what one is setting out to do.'

Before a throng of 72,000 people at the Alexandra Park Racecourse, the cast of eight, directed by Bill Bryden, was received with roaring approval. Bob played the very small role of Buddha, who helps carry in a world-weary Jesus at the play's finale. He only had four lines. 'We'll find another world where they'll accept our priceless gift of peace,' he says in one of them. It was certainly another world from nearby Finsbury Park.

'It was a startling play – all parody – strongly anti-war and obvious in a way and very amusing, partly because Bob was in it,' explained Penelope Wilton, who played the dizzy Queen. Her finger gets stuck on a button while she is planning to unveil a monument (of a crucified pig) and the bomb is dropped instead. 'We were rather under-rehearsed and there were a lot of lines to learn, and we never knew how many people would turn up. We were all a bit astounded by the size of audience and worried whether it could be heard, although we had enormous mikes. It was very successful, so I'm told. It was difficult to tell, especially if it's only done once!'

'. . . If you think this is the sort of symbolic nonsense that half the earnest fools in Britain are writing you are probably right,' went a review in *The Guardian*. 'But the earnest fools do not have Bond's theatrical cunning . . . when Christ appears the dialogue mingles comedy and high anger with absolute sureness.'

Bob would continue his Brechtian education with his portrayal of Azdak in *The Caucasian Chalk Circle* at the Northcott Theatre in Exeter, where his family was to settle. Directed by Jane Howell, who put the Northcott's semi-circular and open stage to good use, the play was a surprising success. 'The students [at the University] use the bar a lot,' she said, 'but a lot of them went to see *Chalk Circle*.'

One of Brecht's 'Parables for the Theatre', it's set in Transcaucasia on the European–Asian border, a fitting location since the characters are members of two collective farms squabbling over land rights. Azdak, the village scrivener turned judge, dispenses his own brand of justice, and the role is a near-perfect showcase, in verse and song, for Hoskins's swaggering, blustering, cynically intelligent man whose judgments announce that he knows it's a dog-eat-dog world and the sooner you learn that, the better.

Bob began rehearsals for the Royal Court première of Bond's *Lear* on 29 September 1971. Bob and director Gaskill would work closely together on the exact interpretation. In this reworked version of Shakespeare's tragedy – not intended to be a mere update – Bond used the myth of Lear as king and the metaphor of 'blindness as insight' to show the character of a society as well as to deal with the fundamental desires and fears that people have.

'I wanted to explain that Lear was responsible, but that it was very important that he could not get out of his problems simply by suffering the consequences, or by endurance and resignation,' Bond told *Theatre Quarterly*. 'My plays are all concerned with the problem of violence because it is *the* consuming problem – the one that will decide what happens to us all.'

Besides Lear, played by Harry Andrews, there are seventy speaking parts, over eighteen scenes, and actors in the smaller roles more than doubled up. Bob played a Soldier, Soldier A, Sergeant, Soldier G, Guard in Prison, Soldier J, Convoy Escort, and other soldiers/workers/strangers, etc. As Soldier A he was responsible for matter-of-factly performing a torture scene. 'Lay off, lady, lay off! 'Oo's killin' 'im, me or you?' he asks the bloodthirsty Fontanelle.

35

'Mr Hoskins was very good as the Soldier in *Lear*,' said Edward Bond. 'Normally such a character would be portrayed as a brute and so dismissed: we punish what we don't understand. He made it clear that the tough character was acting out of weakness; that he was also a victim. Of course, this could be a sentimental reflection. But I remember clearly the way he looked at the people – the members of the ruling class – who were giving him his destructive orders: with total bewilderment and yet with a terrible wish to ingratiate. I dislike it very much when actors portray characters as if they understand them completely, as if they *were* the character – as if they summed up the character. Really a character is several characters, several characters struggling to understand each other. I remember that Bob played the most authoritarian moment of the character on his knees. This is probably a false memory – but the important thing is that he put the idea into my head.

'Also I hate it when actors sing their lines – as they do in RSC Shakespeare. There has to be '"a music" in the actor's voice – it reassures the audience of the humanity of what they're seeing. It's like the slide rule on a mathematician's desk, even when it isn't being used – but it mustn't be music *with* the words. So when he played the Soldier there seemed to be a music from outside or above the voice, which seemed to contradict what he was saying – to suggest: you could be saying something else, you could be understanding these orders instead of merely obeying them.'

For the thirty-seven performances, the audience was filled to over half-capacity. The reviews, however, were decidedly mixed. A Royal Court advertisement ran: 'Edward Bond's *Lear* is magnificent! But some critics have called Bond's *Lear* a "failure", because it "catalogues horrors". Because it "confuses" them. Don't be misled . . . because it is a play of size and wisdom and theatrical daring. . . .'

'*Lear*, despite its unflinching brutality, is not a negative work. It is a poetic indictment of what, in Bond's view, is wrong with our world and our values,' wrote Helen Dawson in the *Observer*. 'Although its tragic world is unimaginable except in the theatre, it is not primarily a play for "theatre-goers" but it is meant for anyone concerned with our apparently hell-bent course towards self-destruction.'

'One ends the evening more bludgeoned than moved,' said *Plays and Players*, although *Lear* was at least acknowledged as 'an imposing and disturbing piece of work'.

Whatever the opinions of the effectiveness of this play, Bob's talent and uniqueness are indisputable. Hoskins would well remember the invaluable experience – especially the close collaboration between Gaskill and Bond – when he portrayed Bond's Lear himself two years later at Dartington Hall. He has said, in fact, that Lear is one of his favourite roles.

In the meantime, he was rehearsing for another violent yet far less mythical story: *Cato Street*. It was first performed in a limited run at the Young Vic (in association with Thistlewood Productions) on 18 November 1971.

Written by Robert Shaw, *Cato Street* was based on *The Cato Street Conspiracy* by John Stanhope (actually John Langdon-Davies); instead of having the male conspirator in the leading role, Shaw made it his 'spirited Jacobin wife', Susan (Vanessa Redgrave), because he felt audiences would be more interested in 'looking' at a woman. The story is based on the Hayloft Plot devised by a group of protesters who survived the Peterloo Massacre of the Innocents at a reform meeting in Manchester in 1819. Susan, who has exhausted all legal means of protest and seen her husband hanged for speaking out, leads the fight against injustice. It was an appropriate vehicle for the fiercely political Redgrave who, as Susan, speaks impassionedly about 'those who have 'gainst those who've not'.

Bob played, as he introduced himself, 'Butcher Brunt from Cheapside'. His lines continued: 'I'd like to have that bastard Sidmouth's [the enemy] neck under my cleaver. So help me. I say I'm Butcher Brunt from Cheapside and I don't care who knows it. I'd cut him in one. Like this.'

Audiences got the message. Although it's not hard to imagine Bob impersonating such a man, Butcher Brunt and the rest of the conspirators would not have a chance, with or without a cleaver. They were betrayed, set up in a sham trial, and hung as Lord Sidmouth gloated over his victory.

'The reviews were quite good,' said Oliver Cotton, who tripled up as A Lieutenant, A Poor Student, and Harold Walters, 'but there was a big row because Robert Shaw hadn't liked it. He thought it was too slow. So either he sacked Peter Gill, the director, or Peter Gill resigned after a big row, and Vanessa took over.' (Gill was still credited in the programme.) 'The main aim was to speed everything up.

'We had a big party after we opened, and the next day there was a matinée for schools, so there were lots of kids around. At the Young Vic, there are only two or three dressing rooms, so all the men – about twenty of us – were in this long, thin room, and the women in another. It was really quite tight.

'Then there was a phone call or something, saying that there was a bomb in the building. We were half-way ready when the whole building was evacuated. We all went out in the street and waited as the police came with their sniffer dogs and checked through in about ten minutes. They gave the all-clear and in we went.

'I remember this very clearly. I was getting dressed next to Bob, and we looked at each other. "Oi, 'ang on a minute," Bob said. "They've only been here for ten minutes. That bomb could be anywhere." He had his trousers down at his knees when he said this. So he pulled them up and marched over to the girls' dressing room. Vanessa was management by this time. Bob told her we were not very happy, and if there was a bomb there were 300 schoolkids apart from us. We cancelled the performance.'

1972 would become a year to remember. Bob's daughter Sarah would be born. He would begin to work in television, even be flown down to Spain for a commercial. But before all this, he would finally get the chance to electrify the Royal Court stage as a nutcase called Bernie the Volt.

5

Veterans

'I wish I'd kept a diary during *Veterans*,' said director Ronald Eyre. 'It would have been the theatrical memoirs of a madman.'

Veterans or *Hairs in the Gates of the Hellespont* is a play about the making of a film set in Turkey in 1870; the veterans in questions were Sir Geoffrey Kendle (played by Sir John Gielgud), and Mr Laurence D'Orsay, known and acting as Dotty, as much for his behaviour as his speeches (Sir John Mills). The author, Charles Wood, had already written the screenplay for Tony Richardson's *The Charge of the Light Brigade* (Gielgud played the one-armed Lord Raglan) a few years before, and he drew on these experiences, his knowledge of the military, and, as he wrote in the Preface to the Methuen edition of *Veterans*, 'I decided to suppose that . . . somebody else had been asked to write a film based on *H* [another of his plays].' It would also turn out to be, eventually, a marvellous vehicle for Sir John.

'It's a brilliant play,' said Gordon Jackson, who played the effete Rodney, the cook who may mince meat but doesn't mince words. 'And a labour of love, really; a story using Gielgud's personality.'

Gielgud had played with the English Stage Company two years before in *Home*, with Ralph Richardson, and was asked to play Kendle by Gaskill, Lindsay Anderson, and David Storey. The Royal Court, Gielgud had written, 'always had a certain magic for me'. Little did he – or the rest of the company – know what was waiting for them before the successful London opening on 9 March 1972. Before that triumph was a month of torture as the troupe wound its way around England, and was met with what one could politely call a little hostility.

Ronald Eyre, an experienced theatre and television director as well as accomplished television playwright, was given the script to consider, and that's when the fun began. 'Nobody felt they could trust the text the Royal Court Theatre sent up,' he explains. 'I don't, however, decide to do a play unless there's a little spark – and I trust that spark. I must respect the fact that when I read it at first I thought it could work, though it was quite a rocky road. The problem with the play is that because it is about a film within the play, the balance is difficult to hold. But the real problem was everyone came expecting to see John Gielgud playing Captain Scott of Antarctica. And he wasn't. It was a real stretch for him and he was very insecure about it. That's fine – it's only natural for actors to feel nervous about such a change – but the end result was that no one was sure if it would work, and that feeling translated to the whole cast.

'I couldn't believe the problems. When insecurity starts weaving its way through the cast and your reputation is on the line, it affects everyone, and their reputations. So as the director you focus on shoring up the positions, even though I felt like coming up with the excuse that my aunt was ill and I must leave immediately for South Africa.

'I cast Bob because you just had no doubts about him. He loved the buccaneering. He always said, "I'll have a go"; he had such an appetite for learning and such enthusiasm – he even enjoyed the stuff that was driving the rest of us crazy.'

Bob played the raucous Cockney electrician, Bernie the Volt, who was singularly unimpressed with the film's stars and just wanted to get his job done in his own way, which was rather earthy.

'His makeup was extra thick so his face was a bright red,' said Jackson. 'It looked as if he'd spent far too much time in the sun. And every other word he said was a four-letter one.'

Bob's first line is, in fact, a shouted 'No, it's all right mate, no fucking shop stewards watching, is there?' He then pins a batten to the ground before grinning up at Sir Geoffrey. 'You don't mind my language, guv'nor, too bleeding bad if you do. . . .' It's not difficult to imagine the shock waves rippling through provincial audiences as this hairy-chested, unkempt, sweating, red-faced blob, clad only in tatty rolled-up shorts, a tool belt with its hammer slung in the most obvious place and his narrow eyes peering through thick glasses, clomped around on stage, utterly indifferent to the great company he was sharing. How dare he? And how dare the great Sir John parody himself so easily or, indeed, John Mills his partner-in-crime, both playing with such insouciance and humour?

Bob wanted to learn everything he could from these veterans. 'It was wonderful to see him watching Gielgud,' said Eyre. 'They were on stage together for about forty minutes, and I can't think of anyone else who could have done it. Even at this, the start of Bob's career, his quality was so apparent. Gielgud quite admired him, and felt safe, which was very important, for, as I said, when actors are nervous the project gets worried. And they were nervous!'

Bernie's long scene with Sir Geoffrey, stuck perched up on a prop 'horse box', proved to be one of Bob's most indelible lessons in acting: timing, reaction, and how to hold himself back (as much as it was possible for Bob to hold back). One line of his in particular was not working, so Sir John told him how best to get the laugh.

'Step back two paces, dear boy,' he advised. 'Count to two, then say it.'

He did, and the audience roared.

'I couldn't believe it,' Bob said. 'Next night I got another round. I thought it must be something Gielgud was doing. The next night I did it again, but spun around to see. He wasn't doing anything. He was just sitting there, giving it to me. He gave me a sort of wink – he can't wink very well. I got a round every night. Ever since then, I've been stepping back two paces, counting to two, and getting nothing.' He also said, 'I learned presence from Gielgud . . . stillness. I had all the lines, and he just gave it to me.'

'Bob was very impressed with Gielgud,' said actor Edward Petherbridge, who would star in one of Bob's plays. 'And Gielgud's technique certainly *isn't* counting, stepping back, and then doing it. Bob hadn't come up against anyone like that before and his acting suddenly got a lot better. Gielgud was a huge influence because they hadn't *anything* in common.'

Yet the audiences weren't laughing at first. 'The audiences were very difficult and very hostile,' said colleague and director Jonathan Miller, 'because it was not reverential poetry speaking. It was perfectly ordinary and real, and this reality offended the audiences who wanted Gielgud and Mills to be like the way they knew they were – on their knees in front of the classics. *Veterans* desecrated their authority.'

'It should have been worse, but nobody chickened out,' said Eyre. 'Anyone else would have jacked the project; I felt like a horse with my bit between my teeth, but we doggedly persevered and we did it.

'At the first performance Moira Shearer came, dressed like a fairy on a Christmas tree. Of all the inappropriate people. . . . Another form of torture was two weeks in Nottingham, at the Playhouse. We received blood letters, and notes were shoved under the door. Once at Brighton we had to play during an electrical strike, so we had car headlights trained on stage.

41

'I never like to see first nights. I'd go to previews and see the actors before, but I thought, I am not going to sit through this farrago. I had a very good assistant director and he said I'd better show up, so I had a drink with a friend and came over about an hour and a half later, thinking that only the night watchman would be on stage, and the cast was popping champagne. I don't know how they got through it.

'A friend of mine, a monk, went to see it, and there was this sort of pained silence from him – you know the kind of regret when someone close to you has done something foolish or regrettable and you feel you must ease them through and ignore that patch, and don't worry, they'll get over it.

'Everyone in the cast wobbled a bit, because the pressure was enormous. People enjoy a failure – watching the great like Gielgud or Mills humiliate themselves. The audiences would often be shaking their umbrellas at the stage. Or else they would be catatonic, gazing at us and pretending that nothing's really happening.'

'Outside London,' Gordon Jackson said, 'people in the audiences were shouting, saying that the play was filth and then walking out. So we all had a meeting, and we sat around depressed and wondering what to do, so we said, "Let's cut out all the swear words." And Bob said, "But I'll have no part left!"'

'The awful thing is that when you actually go through the fire, it does create an undeniable quality,' said Eyre. 'The worst thing was when we would see these glazed people and we all began to believe that anyone in the audience was preferable to anyone of us! I remember at a matinée in Nottingham, the audience was so silent, but there was this one man, and he was laughing so hard we figured he was from a nearby mental institution. But it was Ian McKellen.

'It was hell to do. I felt like I was dragging a mad dog across the kingdom and down into Sloane Avenue and the Royal Court, and then shutting the door and wondering how we'd survived. The cast was incorruptible and invincible by the time we got to London. And they played it brilliantly. At the Royal Court the audience laughed a great deal and we didn't believe it.'

Veterans was a smashing, sell-out success in London. No longer did Gielgud receive mailbags of abuse from fans who'd come expecting a drawing-room comedy.

'It must be the most endearing portrait of [Gielgud] ever drawn,' wrote Ronald Bryden in *Plays and Players*. Gielgud's 'timing of each joke on himself is as perfect as the modesty with which he offers it'.

Irving Wardle wrote in the *Times*: 'The result is a large-scale public work, extracting some marvellous comedy from the interplay of character and situation and touching on issues much beyond its immediate circumstances.'

'I retain a clear image of [Gielgud] in *Veterans*, wrote Michael Billington, 'sitting astride a prop-horse in a *kepi*, surrounded by the synthetic smoke of cinematic battle and listening patiently while Bob Hoskins's Sparks invited him to pop in for a cup of tea back home whenever he was passing.'

'People still remember it,' said Eyre, 'even now, as an extraordinary thing. Much of it was due to Michael Codron, one of the great producers, who believed in breaking new ground. My only moment of real pleasure was when it later went to the West End and I was asked to direct it. And I said no, no thank you. That was my vengeance.'

For Bob, *Veterans* provided many answers. For one thing he had the support and friendship of the actors in the company. 'This is where I've been lucky,' Bob said. 'You only get better by acting with actors better than you. It's like chess. You instinctively come up to their standard, if you can.'

'There's something about being young, when you're learning a lot, and there's nobody in your way,' explained the RSC's Estelle Kohler, who later worked with Bob. 'You steadily go down in your own estimation, your own confidence, because you see around you the most wonderful talented people and the more you learn the more you don't know!'

'Bob would come into my dressing room for little chats,' Gordon Jackson remembered, 'and I seem to recall him talking about how he spent odd days working on something for some Polish people, filming around London, for the fun and experience. Trust the Poles to see the quality before the British!'

'What Bob could do,' said Eyre, 'is make it so you can't deny his humanity. No matter what he does, it couldn't be a caricature, and not have that essential quality.'

Even more amazing was the friendship of this squat hulk of a man, who'd only been working professionally for little more than three years, with the great theatrical knight Gielgud. 'We got along like a house on fire,' said Bob. 'We had a wonderful time.'

'The relationship they struck up was really something,' Ronald Eyre told *Time Out*'s Steve Grant. 'There was no question of Bob being out of his depth, which is sometimes the case with regional or character actors who are brought into the big arena. I remember Gielgud had this chauffeured Rolls, and Bob took especial delight in getting lifts in it, sometimes just as far as Chelsea Barracks, which from Sloane Square can't be more than a stagger. It was great fun.'

Yet the most important results would be the reactions of two people who saw Bernie the Volt steal his long scene from Sir Geoffrey. One was the producer Kenith Trodd, who remembered the hilarious, yet humble electrician when he began casting a Dennis Potter mini-series.

The other was an agent named Sally Hope, who would become an integral part of Bob's life, both professionally and personally, for the next fourteen years.

6

Bringing Down the House

'You fill your mouth with kerosene. You get used to it. The taste isn't very nice and you get indigestion now and again,' Bob explained about fire-eating. 'Just keep the flames moving. I'm very hairy. If I hang about too long it's all up.'

Doing a stint in the circus run by a friend was a piece of cake. Clowning and escapology were hardly more difficult than getting wee on the socks in dodgy pubs, although they were hardly comparable to stealing scenes from the great Gielgud. What the hell, acting was a lark, wasn't it? Or, at least, it was a game. And Bob Hoskins was learning how to play it. Over the next three years he would not have to hunt for work in the theatre and he would also begin making a name for himself in the rarefied atmosphere of television adventures and comedy.

Not long after this dazzling display of hirsute, fire-eating talent, Bob landed a part that would make his mug a familiar one on British television. 'Only here for the beer' went the slogan for Watney's, and that's what Bob was there for, although it was hard for him to recollect much of that episode. 'The company took us down to Spain for a week to film the thing and we were all getting paid a lot of money and living on expenses,' Bob said. 'So we went bananas. After a week, they took us back and poured us out of the plane. I can't even remember filming it.' Luckily, director Dick Clement remembered him and would use him later.

Bob also began playing bit parts on the telly, usually cast as 'the heavy', with appearances on *Villains* as Knocker, one of the crooks; *The Bankrupt*; *On the High Road*; *The Main Chance*; *Her Majesty's Pleasure*; the daytime *Crown Court*; as Eddie Wharton, a bank robber, in *New Scotland Yard*; *And All Who Sail in Her*; *Shoulder to Shoulder*, portraits of the suffragettes; and *Softly, Softly*, the follow-up series to the popular *Z-Cars*. He was also seen in the one-off play by Johnny Speight, *If There Weren't Any Blacks You'd Have to Invent Them*, a symbolic farce originally commissioned by the BBC in the mid-sixties.

And Bob made his first appearance in films: a tiny role as a heart-attack victim in the ruthless farce called *The National Health*, written by Peter Nichols, directed by Jack Gold, and starring Lynn Redgrave and Colin Blakely. Before his date with eternity, the sick man receives, as did everyone in the ward, a visit from a religious and tactless old lady. 'Jesus Christ this day is risen,' she announces to her immobile audience. 'I should hope so,' Hoskins retorts. 'It's half-past three – is he on nights?'

In between television shows Bob was back sharing the stage as Sextus Pompeius with Vanessa Redgrave as Cleopatra at the Bankside Globe Theatre in *Antony and Cleopatra*. Directed by Tony Richardson, it also featured Julian Glover as Antony and a young Julie Covington as Charmain.

The Globe was built on the site of an old Elizabethan bull-baiting ring, and its opening summer season the year before had incurred the indignant wrath of critics who proclaimed it entirely unsuitable in adverse weather conditions, despite the theatre's historically important location on the Southwark riverside. These words must have rung in their ears as this production of Shakespeare's tragedy, opening on 9 August 1973, took a back seat to the drama played out in the skies above.

'It was an unusual production, in modern dress from the twenties, and on many levels it was very unsuccessful,' said Julian Glover. 'The play itself is difficult to put on, although Vanessa – directed by her husband – did pretty well. Only about a quarter of the critics like it. *We* adored the production, though, and I do think it would be much more accepted now. The people who came did so for the right reason – they didn't have the preconceived ideas that others bring with them.

'Bob was comparatively unknown and it was quite brave and inspired of Tony to cast him, for it was right out of Bob's range. I have tremendous admiration for him – he's one of the few really original English-speaking actors in the world. He was totally natural and not overwhelmed by technique. And he was enchanting to work with.

'What happened, though, was that we were scheduled for a six-week run at the Globe, which was a tented structure with an enormous awning over the scaffold. The play had been on for about three and a half weeks – it was a glorious summer with fantastic weather and perfect for us, but then it began to get hotter and hotter and we knew something was brewing. It was so hot I could hardly stand up. One night by the third scene the skies opened and there was so much noise of rain on the tent we couldn't be heard properly. We could also see that the awning was filling dangerously with water. We couldn't keep going, obviously, so Bob got up and told stories right off the cuff, keeping the audience entertained. This must have lasted for over five minutes, and then suddenly the whole of the awning ripped and drenched the whole of the audience, cast and stage with water. No one was hurt, luckily, because with all the electricity there were sparks everywhere. Everybody was screaming with laughter. And no one said anything, but by common accord we all went to the bar and got roaring drunk and had a marvellous time.

'It was so typically Bob, so wonderful, and luckily he was on stage when the crisis hit. I couldn't have coped with it – I would have said, "Right, chaps, let's go and have a cup of tea."

'And that was the end of the Bankside Globe Theatre. We actually brought the house down!'

Captain Harry Flashman in the Royal Hussars is a fake, a rake, an impudent ingrate and a coward, which helps explains why, in Richard Lester's romp *Royal Flash*, based on the *Flashman* books by George MacDonald Fraser, he becomes a hero of Afghanistan and a recipient of the Victoria Cross. As embodied by Malcolm McDowell, Flashy disproves the notion that cheaters never prosper. His fame would save his skin in an early scene when, after a raid by blundering coppers in an illegal gaming house, he escapes over rooftops and ends up hiding in the carriage of Lola Montez (Florinda Bolkan) and Otto von Bismarck (Oliver Reed). The busy-faced sergeant chasing Flashy peers in, ready to pounce on his prey, when he suddenly recognizes the hero and defender of Pipers Fort. The copper throws back his head and lets out a maniacal laugh. Bismarck, however, is not pleased, and demands that this invading trespasser be properly punished.

'I don't care if he invaded Buckingham Palace,' quips the sergeant, mutton chops all aquiver. 'Cap'n Flashman is a British officer, so don't you demand nuffink!' With that he tips his hat and pushes off, chuckling to himself. And with that tiny, nearly unrecognizable part, Bob Hoskins made his second appearance on the silver screen.

While not as successful or as trenchantly witty as Lester's *Three Musketeers*, *Royal Flash* was nonetheless good entertainment. For Bob it was work, it was experience.

His next role, one that had been offered to Michael Gambon, was at the Theatre Upstairs in the world première of *Geography of a Horse Dreamer, A Mystery in Two Acts* which opened on 21 February 1974. It would become a milestone in his career . . . not only because the playwright himself, American icon/sex symbol/film star Sam Shepard, would be directing, but also because it was Bob's first incarnation as a proper gangster on stage, and as a Yank to boot.

America had become too much for Shepard, and this artistic cowboy arrived in London – by boat; he has a pathological fear of flying – with wife O-Lan and young son Jesse, and soon became immersed in the finer points of English culture, like dog racing. 'I loved horse racing before,' he said. 'Then, when I came here, I found dog racing is the second biggest spectator sport in England . . . and suddenly it was all like your romantic childhood dreams come true – only with dogs. So I thought, shit, this is great, and I got involved with it. It's really a sort of romantic impulse, you know. Being around the track, punters, and all that kind of stuff – I like that world.' He even had his own dog, Keywall Spectre (named after an organization in one of the James Bond books).

In his inimitable style, peopled with American dreams and myths, Shepard shaped his English experience into a cathartic metaphor for the dilemma facing all creative people, the keepers and the kept, to conform and belong, or try to be free. The hero of the piece, Cody (Stephen Rea), has lost his knack for dreaming the winners of horse races and has been kidnapped by gangsters (Bob and Kenneth Cranham) who hope he'll regain his magic touch. ('You got the genius,' one of them tells him, 'somebody else got the power.') A captive in his room, he seems to go crazy before switching his talents to the dogs, and is 'saved' at the last moment by his two brothers from Wyoming.

Shepard, notoriously displeased with the direction of his previous works, decided to have a go at shaping this himself, and learned a few valuable lessons in patience and collaboration. Bob would learn a lot, too: a believable American accent and a credible American persona, as he stomped around on stage in his ill-fitting hat, huge overcoat, and large specs.

'Shepard directs his play with workmanlike ease,' wrote critic John Lahr, 'getting substantial support from Rea, Cranham, and Hoskins. . . . All three have the energy and expertise to flesh out these dream figures.' And all three would go on to success in their careers.

Knowing exactly what the playwright wanted on stage would be of great use to Hoskins years later when he starred in Shepard's *True*

West. After *Horse Dreamer* was over, though, he took Shepard's cowboy-mouth myth a little too far and had an awful, although luckily not life-threatening, accident.

'Bob had a prop shotgun,' Oliver Cotton related, 'and it went off near his eyes so he was temporarily blinded and had to go to hospital. I went to visit him, and he told me this story: "I'm lyin' in this fuckin' bed – they put this band round me eyes – after twenty-four hours I was completely disorientated, and I was dyin' for a piss but they wouldn't let me out of bed. So I wanted a bottle, anything to piss in; I was dyin', lying there. I know it sounds ridiculous, but I couldn't get my cock in this bottle they gave me, but at the same time I fell out of bed and I fell on to the *next* bed and nearly broke my nose. And I'm lying there practically unconscious, groping around for this bottle, and what do I hear? 'Nurse, nurse, he's pissing my drip!' " '

It was back to cheeky Cockney chappies after this one, and Bob prepared for his first major West End production: as Alfred Doolittle in *Pygmalion*. It opened on 16 May 1974 at the Albery Theatre.

George Bernard Shaw, who wrote *Pygmalion* mainly as a vehicle for the wonderful Mrs Patrick Campbell, described his play as 'a shameless potboiler', and was astonished when it became a commercial success. Based on the legend of a statue come to life, it is actually one of Shaw's less polemical plays about the failures of the English. 'The English have no respect for their language,' he wrote, 'and will not teach their children to speak it.'

'If ever there was a play about language, and the ability to *express* oneself in language, without trivialization, that play is *Pygmalion*,' claimed Peter O'Toole, who played Henry Higgins on Broadway. 'The most eloquent man in the play, the philosopher – Alfred Doolittle, the dustman – speaks in Cockney. But he *speaks!*'

'I think Doolittle is one of the most marvellous parts Shaw ever wrote,' said Sir John Mills, who played him on Broadway. 'He's a cunning, very funny fellow.'

It was a terrific role for Bob the comic, and he more than held his own on stage with far more experienced and venerated actors, in this case Alec McCowen as Higgins and Diana Rigg as Eliza. 'Bob Hoskins's Doolittle is all there from the moment he takes the stage, a philosophical walrus who puts a curve on his rhetoric rather as sealions curve their torsos to catch a fish,' wrote one metaphor-strained critic.

'*Pygmalion* ran for six months and was sold out for the entire run,' said Alec McCowen. 'They wanted us to take the production to

America, but Diana and I were already committed to *The Misanthrope*, which we did in the USA instead.

'We played *Pygmalion* as if the play had been rediscovered, especially the last act, which has the seed of *Who's Afraid of Virginia Woolf?* It was very tough stuff indeed. Jocelyn Herbert designed it beautifully. John Dexter directed, as you must, by sticking to Shaw's directions. Any director who tries to do a remake or a reworked version will usually have a disaster. Shaw is unique inasmuch as if you stray from his stage directions you are immediately sunk. He writes all the movements and descriptions, and you have to follow them; he's done the work for you, and that's great. But in that sense – dare I say it – playing Shaw is a little boring because you cannot do it your way.

'In addition, we had one of the most authoritative directors in the world. No one had to look anywhere but to him for direction. John is quite easily displeased, but I don't remember any evidence that Bob needed special attention. There was this extremely young man of thirty-two, playing Diana Rigg's father! Nobody thought about his age; he fitted into that show so easily. He was so refreshing – to see this absolutely natural talent. And backstage he would chat quite happily about his family. His head was so properly screwed on.

'Years and years ago I waited outside the stage door to meet the wonderful American actress, Ruth Draper. And I asked her, "Miss Draper, how do you do it?" And she said, "It is a matter of seeing the world through the eyes of a child." *Bob* has the astonishing ability to look as if everything is brand-new – he seems to register this acting with the delight of a child, so that his acting is always fresh and original. This translates into everything he does, and is one of the reasons why he has become so successful.'

Perhaps, though, a taste of this success was beginning to go to Bob's head after all. 'When *Pygmalion* opened,' said a friend, 'only the upper echelon of the cast was invited to the party. Bob, of course, went along. But it was very interesting that there was not this dissenting voice to say, "*I'm* not going to go if you don't invite the rest of the cast." You'd have thought he'd put himself out . . . but he can be quite insensitive to other people.'

Dick Clement has a good memory. He remembered a saucy young actor who quite enjoyed mouthing 'Only Here for the Beer' in take after take. In fact, he thought he'd be rather appropriate in his new comedy series *Thick as Thieves*. The part he had in mind for him was Dobbs, a petty thief who returns home from prison to the loving arms of his wife, only to discover that his best mate has moved in with her. Sounds like a perfect formula for a disastrous sitcom . . . but it wasn't. It was an excellent, far-too-short-lived success, because Dick Clement and his partner Ian La Frenais are two of the most talented comedy writers around. The cast also included Pat Ashton as the fickle wife Annie, and John Thaw as Stan, the 'mate', who contrives to fall down the stairs when Dobbsy throws him out, so, of course, he has to stick around while he recuperates. 'I never thought you'd turn from petty larceny to grievous bodily harm,' says the indignant wife to her husband.

'It was a fantastic success,' said Pat Ashton. 'The write-ups were unbelievable. We thought it was good, we had the top comedy writers, and you couldn't go wrong with Bob and John. It was so right for Bob – he is so funny and down-to-earth, and we'd all put in a bit of our own stuff, because the more real it was the funnier it became.' In one scene, for example, Bob is annoyed at finding a cup of tea as a peace-offering from his two-timing spouse. 'That won't erase the bitter evidence of betrayal,' he says before adding in the same breath, 'Two sugars, please.'

The rounded, bespectacled Bob hardly looks like a menacing thief. He 'has an anonymous face, apparently assembled from Identikit parts,' wrote one TV critic. 'His accent is standard outer London, and would pass without comment either selling insurance in the most respectable surroundings, or nylons which had fallen off a lorry.'

'Hoskins played the husband as a sawn-off Eric Morecambe,' wrote another. 'He walked and talked with the aggressive despair of one of life's perpetual put-upons. His face was a study. It was also richly comic. . . .'

Why, with writers, producers and directors (Derrick Goodwin and Mike Gibbon, now directing *EastEnders*), actors, critics, and punters happy with *Thick as Thieves*, did only six episodes appear?

'LWT was a bit nervous,' said Pat, 'and it was also brought out at a bad time – during the summer – which was naughty. But everybody went potty about it anyway. I'm sure it would work now and get the same attention.'

'The intention, I think, was to develop those three characters into a series where eventually the two of them would go into prison,' claimed Mike Gibbon, director of two of the episodes. 'That was going to be called *Porridge*. But LWT couldn't make up its mind. Because the writing was so good, they almost thought it'd go over everybody's heads, but it didn't of course. It *was* so beautifully written, and the public loved it.

'So what happened was LWT only ran the six episodes, and then they prevaricated. Meanwhile John Thaw had been given the opportunity to do a cop series with Dennis Waterman, which ran on and on, so he wasn't available. And the idea for *Porridge* was taken to the BBC and they got Ronnie Barker and Richard Beckinsale to do it, changing it slightly to accommodate those two characters. It caught on because the BBC let it run, let the public get used to it. But it was awful that LWT never bothered to make it a proper series.'

Ironically, *Porridge*, written by Clement and La Frenais, became one of the top comedies, running from 1974 to 1977. It won BAFTA awards as best sitcom in 1974 and 1976 before spinning off into *Going Straight* in 1978. LWT blew it. But for the millions of viewers who saw *Thick as Thieves* and laughed themselves silly, those three losers in the show were winners at comedy.

For the rest of that year, Bob stayed busy. He worked on his own plays: *All for the Nation, Rubber Love,* and *Dog's Dinner*. He played the Common Man in *A Man for All Seasons* in rep with the Manchester 69 Company. He appeared again on television in *Gentle Rebellion*, and then, in his first association with the acclaimed playwright and critic, Dennis Potter, in *Schmoedipus*. It is a play about a man who shows up on the doorstep of a housewife's home and announces that he's her long-lost son. In truth, he's but a fantasy. The title stems from an old Jewish joke, 'Oedipus, Schmoedipus, what does it matter as long as he's a good boy and loves his mother?' But the real message, of how a figment of the imagination can mutate seemingly effortlessly into reality, is something that would hound Bob Hoskins in years to come as he became more popular, more in demand, more sure of his gifts, and less happy with his marriage and himself.

7

Big Mac, Hold the Fries

'We are not some pack of degenerates smearing some slime we shot in a seedy motel room across the stag party screens of America!' says the Boy Wonder as he prepares an actor for a scene. 'We are *pioneers*! Pioneers of the neo-plastic arts! Ever searching for that excuse to extend the boundaries of those arts beyond the limits of urgency! . . . I'm talking about subtlety! Poetry! Strangle her with the fucking ascot, you orangutan!'

And then there was *Inserts*, which provided Hoskins with his first major film role.

Created, written, and directed by John Byrum, *Inserts* is a one-set, one-act 'play' with only five characters. Holed up in his once-fabulous Spanish-style bachelor pad in a neighbourhood soon to be demolished for a freeway is the Boy Wonder (Richard Dreyfuss), genius director of the Silent Age turned alcoholic has-been at thirty. He makes porn flicks for a bootlegger named Big Mac (Bob Hoskins) who has a mistress named Cathy Cake (Jessica Harper) who's willing to do anything to be in 'real movies'. Boy Wonder uses a talented, former starlet-turned-junkie, Harlene (Veronica Cartwright) and an egomaniacal pretty boy, Rex (Stephen Davies) as his porn stars. 'Inserts' are filler shots. *Inserts* was ninety-nine minutes of wisecracks, *petit mort* and *grand mort*, drugs and drinking, fears and failures. In essence, about Hollywood.

That the film was even made is a story of hilarious coincidences every bit as fantastic as Bob's discovery in the bar of the Unity Theatre. John Byrum, who now lives in New York, told the tale: 'I was a cab driver in New York, then got a job for the Muppets, working sound on 16mm films of Kermit the Frog handing out trips to Hawaii at the IBM convention for whoever sold the most Selectrics. I quit that, went to London for a year, started writing, came back and got a call from a friend who'd been contacted by a man who owned a massage parlour on 42nd Street. The guy had $30,000 and he wanted to make a porn film. So he asked me if I had a script and I said I'd speak to my agents. I didn't have an agent. I wrote it literally over the weekend, just sat up all night. I'd never seen a porno film but I knew it had to be cheap, set in one room for $30,000. So it became a script about a guy who is forced to do porno because that's the only thing I knew about. I wrote *Inserts* and the guy read it and said it wasn't what he had in mind!

'Ultimately I wound up getting an agent and being in Hollywood proper, and I wrote a script called *Harry and Tonto Go to New York* for Tony Bill, who'd just done *The Sting*. One week I was selling blood because I was so broke and the next week – after *The Sting* won all these Oscars – I was the hottest young screenwriter around. So I did a couple of screenplays, and then finally United Artists offered me some films to write, and I told them I wanted to direct. I gave them *Inserts*, since it was lying around. They said, "We're interested in this – how much can you do it for? And you can direct it because we had luck with Bertolucci's *Last Tango*." You see, this is how decisions are made in Hollywood. They had an X-rated film, they read my script, they just assumed it would be controversial. . . . I said I needed $500,000 and they said fine. So we did it.

'Through the producers, Davina Belling and Clive Parson, I met Richard Dreyfuss. I thought he was a great actor with such intelligence and a unique style, which is what I was looking for as a novice director. But how I really got Dreyfuss to do it was because of *Jaws*. *Jaws* was really bad. I can't believe it now, but I turned it down – to write. They gave me the galleys and I thought it was shit. So I told Dreyfuss that I *could* have made *Jaws*, but I was no whore – which was a complete lie – and he fell for it. It was being in the right place at the right time. I don't think a month earlier or later he'd have agreed, and he also wanted to get out of the country for a while – he was just starting to get famous – and we shot the whole thing on a set in London.

'He taught me a lot, about directing, about Hollywood, about actors and acting. If one of the other actors would have a problem he'd come over and stroke them. I had to use English actors playing Americans, because the financing had come from England. Veronica [Cartwright] and [Stephen] Davies were both British citizens. And the Hoskins part was going to be played by Nicol Williamson.

'When I met Nicol he was going to do the whole thing as an impersonation of Mike Nichols, the director. It was funny and it would have been interesting. But about a week before we were

54

going to film, Nicol's mother died, and he got all freaked out, and I never heard of him again, for years. Hoskins was second choice – he'd come in and read and he was great. In fact he was better than Nicol but I thought to myself that since it was my first movie . . . if I could have Nicol Williamson in it . . . Bob certainly was a lot earthier. I liked him in the movie so it doesn't really matter.'

Big Mac doesn't know much about the mechanics of film-making – he just knows there's money to be made. He has a scheme to build a 'mess o' hamburger stands and a mess o' gas stations' exactly alike, so hungry drivers can get confused and spend their hard-earned money anyway. 'Well that's what I'm talkin' about here, buster!' Big Mac says. 'If you don't get 'em comin', you get 'em goin'! After a while, they're just gonna roll down the windows and throw out the dough without even stoppin' the car! Freeways, what a gimmick! If these freeways don't end the Depression, nothin' will!'

'Bob looked the part,' Byrum continued. 'Those glasses were a nice touch – he looked like Louis B. Mayer, which is what he was trying to do. A lot of people thought he *was* American. And he and Davies had a good thing going – this comic relief, all these little asides. They were very funny together and really hit if off.

'We rehearsed for three weeks and shot it in fourteen days, about ten pages a day. This group liked each other, and it was very controllable because there was just this one set, and it's an actor's movie. It was one of the nicest experiences I've ever had. The actors didn't try to change anything, which is, as I understand it, how it is in the theatre. When you're working with an actor in that enclosed situation, even if it's a big star, and the film is *just about acting*, no one gets temperamental.

'It was like a real hothouse when we were shooting – they were just a bunch of animals! Bob was preoccupied with the other things he was doing. It was always like he would show up; he was always catching a train to be in a play somewhere, and on weekends he'd go to Exeter. Yet he always had plenty of energy. I know he was drinking in the evenings, but never at work – God knows, he didn't have enough time to drink between jobs! So it was like he wasn't there a lot. He was always on the run, but he always had plenty of energy. He was ambitious, but he didn't seem driven.'

Byrum explains the film's unexpected media attention. '*Inserts* is basically a dick-joke movie, and it's funny. It was just a tiny little movie and should have just gone into a couple of tiny little theatres. What happened was very simple, as these things usually are. Bertolucci was out of control – he was doing *1900* like it was Kurtz up the Khyber and he wasn't ready; it was a year overdue – and United Artists had booked all the theatres for it so they needed a picture for his dates. So all of a sudden *Inserts* opened in 800 theatres – this teeny art movie with the guy from *Jaws* in it. It was porno being played in what only should have been art houses in New York and Los Angeles. It was on Broadway in one of those 1200-seat houses with Dolby sound.

'When it was rated "X" I asked the censor why, because that meant commercial death, and he said there was nothing to cut; the whole thing was prurient! In Los Angeles you could advertise in the *Herald-Examiner* on the "X" page, so we had an ad between *Debbie Does Dallas* and *Barbara's Blowjob*. Dreyfuss and I went to the theatre the first night in Westwood, and we could see all these guys going in and we wanted to say to them. "Look, save your money – it ain't gonna happen! Take off the raincoat!" Of course they didn't go for it and the critics pissed all over it. They didn't like anybody, and what was offensive to them was the language – there was no fucking, really – and ideas.'

'I didn't feel like *Inserts* was showbiz – but it was *treated* like showbiz, and that was the lesson I learned. When you release a movie in a movie theatre, it's *showbiz*. You're being compared to *Star Wars*, James Bond, and *Jaws*. *They do not make allowances for your intentions*. That's a hard one to learn.

'Dreyfuss never mentions it now, although he championed it at the time. Bob never talks about it either.'

'Byrum created an atmosphere from the start,' Bob would tell the *Times* in March 1977. 'There are only five parts and the six of us became enmeshed immediately. An English director might have asked you to stand back and look at your work. Byrum never did that. He insisted on working at fever pitch the whole time. He taught me confidence in confusion. He'd stick me out on a limb and then push me off on to a totally different limb. "Do that! Now do it in reverse!" I think he knew precisely what he wanted' – though, of course Byrum claimed he didn't; it was only his first film – 'and was simply out for the right tensions. Certainly at the end of shooting everyone was exhausted and we could not have gone on any longer.'

In another interview five years later, while promoting another gangster role in the successful *Long Good Friday*, Bob would make a point of disassociating himself from *Inserts*. 'I got the part in *Inserts*,' he fibbed, 'because they couldn't afford Rod Steiger.' Quite a leap from Nicol Williamson. 'It was a lousy performance.' Not true. 'But nobody spotted that I wasn't American.'

'I just assumed Bob was what he was,' Byrum remarked. 'He's a very powerful presence. You meet a lot of actors and you think, my God, the camera is two-thirds of this guy's trip. But Bob would walk in the room and you just knew. He's like a blotter, sucking all the energy out of the room. It was fantastic to watch him. He's got that voice, and you just knew that this guy was a heavyweight. Because he's a little short balding guy you wouldn't expect him to be so squishy-soft inside like he is. In the last scene of *Inserts* he's almost crying. He's very sentimental, with a heart of mush, and it comes out in funny ways. Everyone felt very protective of him, and he exploits this. He was real congenial. I'm not saying he's too nice, because he's not, but there's a way to not invite any questions about yourself. And the way to do that is to be disarmingly pleasant and convivial, like a good-natured bartender. You don't ask him and you wouldn't know how and he doesn't leave you any openings. You almost feel they're putting you on the whole time.'

Although *Inserts* was too clever for its own good, it provided Bob with the prototype for the gangster character with the soft spot, which would, eventually, lead him on to success and accolades far beyond any of the wildest imaginings of a bootlegger named Big Mac.

8

TV, BBC, RSC

Edward Dowden, the critic, may have said that Touchstone is the daintiest fool of the comedies, but Bob Hoskins is not one actor normally associated with simpering refinement. 'I was an awful Touchstone, terrible,' Bob confessed. 'I don't think I get Shakespeare's gags. Tony Sher gets them and he's brilliant at them. I'm good at making the serious stuff a bit funny, but getting a laugh out of them gags is hard.'

'Touchstone is one of the unfunniest characters in the world,' said Colin Bennett, who was a member of the Oxford Playhouse Company in the spring and summer of 1975 with Bob, when they performed *As You Like It*, 'and here it was being played by one of the great comics in the world. Every night Bob would try to make it funny, he actually did as well as he could and had some good moments, but Touchstone is not a part that can be made a great deal of.'

From that hapless and thankfully shortlived role Bob threw himself into preparation for Bill Cracker in *Happy End*, the Chicago hood of 1919 whose 'tough exterior concealed a heart of stone'. He will be, nonetheless, seduced and 'saved' by Lieutenant Lillian Holiday (Hallelujah Lill). It is not the most succinctly conceived character and a difficult play. The second major collaboration of Bertolt Brecht and Kurt Weill fell flat; audiences arrived at Berlin's Schiffbauerdamm Theatre in 1929 expecting another *Threepenny Opera* and found instead a melodrama with songs.

Happy End had only been staged once before in England, a production at the Royal Court in 1965. With a new translation and adaptation by the American dramatist Michael Feingold, the Oxford Playhouse Company's director, Gordon McDougall, decided to have a go.

'We began rehearsing while on tour with *As You Like It*,' Colin

Bennett explained, 'so they were fairly fraught rehearsals. We were living in grotty digs, working in an extremely long play, and it was all a bit tough. We could only rehearse for three weeks, due to the tour. If only we could have afforded more time, although I must say the tendency at the big national companies is usually for too *much* rehearsal. Actors don't really know their parts till they're shown to an audience. The longer you work in a void the more it can affect your performance in the show, and actors must be a source of energy, to relate to the audience and to the other actors. But with *Happy End* we had a good director and a good cast.'

Bob had already cut his Brechtian teeth in *Man Is Man*, but Bill Cracker was a more demanding role, one many say is a precursor to Nathan Detroit in *Guys and Dolls*. For one, he has a solo number and for foghorn Bob to face the West End with the comic number 'The Song of the Tough Nut' – telling everyone never to get soft – took a lot of courage. 'Bob's singing was great singspeak, really,' said Bennett. 'When you're not really a singer, if you are focused and convey the *thought*, then the notes aren't as significant as they would be in another production. Under those circumstances Bob did a great job. And the *band* played the notes!*

The *Plays and Players* critic, David Zane Mairowitz, argued that this production 'takes *Happy End* on its most superficial terms and serves up *Guys and Dolls* after all. Relying on caricatures of American film gangsters [admittedly a trap set by Bob himself], there is no effort to turn them into potential lieutenants in the "army of the poor". This is especially true in the misconception of Bill Cracker as a Capone-type two-bit hood.'

Director McDougall protested this review several issues later. 'In its use of song for this dual role of release of latent emotional potential and deepening of character, *Happy End* is the first great musical, and its structure and style were very influential on many Broadway composers. . . . To suggest that the solution [to staging this play] is to seek out actors who are "slightly frayed at the edges" and who "never get soft" seems to me woolly thinking of the sort that Brecht would have thoroughly disapproved.'

So even if the play's text borders on the ridiculous, the songs are terrific . . . but in this case not terrific enough to pack them in at the Lyric.

Playing two American gangsters, one of them singing, in quick succession would try the patience and test the talent of any actor, especially if he's English, and Bob's next assignment took him back to the BBC where the end result would be as far removed from menacing toughies as Mother Goddam's Mandalay dive in *Happy End* is from a porcelain exhibit at the Victoria and Albert Museum. For once Bob was going to play an ordinary, contemporary Englishman. As Alf, the Cockney lorry driver, Bob was pretty much the stereotypical, good-natured yob. In fact he could have been any of Bob's less talented, intelligent, and fortunate schoolmates in Finsbury Park. Or Bob, for that matter, if Bob had not been so talented, intelligent, fortunate, and well-motivated. Alf, you see, can't read. 'If I can say it, why can't I read it?' he wonders. He made countless millions of viewers wonder too.

In 1973 it was estimated that two to three million adults in Britain needed help with reading and writing, and that there could be as many as ten million illiterates as well. The British Adult Literacy Campaign was launched to encourage people to come forward for help, so *On The Move* was conceived by the BBC's Further Education Department. In a series of fifty ten-minute skits which began showing in October 1975, using animation and vignettes, Bob and his co-star Donald Gee helped make TV viewers aware that illiteracy was so commonplace that it was nothing to be ashamed of or embarrassed about. A thoroughly sympathetic and likeable guy with long sideburns and awful taste in clothes jokes about football as well as his own disability. Bob was so convincing that many viewers wrote in offering to help teach him his ABCs, and many others who were perfectly capable of reading tuned in just for a laugh and a look at this adult version of *Sesame Street*.

'We knew it had to be a family show,' said producer David Stargreaves. 'Illiterates are frightened to admit they are not like other people. They have to bluff their way through life. So it had to be light, entertaining, with no teacher, and able to bring up points for discussion. We did a great deal of field work for the pilots.'

At first, he and comedy writer Barry Took had problems when they realized they weren't tackling the subject with the sensitivity it deserved. Once they had established the format of Alf and Bert driving across England in their large removal van, with pitstops in pubs and cafés, discussing the hows and whys (and why nots) in perfectly scripted, everyday conversational bantering, the series really hit home.

On The Move was so popular that it was succeeded the following autumn (without Bob or Donald, unfortunately) with a new series, called *Your Move*, for more advanced beginners, which won a BAFTA award as Best Special Programme of the year. A third series followed in 1979.

Bob was naturally pleased at the immense viewer response and the good it was doing. He has claimed that he'd already acted as a tutor back in his Covent Garden porter days, helping a seventy-two-year-old workmate. 'I began by writing the alphabet in rows across his fingers and he soon started to learn. It was a great triumph for us both when he finished [a book] after about six months.'

Bob made a few more television appearances over the next year: bit parts in the *Thriller* series, *To Kill Two Birds; Van der Valk*, the continuation of the 1972 series about a Dutch policeman that failed to reach the popularity of its predecessor; *The Crezz*, the soap opera that blew bubbles instead of sparks; *Three-Piece Suite*; and in two showings of *Omnibus*, the cultural documentary series. One was on Brecht; the other a more light-hearted edition in December 1976 called *The Story of Pantomime*. Playing the celebrated Regency clown, Grimaldi, famed for his on-stage appearances with pigs and geese in what you hope were copious pockets, Bob had a few problems with a piglet named Humphrey. 'He started squealing and kicking up a fuss as soon as I tried to put him in my pocket,' Bob said. 'I'm rather soft-hearted so I couldn't force him. . . . In the end I spent ages sitting around with him, getting to know him.' Poor Bob also had his finger bitten by an ungrateful goose named Tildie.

Luckily, he received an offer to join the Royal Shakespeare Company.

'I hesitated over that RSC invitation,' Bob said, 'but I was assured it was a nice family place once you forgot about the capital letters of the RS bit. So I had a go. I've always tried to do everything. I've never been to drama school, so I have to learn from others, and actors like John Wood and Norman Rodway are worth watching. My art is myself, and my pleasure comes from doing what I fancy at any given moment, whether it's cinema, Shakespeare, or being a clown in the circus.'

'I was quite insistent that Bob do roles with the RSC, and at the National,' said Sally Hope. 'You *need* to show how versatile you are.'

Whatever the reason, Bob spent the summer of 1976 in rep with the RSC: as Rocky in *The Iceman Cometh* (opening 25 May), the sergeant in *The Devil's Disciple* (opening 8 July), and Borkin in *Ivanov* (opening 2 September). If nothing else, it was an opportunity to improve as an actor while in the rarefied atmosphere of a national institution. He was working with friends like Ken Cranham, and he shared the stage with Patti Love, who would play a far more personal role in Bob's life a few years later. And in two of the three plays he was cast in roles that were suitable vehicles for his particular brand of look-at-me, Ma! talent.

'The past I have chosen is the one I know,' wrote Eugene O'Neill. 'I've tried to show the inmates of Harry Hope's saloon there with their dreams. . . . All I can say is that it is about pipe dreams. And the philosophy is that there is always one dream left, one final dream, no matter how low you have fallen, down there at the bottom of the bottle. I know, because I saw it.'

The Iceman is a very long play, filled with the dregs of society who congregate in Harry Hope's saloon to ward off their disillusionment, and it is demanding for the participants. Director Howard Davies described Bob to *Time Out*'s Steve Grant as 'an emotional black hole . . . the focus of the company. Funnily enough he never seemed to think he was of the same calibre as the rest of the actors – people like Ken Cranham and Ian Holm – but his performance was marvellous. He's a very humble and sensitive guy under all that hardness. And a great storyteller. In fact we sometimes had to tell him to shut up when he was starting on another story, but he never took it the wrong way.'

One critic wrote, 'Only Bob Hoskins as Rocky looks completely comfortable with the sense of *place*.' It *was* set in a bar, after all, and the lowlife booze-hounds were not all that different from Finsbury Park pub crawlers. Furthermore, O'Neill's anarchist/Syndicalist leanings were dear to Bob's heart.

'Bob is very attracted to the anarchist movement,' said T. P. McKenna, who starred as the Reverend Anderson in *The Devil's Disciple*. 'He often lectured me on the anarchic contructivist movement, and he was very eloquent about it. He'd seen a lot of that in the Paris student riots in 1968. And in the kibbutz he lived in he'd been exposed to anarchist ideas as well. The core of his philosophy about it was how keen he was on the small community and the self-governing.'

Collective farming would have been an idea close to the heart of the conniving, vodka-drinking prankster Mihail Mihailovich Borkin, steward to the estate of Ivanov. 'What I want to know is: are the workmen to be paid, or aren't they?' Borkin asks the moping Ivanov. 'Oh, what's the use of talking to you? Call themselves landowners, the devil take them! Rationalized farming! A thousand acres – and not a farthing in your pocket. It's like owning a wine cellar without a corkscrew.'

Chekhov's first play has its flaws – trying to construct a tragedy on the sympathetic portrait of a spineless neurotic – and the production had them as well. The brilliant John Wood was perhaps

62

miscast as the whingeing, much younger Ivanov; angel-faced Mia Farrow was too timid a Sasha. And, wrote critic Stephen Gilbert, 'David Jones's production has a central dilemma of its own. In due deference to Chekhov's youth when the play was written, Jones has rendered the stage a lively place, making of the dreadful Lebedev household a scene of high, almost zany, comedy. Bob Hoskins, though he can never quite escape suggesting the life of White Hart Lane's Paxton Road End, brings exuberance and athleticism to Borkin. . . .'

'Bob did talk a lot about his director in *Ivanov*,' said a friend and fellow actor. "Poor old David, he does try, doesn't he," Bob said. "He's done a lot of good work; he does try very hard." '

The play that was the most successful of the three, however, was the one in which Bob had the smallest part. *The Devil's Disciple* was, actually, a melodrama of soul-searching exposed hypocrisy and mistaken identity, and it became a huge hit, due mainly to Tom Conti's swaggering hero, Dick Dudgeon, who created a marvellous rapport with the audience and made the girls scream as if he were a rock star at Wembley Arena.

'Conti used to ogle the girls like there was no tomorrow,' explains McKenna, who saw it all.

Jack Gold, who had directed Bob in his bit part in *The National Health*, made a memorable debut as a stage director with this play. 'He has a very good visual sense,' says McKenna, 'and we had a magnificent set.

'The problem for Bob was, this was done in 1976 during the longest and hottest summer in living memory, or so it seemed to me, under unbelievable skies. And Bob was in uniform, wearing a very heavy red coat and white trousers with high black boots and all the accoutrements, and he had to stand at attention in all that heat. We shared a dressing room and he'd come backstage after one of his scenes and shout, "Fucking cunt show!!" as he'd kick off his boots.

'So we invested early on in an ice bucket, because we both drink vodka, and we'd smuggle in the ice in plastic bags, packed into a briefcase.

'The sergeant is not really an ideal part for Bob. Shaw, you see, is concerned with ideas, the nature of good and evil – which is why the play has this title – with women's romanticism, with the Puritan ethic in America. And his speeches are endless. I had a ferocious part as a preacher-turned-burglar. And Shaw is not so good at writing for women. My "wife" is a real bitch of a part. Luckily Estelle Kohler played it; she's a marvellous instinctive actress.'

'The play was a great deal of fun,' says Kohler, 'although I didn't actually love Judith Anderson that much because she is so serious while all the men are having the fun. Bob's role was very small. It certainly is the most humorous, and I remember it as being extremely funny. Bob seems to arrive at something very instinctively, very quickly; he doesn't seem to have to struggle. It's such an enviable thing because others of us have to dig around. But that's the joy of acting as well.'

McKenna, however, had his doubts about the performance which stole the show: 'The ideal actor to demonstrate knowledge about how *not* to play a Shavian character is Tom Conti. With Shaw you don't act *between* the lines. John Wood, a superb technician, was interrupted by Tom's machine-gun delivery, and John's lines would be ruined. There Conti was, ogling the performers and the audience with those Jack Benny-type muggings for a cheap laugh. Of course the audiences loved him and the critics didn't know the difference. It was like top-class tennis, when you're playing long volleys. If you constantly play drop-shots there are no long volleys. Conti plays the drop shot and no net.

'Nor did he socialize with the rest of the cast,' McKenna continues. 'We all know the Scots are famous for their parsimony, but, well, Tom bought a chain from the hardware store and he'd lock up the handle of his transistor radio and the electric kettle in his dressing room. Now these items do tend to disappear, but we all fell about laughing.'

Those summer months with such a company had been a shrewd professional move for Bob. Whatever his initial doubts about fitting in, he had proven his versatility after all.

Estelle Kohler explained the value of the experience: 'It gives you a huge basis, a wonderful skeleton for the rest of your life, with *language*. If you can deal with that, conquer Shakespeare and the classics and have that and your *own* language, I don't know if things can scare you much afterwards!'

By the time the RSC season wound to a close all was not well on the home front. Bob and Jane's marriage, a meeting of two highly intelligent and creative people with dominant personalities, had been problematic from the start. They had had the dual pressures of poverty and a handicapped child. Despite his delight in his children, Bob was hardly the model father, and like many people who are all for 'just causes', the needs of those who love them most tend to be overlooked. For one thing, Bob was rarely home; commuting back to Exeter at weekends or when he was off work may have been satisfactory to him but was immensely frustrating for Jane. She still needed to spend several hours with Alex every day in exhausting physical therapy, as well as having a lively four-year-old daughter to look after. For another, Bob liked the ladies and his liquor, and his erratic schedule in London undoubtedly served as a handy alibi for extracurricular dalliances. So did the nearly unarguable excuse, 'I have to work' – which gave him a useful escape route from the responsibilities of everyday family life.

'Once Bob told me Jane was coming up from Exeter and I had never seen him so rattled,' said McKenna. 'He almost completely lost his composure. It was very interesting. He invited me for supper but I didn't want to stay because I didn't think Jane would have appreciated me, but Bob's eyes were pleading, like a child, as if to say, "Don't leave me alone with her." But Bob at that time would screw anything. He would screw in the wings between scenes, when he was in *The Iceman*. I couldn't manage that even in my heyday and I was green with envy!'

A wife could hardly regard such activities with the same bemused indulgence. 'He always had to have two people – a foot in each camp,' said Jane. 'So then if life becomes too intolerable, he has somewhere to go.'

As Bob occupied himself with whatever television work he could find, the troubled Hoskins marriage went from rough to untenable, and under all the pressure, the doubts and delusions, mostly about himself, Bob cracked. 'I had a nervous breakdown,' he said. 'I was under a psychiatrist and everything. It was hell.'

'He was in a bad way,' says Sally Hope, 'so we shipped him off to a doctor. And then I got him the very small part of Johnny Britain in two episodes of *Rock Follies*.' The series was about three young rock'n'rollers – Julie Covington, Rula Lenska, and Charlotte Cornwell – and incorporated fantasy sequences of musical numbers with the plots themselves. It won a BAFTA Award as Best Drama Series of 1977. (Its format, mixing fact and fiction, would be seized upon by the audacious mind of Dennis Potter and soon give Bob the role of a lifetime.) 'It was shot from 15 February 1977 to 11 March. It was not the kind of part he normally played, but I thought it would be a good thing to do to get his confidence back.'

Bob has since scoffed at shrinks. 'I went for psychoanalysis and all I learned was how expensive it is,' he said. 'They gave me some tranquillizers but they made me feel dizzy so I said to hell with that. I know too many actors who get hooked on tablets because they get all hyped up for the night's performance, then they can't sleep so they take those things and get addicted.'

He found work a much more effective drug than any prescribed by his doctor, and his spirits were buoyed no end later in March, when one of his plays, *Dog's Dinner*, was chosen to be staged by the prestigious Cambridge Theatre Company under the direction of Jonathan Lynn. Bob had been scribbling poetry and stories since he was a youngster. He began writing in earnest – short, funny skits – in collaboration with Ken Campbell, and continued on his own after he left the Road Show, using the nom de plume of Robert Williams.

'I came home a bit sloshed one evening,' Bob related, 'and wrote this play overnight. A mate came round in the morning and started reading it. "'Oo wrote this shit," he said. "Er, Robert Williams," I said. I wrote as Robert Williams for ages. I don't want to admit I'm responsible in case it's a load of rubbish!'

A pen name is, of course, an easy way to adopt yet another façade behind which one can hide, so is playwright Williams really the same person as actor Hoskins?

In 1970 Bob wrote *Sunday with the Family*, clearly inspired by *The Homecoming*. His colloquial dialogue was even more convincing in *Onions*, the saga of two charmless gits named Spud and Whistle. There was *Rubber Love*, about one man's affair with his blow-up doll; and *All for the Nation*, an extended skit about a dole office that bears a close resemblance to Dr Frankenstein's laboratory. (It would be performed at the National Theatre in 1984.) And even if Bob's early attempts failed as cohesive or entertaining plays, it was certainly with no small amount of talent and courage that Bob tried to tackle the medium and kept at it even as his fame as an actor grew.

He has also said: 'I write very quickly to get rid of it. It would never be a full-time career. It's too lonely.' His wife Jane, the former drama teacher, would help him to polish and edit the scripts. *Dog's Dinner* was by far the most accomplished of Bob's efforts thus far. It took the basic premise of Ken Campbell's *The Man Who Tossed Himself Off* – an attempted suicide aided and abetted by some tramps – but expanded it into an extremely funny meditation on the value of life.

It opens with Charles Dobson, a city gent, peeping (or 'blimping', as the tramps call it) from a derelict building at two lovers in a nearby flat. The floors suddenly give way and Charles falls down to the cellar, bringing the house down unceremoniously on the head of poor Barney, who lives there. Dobson survives with a nasty gash on his forehead and sprained ankles, but all he wants is to die, having already botched several suicide attempts. Barney is horrified, until

Dobson offers all his worldly possessions in exchange for a little murderous help. The tramps then decide to give him a 'send-off'. But when Dobson understands that a send-off means an evening of cannibalism, he begins to have second thoughts. Once he is convinced, however, that suicide is a 'mortal sin' and that unless he finds a method of atonement he will suffer eternity as a 'tree in torment', Dobson opts for a final act of martyrdom. He decides to be crucified. A gigantic support strut from the collapsed house is set up in the toilet; Dobson is tied on, crowned with a ring of dandelions, and sent off with the lovely hymn, 'Jesus Wants Me for a Sunbeam'. But there's a twist. (Hoskins had learned his Road Show lessons well.) The entire house collapses and everyone dies . . . except Dobson.

'Bob was writing the play incognito,' said Edward Petherbridge, who starred as Dobson, 'but we all knew it was him because he kept turning up at rehearsals. He came in at least three or four times, which is not really all that often, but he found it all so amusing and intensely delightful. He was like a child at his own birthday party.

'I was invited to do it by the director, Jonathan Lynn. There was obviously no money involved. One does it for art,' he laughed. 'It was an interesting part and play, even if it was slightly depressing to do and difficult in parts. It was a marvellous set. As my effigy fell those three floors, I would hurriedly nip down to the basement amidst a great deal of theatrical smoke, and I'd have to crawl so when the dust cleared there I was with a nail up my nostril. It was meant to be done precisely but can't be, but it was well worth it for the effort. I had to hobble around with two sprained ankles, which was like walking on pointed elbows. Acting *has* taken its toll!

'On Easter weekend we played in Harlow New Town, outside London, which is not famed as a mecca of culture. But when we went on that evening the audience was so lively and enjoyed it and had a good time. Actors can always tell on these occasions when a play feels exciting. I do believe I am the only actor to be crucified on Good Friday in Harlow New Town.'

Jonathan Lynn wrote in the Cambridge Theatre Company's hundredth production brochure: 'We were able to cause a stir with a play by Bob Hoskins. The press weren't wild about the play, perhaps because the amazing settings of the three-storey house which collapses at the end of Act Two upstaged the play itself.' Or perhaps, as one critic put it, because, 'It remains a series of slightly sick but very funny jokes.'

Equally strange was Bob's second play to be staged that year, this time at the Soho Poly from 18 to 30 April, and directed by the late, great Verity Bargate. It was based on a small story in a newspaper. A Miss Carol Hormer died from an internal haemorrhage; a man who lived at the same address died four months later, evidently of starvation. From that gruesome and unexplained true story, and, like *Dog's Dinner* using blimping as a central theme, *The Bystander* by Robert Williams was shaped.

Mr Grant is a lonely, solitary office worker who talks to his plants and is in love with Carol. He spies on her through a hole in the wall, watching her every move – not in a salacious way, but out of devotion. And as Carol's life begins to fall apart and her boyfriend deserts her while she is pregnant, Grant deteriorates as well. Bob described him as having a 'certain nervous lightness about him; a brave face that covers an underlying hysteria. He is calm but one is aware he is very close to the edge. A man conscious of invisible ghosts.' Perhaps like Bob himself. Grant loses his job and then watches in horror as Carol has an abortion, like the one he'd seen his own mother have, and he feels closer to her than ever before: he is the 'unknown bystander to her life'. But she bleeds to death and he dies not long after of melancholia.

It is a one-man tour de force, Grant touching and terrifying in his tormented isolation. He was Bob's first fully realized and sympathetic character. 'When you're writing you have to think about characters,' said Jane Hoskins. 'Bob did talk out the role in *The Bystander*, and I helped him write and edit it.'

Bob has, quite often, told of how he had his nervous breakdown at this time. 'My biggest problem was that I couldn't take the joy in people. I was a sad little feller. It was the worst time of my life. The person who got me out of it was Verity. After I'd been to Harley Street, I'd go over to see Verity and have a jar and a chat, and she said, "You're wasting all your best plots giving them to your psychiatrist. Put them on stage."' That way he could have his nervous breakdown in public and the performances would act as catharsis. Maybe they'd even make some money out of it. Work was always the best therapy for Bob, after all. 'Anyway,' he continued, 'I wrote this one-man play called *The Bystander*, about a guy who sort of disintegrated. And I got it together.'

The only discrepancy with this story is that Bob had written *The Bystander* two years before – in 1975. Nevertheless, his mental state was still precarious, and on the opening night he felt he couldn't go on. 'I was terrified because I was exposing so much of my inner self,' he said. He ran from the theatre out to Regent's Park and had a long involved discussion about the meaning of life with the ducks in the pond. Verity was hot on his heels. 'Not one of those fucking ducks has bought a ticket, and there are a dozen people who have, and they're getting impatient,' she reportedly told him. 'So get your arse in there now.' Bob got his arse back in. 'By the end of the show I'd beaten the breakdown,' he related. 'It just broke. It was like my ears popping and I just came out of the breakdown and that awful feeling of grief.'

Why has Bob felt the need to fudge the dates of his breakdown so that in timely B-movie fashion it coincided with the debut of his play at the Soho Poly? His life and work have unquestionably been melodramatic enough without exaggeration. 'Frankly,' said Sally Hope, '*The Bystander* was *not* what precipitated his crack up. It was part and parcel of getting *over* it.'

'Bob claimed he went to a psychiatrist at the time,' said Jane, 'but I think he was looking at the character for *The Bystander*, and the breakdown he had was related to that character. He used to say that he wouldn't go to a therapist because he might lose his abilities as an actor.'

Certainly the after-effects of a breakdown do not disappear overnight, and the problems with the Hoskins marriage had not been resolved in any satisfactory way, although the divorce itself did not take place until years later. Bob spent most of his time in London, as ever, with weekends or time off spent in Exeter with the children. He was not denied access to them in any way. The real crisis with his marriage was still to come.

But the intensity and concentration demanded by the play and its depressing subject matter would make even the most stable and well-adjusted male feel like locking himself in the loony bin. How ironic and even self-defeating for Bob to draw attention to a pre-existing situation and in the process denigrate his own astonishing ability to pull off a major one-man stage achievement.

In the long run, however, what is most important about this period of Bob's life is that the breakdown, whenever it was and however long it lasted, liberated something deep inside his pysche. 'Bob talked about having broken down at a certain point in time,' said A Martinez, one of Bob's co-stars in *The Honorary Consul*, 'of how he lost control of himself, but in that breakdown was the key to freeing up his talent.'

Bob remained busy with television work after his play finished its run: a small role in *In the Looking Glass* in May, and then playing the lead in *Napoleon* for BBC Bristol in June. It's a part he's never talked about; at least he was cast to *physical* type. His next role on stage would have him playing a type he knew very well indeed.

'Emile Durkheim said that we are all murderers and prostitutes,' playwright Snoo Wilson once said in an interview. 'I'm interested in crime because it relates to our ideas about property. As soon as you own something you're in a position of being robbed of it. That means someone is at potential war with you.'

Those someones could easily have been the Kray twins, Reggie and Ronnie, who rose out of the East End and ruled their kingdom until they were brought down by a myth of their own making. Snoo and rock musician Kevin Coyne took this history/myth and twisted it into a sadly short-lived musical with twenty original songs. *England, England*, performed by the Bush Company at the Jeanetta Cochrane Theatre, opened at the beginning of August 1977.

'At the heart of the twins' extraordinary and ultimately doomed career lay one important fact which will mark them out from other murderers and gangsters,' wrote John Pearson in his biography of the Krays, *The Profession of Violence*. 'In essence they were not ordinary criminals but criminal performers, consciously acting out the crazy drama of their lives. The East End was their audience, the members of "The Firm" were their supporting cast, and the celebrities and public figures they befriended helped confer a sort of glamour on their lives . . . even the murders they committed were essentially dramatic acts.'

With such a potent brew it was a shame the play did not succeed, especially with Bob as Jake (Ronnie) and Brian Hall, who was well-known to the real Firm, as Jim (Reggie). According to jail-free brother Charlie Kray, Brian was a 'nice lad'. 'I've told Ronnie and Reggie about the play,' Charlie said at the time of its staging. 'They didn't mind and I plan to come along and see it.'

Bob had known of Finsbury Park criminality, of course, and had played criminals before, too, but Bill Cracker or Big Mac or Beaujo in *Geography of a Horse Dreamer* were hardly more than scurrying ants to be squashed under Ronnie Kray's highly polished shoes.

Steve Grant described the time Bob lost his temper while rehearsing: 'There were continual noises and off-stage interruptions caused by a group of builders and technicians. Director Dusty Hughes finally remonstrated with the noise-makers. There were chortles from the circle – and then it happened. Hoskins, already primed for his role as the man who calmly walked into the Blind Beggar pub in Whitechapel and shot George Cornell in the head at point-blank range, suddenly lost his temper. "What do you think you're playing at, you cunts? I'll fucking have you!! What are you fucking well laughing at?!" Silence. All around Hoskins was an almost visible force-field of sheer naked aggression. . . . Yes, I thought, this really could be Ronald Kray.'

'Bob was hired because he's a very strong actor, from Finsbury Park, and could sing – and he's got very quick access to very straightforward emotions and can magnify them,' Snoo says. 'I don't remember having any trouble making him get that across. In a number of scenes Ronnie loses his marbles and Bob rose admirably to the challenge of playing somebody over the edge. He has a consummate skill at that kind of thing and he was a joy to work with.'

'Jim and Jake,' wrote one critic, were 'above all, inevitably Cockneys – two sentimental, illogical, unscrupulous, extremely large Cockneys.' Easy enough for Bob to play, especially the sentimental bit, although it was harder to appear immense when you're built like a fireplug.

'As far as criminals go, they were both bad, but they're our gift to civilization,' Snoo says sardonically. 'People thought that *England, England* glorified the Krays, but what they failed to realize was that they weren't big villains like Hitler but small ones striving to be English gentlemen.

'We got a telegram on opening night: "Good Luck from the Krays." They thought it was going to be recognized, but it turned out the wrong way. It was under-rehearsed – Bob and I always said we'd do it properly some day – and we got a ticking off by the press. At the time, this musical was about a taboo subject – and it was simply not on to treat villains as real people. Given all the confusion about stars and showbiz, I tried to make it a warm-hearted, understanding portrait of why people fall from grace.'

The failure of *England, England* may have been depressing and frustrating at the time, but secretly Bob could not have been too disheartened, for if he had been committed to the play it might have prevented him from playing a character whose fall from grace would change his career for ever. And nothing was going to stop those pennies from heaven from raining on Bob's parade.

9

Someplace Where the Song Is for Real

Arthur Parker, what a role. A sleazy, naughty, vulgar, and shamelessly pathetic lout of a song salesman, with sex on the brain and a cheap lyric on, as creator Dennis Potter put it, his 'soft and squelchy' heart. But – and what a big *but* it was – his banality was tinged with an underlying unquenchable need to be needed, a desperation fuelled not only by sexual despair but by the inescapable knowledge that the dreams he lived and breathed would not come true, at least in this lifetime. Bob Hoskins *made* Arthur Parker human, made him sentimental without veering into the maudlin, made him an object of pity rather than scorn even as the lies poured from his lips. And in doing so, Bob Hoskins made himself a household name.

Arthur Parker's creator, Dennis Potter, is arguably television's best playwright. It was while working in 1969 on *Moonlight on the Highway* for Independent Kestrel Productions, set up by Kenith Trodd, who would become his partner in Pennies from Heaven Productions, that Potter first tackled the importance of popular music in everyday lives. *Moonlight*'s hero was Al Bowlly, the velvet-voiced crooner who perished in the Blitz. The soundtrack of Bowlly songs shaped the action of the programme as much as his lyrics did.

'I write dramas as opposed to essays about beliefs,' Potter said, 'because I think we see the world in terms of metaphor and images.' And what more potent images than the often banal, rhyming lyrics of the popular music of the thirties that reverberated like jungle tom-toms for millions of ordinary people during the Depression; enjoyed by those who had little fortune to anticipate and few hopes to cherish. From thinking about a play on Bowlly, Potter began to write his most ambitious work yet – about the *music*, not the singer – a 'play in six parts with music'. His leading man would not be a romantic hero like these tuxedo-clad dispensers of savoir-faire portrayed in the Hollywood musicals of the 1930s. Arthur Parker would be a skunk, yet one whose yearning for what was inexpressible beyond the triteness of 'Down Sunnyside Lane' made him utterly sympathetic.

'It was the nature of the songs which interested me,' Potter said, 'their sweetness, their banality, their sugariness . . . and yet they have this tremendous evocative power . . . which is much more than nostalgia.' In an interview shown on *Arena*, Potter also said, 'The songs he was peddling were in a direct line of descent from the Psalms. They were saying, no matter how cheap or banal or syrupy or syncopated, that the world is larger than it is . . . the world is better than this. Arthur Parker believed in them and that was his tragedy.' In the novelization, released to coincide with the MGM version of *Pennies* in 1981, Potter wrote: 'Arthur hoped against hope that somehow, someplace, *everything* was going to work out *all right*. Around the next corner, or the one after that, the cruel and misshapen old world was going to put on its dancing shoes.'

Poor old Arthur was in for a big surprise! So were viewers. Potter had found the perfect method of incorporating his fascination with the music of the thirties with his portrayal of the paltry lives of his imagined characters. It was the first drama ever to be written around pre-exisiting songs. They, as Potter explained in his script, 'step sideways into another convention. . . . In the "real" story, the people are well and truly *this* side of the rainbow, earthbound and troubled, but the action regularly zooms off to the other side of the rainbow – to the land of song, of dream or of Arthur's inner life.'

The catch was, of course, that these characters 'mimed' to the original songs, even if they happened to be sung by a member of the opposite sex. Who can forget Bob's opening number: his frigid wife Joanie (Gemma Craven), who never wants a 'bit of the other', rejects his advances and he bursts into Elyse Carlisle's 'The Clouds Will Soon Roll By'. That device made *Pennies*, as Potter himself wrote, 'a genuine period musical, lovingly recreating, as well as obliquely commenting upon, the marvellous old musical picture zest, style, panache, dream'.

The basic storyline of *Pennies* sounds simple: hopeless romantic Arthur, married to hopeless middle-class prig, falls in love with repressed schoolmarm Eileen Everson (Cheryl Campbell). She returns his affection but unfortunately becomes pregnant. Arthur, the cad, abandons her and she leaves her Forest of Dean home for the bright lights of London, only to find that no work is available. She becomes a prostitute, and good at the game as well.

Meanwhile, Arthur has convinced Joan to subsidize one of his dreams – his own sheet-music shop – yet it's not a success. When Arthur spots Eileen in a pub, they smash up his shop and run away together, supporting themselves on her illicit earnings. But the enigmatic Accordion Man (Ken Colley), who has touched all their lives in a seemingly random yet unforgettable manner, has killed a beautiful young blind girl whom Arthur had also seen (and fancied). Circumstantial evidence (and his wife's confession that he is a 'sex maniac') lead the police to Arthur. He is tried, falsely convicted, and hanged. At the moment of the hanging, Eileen drowns herself in the Thames. Cut to the little bouncing ball over the lyrics of 'In the Dark', and then, inexplicably, Arthur and Eileen are reunited on Hammersmith Bridge. After all that, they couldn't let the viewer switch off the set without a happy ending. 'The song has ended, but the melody lingers on,' they say in unison. Strike up 'The Glory of Love'. Roll the credits. Run off together into the sunrise.

As the script for *Pennies* took its final shape, producer Trodd remembered one evening spent in the Royal Court several years before. He remembered a greased-up, blustering electrician who'd held his own against the incomparable Sir Geoffrey Kendle. And he remembered seeing the same actor in *On the Move*, where the Alf that he played was as sweet as Bernie the Volt was brash. Bob Hoskins was invited to audition.

'I turned that part down about three times,' Bob said in a hyperbolic interview a few years after *Pennies* was first shown. Actor Hywel Bennett had originally been offered the part and turned it down due to scheduling conflicts. 'I was doing a television series and a musical at the same time, and these guys gave me about nine hours of script. I said, "You've got to be kidding, that's a month's reading." I just took it home, put it in the middle of the room, and kind of kicked it. Then the director, Piers Haggard, told me to read three scenes. When I read them, I realized how good it was. I stayed up all night reading. The next day I gave the audition of my life. If they had turned me down, I would have jumped out of the window. It was a great part. It had humour, humiliation, weakness, strength. Everything. Arthur Parker is everybody.'

And so dark-horse Hoskins became Arthur Parker. Producer Trodd told Steve Grant that 'Hoskins told a lengthy anecdote about a couple in a bedsitter [a scene from *The Bystander*] and he was so incredibly natural that he won everyone over.'

'You can't play Arthur Parker if you want people to like him,' Bob told John Powers of *L.A. Weekly*. 'The point about Arthur

74

is that one minute you hate him, the next you loathe him, the next minute you feel sorry for him, and the next minute you love him. Arthur's like *all* the characters – they all switch and change.'

'I played a lot of myself in *Pennies*,' Bob told *The Face* in 1985. 'I'd had a nervous breakdown just before that. I got a divorce.' He hadn't yet, although he and Jane were separated and he went to Exeter only to see his children and when he could squeeze in the time. 'The point is that by the time I got to *Pennies* . . . I knew what a man in that state is like. It wasn't an easy part to play, but I knew where I was coming from. Because most of Arthur Parker was *pain*.'

'Arthur is oversexed, overimaginative, and undercourageous,' Bob also said. 'As soon as I read the script I knew playing him would be painful, for there are things about Arthur that no man wants to admit. He has sexual fantasies, he's weak, he's a fool – a terrible fool – and a lovable loony. To play him honestly I knew I'd have to find these things in me. We're not unalike. If I'd been repressed as I grew up, I'd have turned out like him.'

Less melodramatic was a revealing comment made by Bob to reporter Ivan Waterman in April 1978, as *Pennies* ended its run, one in which he actually admitted his flair for a little mendacity, and one in which he hinted all was not well with his marriage: 'Before I met Jane I was a bit of a rolling stone like Arthur,' Bob confessed. 'If a bird . . . was looking for a bit of adventure, then she'd get it from me. And like Arthur I told them whoppers all the time. The difficult bit of playing him was showing bits of yourself you don't want to show. The weakness, foolishness, and cowardice. I was hell to live with, because I was so much into him. But my wife just turned a blind eye and let me get on with it.'

It isn't hard to turn a blind eye, of course, if the man in question is hardly around.

Whatever the depressing reality of Bob's private life in the summer of 1977, his professional life couldn't have been more exhilarating. Filming *Pennies* took from 26 August 1977 to 30 March 1978. Spencer Banks, who played Eileen's younger brother, described rehearsals.

'Potter was at the read-through, which was mammoth, because we read all six episodes – bypassing the songs – at once. We were in the Acton rehearsal rooms – the Acton Hilton, we called it – and it was just like going into a sort of village hall, really, because the chairs were laid out in sort of audience rows, and there was a top table where Piers [Haggard] was standing or sitting with Dennis.

Then Piers gave us a preamble on the overall structure. I remember Gemma [Craven] arriving at the very last minute and sidling up to me and whispering, "How far have we got?" Then with absolutely no preparation, off we went. It was phenomenal.

'I also vividly remember Bob saying, "If I don't score after this, I'm going to jack it all in." And he said that more than once. Something else that Bob used to say during rehearsals was that his mother would love it. She'd just love it! So we used to tease him that when he picked up his BAFTA, or whatever, that's what he would say. He'd laugh and say, "That's not a bad idea."

'There's an expression you hear in the business: It has a flavour to it. When we were doing *Pennies* we all kept thinking, maybe it's going to be something special. Usually that's the kiss of death – if the pros love it, the public will hate it! Or it becomes indulgent and maybe doesn't score. But because it was so original, especially for a television drama, as Potter's work always is, there was a different feeling in the cast that was like electricity. It just gets passed around. For the months we were making *Pennies* there was a constant charge of excitement.

'I've always found Piers delightful to work with. He is demanding only because he knows precisely what he wants and he won't stop until he gets it. I remember particularly a scene we started shooting at nine-thirty at night, and Bob and Cheryl had been at it since dawn. You would think anyone would say, "Why can't we call it a day?" But Piers will always press on.

'Bob and Cheryl were living and breathing the show fourteen to fifteen hours a day: it must have been mind-boggling for Bob, I should imagine, especially playing this Everyman . . . the energy it demanded!'

Another sapper of energy was the dancing. Of all the principals only Gemma Craven had had any professional dance training. Luckily, Tudor Davies had been hired as choreographer, and he turned a bunch of heavy-footed thespians into passable hoofers. 'Tudor is the closest thing to genius I have ever met,' Bob said. 'He convinced me that I looked like Fred Astaire. And I never doubted it. But when I saw the film I was so ashamed. I thought I looked like a little hippopotamus shaking its hooves.'

'I'd had no training in singing or dancing,' Spencer said, 'and that he got performances out of all us was stunning. He stitched it all together. He always maintained that if you have enough bravado and actually believe in what you're doing, you'll get away with it. That's how he pulled it off. It was great fun to do. We all had cassettes which we took home with us so we could rehearse.

76

'Our big scene with Bob in the Forest of Dean – we're about to do a number on Arthur because we've caught him with Eileen – was full of menace as we walk towards him, then the music strikes up and off we go. They actually built the glade because the space in the Forest of Dean didn't fit requirements, and I remember a family, after a quiet country walk, appearing over the brow of one of the hills. They could obviously hear the music on the playback and see the lights. To emerge into this glade, which had just appeared out of nowhere, and see us all jumping around must have been shocking!

'The first time we did the scene – we had deliberately kept Bob out of rehearsal – he just fell about laughing. It was wonderful.

'One of the most endearing scenes, also shot in the Forest of Dean, was in Potter's actual junior school, with all those wonderful little English faces of the schoolchildren at their desks, breaking into song. There was a hell of a row when they got a hold of the script, as you can imagine!' By then, thankfully, the shooting was already over.

'Most of the burden of *Pennies* was on Bob's shoulders,' said Ken Colley, 'the pace, always keeping it alive. Those songs about America, the Depression, the endless roads, this longing for something you can't quite find – Bob summed it up perfectly. What is so marvellous is how Bob reacts. A great deal of acting *is* reacting to what somebody else is doing. And a lot of actors act *at* you. Bob plays *to* you, and that's all the difference. It's so important, whatever you do. And he's exciting because you know he's going to do *something*, but you don't know what it's going to be. Nothing you're going to do is going to phase him. He'll take it. There's this presence, and his great humour – it's so black – but there's not a negative thing in him; it's all positive. This is Bob's great skill – to seem as if you just came off the street. You don't see the actor; you just see this person from the street. But of course it is all an illusion. So much of the best acting is not slogging out to the best expectations, but *confounding* those expectations.'

Without doubt Bob's seemingly effortless illusion as an actor in *Pennies* was due to the skill and direction of Piers Haggard. 'Playing Arthur wasn't as easy as Bob wanted to admit,' Sally Hopes explained, 'and Bob had a very difficult time at first. Piers is a perfectionist at film technique whereas Bob works so instinctively. He *needs* a strong director.'

'Sometimes,' said Spencer, 'a role comes along that fits a person like a glove, and *Pennies* was one of those cases for Bob. There are certain people that, when they're on the screen, whoever they are

77

you can't take your eyes off them. Bob is like that. He's going to be the one you're going to watch, just because of the sheer power of the guy. Maybe it's a little bit of a cliché to say that, but Bob's talent is totally natural, and understated. You can't just say, "I'm going to make you an actor." That spark, the natural instinct . . . you simply can't teach it.'

Bob's activities even before filming had finished managed to create headlines. One read: 'Pennies Star Bob Gives Nude Scene Peeper a Pounding.' It seems that word had got round the BBC that Gemma would be baring more than usual and so a few undesirable blimpers wormed their way on to the set. A furious Bob struck a particularly stubborn intruder. He also threatened another by threatening to slice his ears off. 'Bob is good at handling tough situations,' said Trodd. 'He's a mature little number.'

By the end of the nearly eight-month shoot, everyone was exhausted, especially Bob and Cheryl, and the cast fully enjoyed their huge party. They deserved it. 'I think if I hadn't had [a breakdown] before,' Bob said, 'I would have had one afterwards.'

'It was a kind of breakthrough in television – they'd never *seen* television like this before,' he also said. 'And a very big break-through for me, to perform this mixed-media kind of stuff. . . . And all these schmaltzy songs were part of a heavy, black theme. It was an extraordinary conception.'

The series provoked an immediate response from the twelve million people who tuned in to the BBC for the first of the six one-and-a-half hour episodes beginning on 7 March 1977.

'You've only got to say Dennis Potter and the pens are out before it's even started,' said Spencer. 'I wasn't surprised that people felt so strongly, because Potter's stuff is nearly always controversial. I fear he gets attacked for the wrong reasons, and people seem to totally miss the point. There will always be the Mary Whitehouse school of thought. People will say it was very original, or they'll say they hated it.'

While nearly all the critics praised the acting, talent, and ambitious scope of *Pennies*, reviews of the piece were mixed. The programme was undeniably long, and some of the musical sequences did seem to be slotted in more for reasons of Potter's personal taste than to move the plot along or shed light on a character; it is also true that the miming loses its novelty after a few episodes. Some felt uneasy with the mixed genres as it changed from a domestic comedy to something much, much blacker. Arthur and Eileen 'were in fact a pretty disagreeable pair bound together by some similarity in themselves,' wrote critic Dilys

Powell. 'But also [bound] by something like love. It is a measure of Mr Potter's skill that one still felt for them.'

Others railed against the fairy-tale ending. It was confusing – had Eileen really committed suicide? Why did Arthur show up at her side? Was it an author's cop-out? Philip Purser, in an essay on Potter's work, explained it this way: 'It is, of course, an old dramatic get-out, used by John Gay in the original *Beggar's Opera* long before the Brecht version, by Anouilh in *L'Alouette*, and . . . in the movie *Cat Ballou*. The author shifts into the Great Key and the players step away from the scoffold. Why not?' Why not indeed?

'The genius of the controversial Potter, with producer Trodd and director Haggard, has wondrously created what may be a new art form,' wrote James Murray, 'a magical welding together of popular music, trenchant humour, high drama, and all the tricks of television technology. It's all so refreshing I think it will galvanize the whole country.'

'Slighty-below-par Potter – i.e. it was pretty good,' said Martin Amis. 'Arthur Parker is played with unflagging, nonspecific vehemence by the excellent Bob Hoskins.'

'Bob Hoskins gives a wonderfully subtle performance,' wrote Hazel Holt, 'every nuance of which commits us to caring what becomes of this yearning, child-like soul. Arthur is one of Mr Potter's most moving creations.'

Pennies from Heaven won two BAFTA Awards and the British Press Guild Television Award for Most Original Contribution to Television. Bob did not, however, get his chance to tell the world how much his mum loved *Pennies*.

Pennies had a resounding and lingering impact. One rather unwelcome repercussion for Bob was that he was occasionally attacked in the street by people mistaking him for Arthur. More welcome was an LP containing sixteen of the sixty original tracks heard in the programme, which sold over 75,000 copies and reached number ten in the LP charts; its popularity led to the release of a second album with eighteen more tracks.

Potter and Pennies from Heaven Ltd would go on to buy the rights back from the BBC for £50,000, and claim half the profits (if any) from the eventual MGM Hollywood version, for which he wrote the screenplay, on the condition that the original *Pennies* never be shown again on the screen for which it was intended. Or anywhere else. When the National Film Theatre planned a Potter retrospective in 1980, *Pennies* was banned. Potter was nonplussed. 'Quite honestly,' he said, 'I can't imagine anyone wanting to go and see it anyway – three men and a dog, perhaps.'

Bob's reaction years later is typically over the top: 'We all had a go about that [the rights being sold] and everybody was really pissed off. It's like eight months of my life down the pan.'

It seemed that three men and a dog represented the film critics in America, whose reactions to the Hollywood version of this series were violent. Bob *would* have been a much better Arthur Parker than comedian Steve Martin, who co-starred with Jessica Harper (Bob's co-star in *Inserts*) as Joan, and Bernadette Peters as a sensual Eileen. The action was transposed to Illinois, and the intimacy of the television version and the engaging maladroitness of its performers were swallowed by the big screen. 'In the end,' said one review, 'Potter seems to have spent a great deal of money [$19 million] in order to say very little, but like many of the songs it contains it is certainly hard to get the damned thing out of your head.'

Arthur Parker would remain one of the best performances of Bob's career. And he was the character closest to Bob in every form of emotion and experience, the man ruled by his heart even as his head rebels. 'I'm lucky to have got the role,' Bob said. 'If I gave up the business tomorrow I would always know that I had fulfilled something special.'

Bob had no intention of giving up the business. It was finally beginning to turn his way. After all, twelve million viewers can't be wrong. Besides, he had a date in Babananga.

10

Rondavles and a Girl Named Sue

'Before we even got on the plane Bob was pacing, saying, "Cor, fuckin' hell, flyin' all the way to fuckin' Africa, fuckin' hell",' said Nicholas Clay, who remembers it well. 'And having got *on* the plane he walked up and down the aisle; he did not stop during the entire journey saying, "Cor fuckin' hell, look at that, it's fabulous, look at it."'

Bob was flying to his location after accepting a part in *Zulu Dawn*. 'On the advice of a Nigerian friend I decided to take the part and go to South Africa to see what it was all about,' said Bob in a characteristic bit of nonsense. 'Bob Hoskins as the Colour Sergeant was cast specifically because of his Cockney background and accent,' explained Jeff Freeman, who was the unit publicist for this film as well as its predecessor/sequel, *Zulu*, which had made a star of Michael Caine and was also written by Cy Enfield.

'For the savage, as the child, sometimes chastisement is an act of kindness,' says the smugly condescending General Lord Chelmsford, played by Peter O'Toole, in 1879 just before his entire regiment of 1300 British soldiers is wiped out by the combined wrath of Zulu spear power.

'What a wonderful adventure,' says one English officer. 'What a marvellous spree.'

'We must fight to survive,' says the Zulu chieftain.

The Battle of Isandhlwana was the worst defeat ever recorded on a modern army by native troops, and *Zulu Dawn* was a magnificently shot historical epic where the ending is moot, but the skill lies in the unfolding of the battle. It was full of famous faces – O'Toole, Burt Lancaster, Denholm Elliott, Christopher Cazenove, Simon Ward, Phil Daniels, and our hero as Colour Sergeant Major Williams. *Zulu Dawn* may also claim to have set a record for the most drawn-out killings ever recorded on celluloid for an unsuspecting audience. The more important the star the longer he took to die; Burt and Simon tied for first.

'Bob was always trying to outdo Burt,' said Clay. 'He and Phil Daniels rehearsed their death scenes for a week with twenty black South African policemen. He would say things like, "If Burt thinks he's gonna get the best fuckin' death scene, he's got another fuckin' think coming!"'

Bob was extremely glad to be in Africa, for both the adventure and the billing alongside the many great actors in *Zulu Dawn*, even though his role was small. Once *Pennies* had finished showing in April, Bob had grown a beard and was hired to be a boarding-house landlord in Alan Bennett's play *All Day on the Sands*, for LWT. He pulled out and got the film instead, where the beard came in handy. His marriage was still on the rocks and it was time to get away from England's weather and problems. He was going to have some fun.

'We all socialized to begin with until we had a major disaster in a modern hotel room in Pietermaritzburg,' Clay said. 'There was a great deal of storytelling by Peter O'Toole, who is the most wonderful raconteur. We were all in Bob's bedroom sort of looking out on Pietermaritzburg, which is not a very big town, parochially quiet after eight o'clock at night. And we were sitting there, having bags of Durban poison – dope, basically – and a lot of beers, having a very good time. There were maybe ten of us. One of the people was Mike Jayston, who didn't smoke.

'You see there is this wonderful thing when you've got a lot of egos about – they can often become competitive in one way or another. So, Mike decided he wanted to blow Phil Daniels' bugle. Bob was saying, "You fuckin' put that down, Jayston," so then we were playing the game of Where Was the Bugle, as O'Toole kept telling his stories. We were being terribly childish, but nonetheless very funny. Jayston kept finding the bugle, and eventually blew it out of a window. As this window was being opened, there was so much smoke in the room anyway that it went Whoosh! rushing out, and you could see all the lights in Pietermaritzburg going on.

'Bob "I Shall Shove This Bugle Up Your Fuckin' Arse, Jayston" Hoskins grabs the bugle. But a few minues later there's a knock on the door. A voice says, "*Open up, South African police!*" Total panic from inside. O'Toole was on the bed, and he suddenly went "Wheee!" as indeed did we all, you know: International incident, end of film, asked to leave, thank you very much, with a stiff prison sentence . . . if we're lucky. That's what flashed through our minds.

'As the knocking on the door became more insistent, there was terrible pandemonium in the room; Keystone cops time. It was serious. And it became obvious that all of what I had, which I was trying to flush down the loo, wasn't going to go. Bob says, "Oh well, there's no way out, we're on the third floor, that's it," in between howling deep recriminations on Jayston's back for waking up the town to this bloody bugle.

'So we opened the door, and there indeed were these short-haired moustached South Africans, who were extras on the film.

'"Hey," they said. "We heard there was a party."

'We nearly killed them and Peter O'Toole went straight out, Whoosh! Gone! and that was the last time we really socialized with him. I think quite rightly too.'

Bob also nearly got into trouble with a police chief for dope smoking in a provincial farming town en route to the Zulu mountain location. He got off with a caution, although it can be a hanging offence in South Africa.

When they moved on to Babananga, Bob had a specially ordered treat waiting for him . . . and another soon to come.

'From Pietermaritzburg, we actually followed the route taken by the British expeditionary forces sent in to quell the Zulu warriors,' said Freeman, 'crossing the river at Rorke's Drift, the site of *Zulu*, into Zululand, where we trekked on to the mountain where they fought the Battle of Isandhlwana, which means two stomachs of a cow. There are piles of stones marking the mass graves – the hyenas picked the bodies bare. Well, one couldn't clear that to shoot a movie, so we shot on a hillside sixteen miles away.

'We came to Babananga, which had a population of about ten. It was only a trading stop for the Zulus. We could have been stuck there in downtown Babananga for the three or four months we had to be on location while the battle scenes were shot, but the film company built a town just outside, a tented city for the English students who were playing the redcoat extras. They had started several months before we arrived, putting in a telephone exchange, running water, flush toilets, electricity, all mod cons for crew and cast. The days were hot and dusty, but the nights were so cold you could break ice on your way to the showers in the morning. It was winter in South Africa, after all. Then they constructed these skid huts, mounted above ground to keep out the rain. So what we stayed in was rather lovely.

'The locals lived in huts, called *rondavles*, made of clay, and mud, with a straw roof and a hole in the middle for the smoke from their fires, which left straight up because of the fantastic engineering by these people. Bob, being Bob, opted to stay in one, and moved in his ground sheet, mattress, and sleeping bag. He went native – except a phone was installed and you could ring up at the drop of a hat. Bob was often ringing up his mates.

'What Bob had told me,' Clay elaborated, 'was, "If I'm going out to fuckin' Africa I wanna live in a fuckin' grass hut." Someone in Production thought, well, we simply have to build one for this guy. So they did, and built three mud huts which would be good for press purposes and anyone who wanted to stay in them. One of the producers thought, great, he'd stay in one, but he found it so uncomfortable and dark and so absolutely unacceptable that he got out to a luxury mobile home.

'Before you could say *bwana*, Bob had a family, somebody who was going to collect wood for him, somebody who would sweep his floor for him, somebody who would be his maid before he moved in . . . he suddenly had three retainers. It was very typical of Bob – people flock to him like that, asking, "Oh, would you like me to do this for you?"

'Africa was fabulously inspirational. To sit under those stars was actually very therapeutic and extremely wonderful. We were a tight-knit group. The riotous laughter and poker games in Bob's hut, which was the centre of our world, were terrific.'

'Bob was extremely popular with everyone,' said Jeff. 'If you're going to be in Zululand it's nice to have someone like Bob in the cast to keep everyone sane and smiling. He was worth his weight in gold both on and off the screen. Every night there would be cards, drinks, a smoke in his hut – what we didn't have was television. He was such a clown we didn't miss it.'

It was a good thing that Hoskins was doing his best to entertain the troops, because there were problems looming.

Political and finanacial squabbles caused the three producers to fall out. Their case went to court and as a result an American bank was left to pick up the pieces. It brought in its own editors and produced a film quite different from the intentions of director Douglas Hickox. The film completely lost its edge. There was also controversy over the payment of the Zulu extras whom the western press reported as being exploited. In fact it had been King Butalezi's suggestion that they be paid the wages they would expect for working in the field.

Logistically staggering, educational for battle-film enthusiasts, emotionally satisfying when the imperialist aggressors are put down by superior strategy, *Zulu Dawn* made a great morality play but a film that was rather dull – the *Natal Witness* referred to it as *Zulu Yawn* – unless you are the sort that enjoys seeing red badges of courage on familiar film-star faces, and row upon row of neatly pitched army tents disappearing into the African sunset.

'For all the mayhem in the movie, there isn't much emotion, even when the fighters are dropping like flies,' said the *New York Times*. 'But the scenery, the top-flight cast, and thousands of African extras make this an eye-catching film, even if it isn't a particularly dramatic one.'

Naturally, Bob was singled out: 'Mr Hoskins wears a full beard and barks his orders jauntily, maintaining his aplomb. He even goes so far as to wink bravely at a comrade just as hordes of Zulus come rushing over the hill.'

Seven years later, in an *NME* interview, Bob referred to the film in an unwarrantedly hostile manner: '[It was] an appalling piece of garbage. The guy who directed it was . . . a fucking idiot. . . . Anyway, I said I wouldn't go to South Africa unless I could live with the Zulus. So they fixed it up.' He also claimed that because he placed calls for his black friends – white South African operators being bigots over the phone – he was made an 'honorary chief'. Because he ran up a huge bill, he said he 'had to leave eventually, run out of the country, or they were going to do me; a police officer told me I'd be in the clink if I didn't go immediately.' Whether or not that's true, Bob *did* have to leave, and not because he talked too much on the telephone.

Absence had made the African dawn grow longer, and Bob missed his London girlfriend, Sue Carpenter – they'd met the summer before at a party and, according to Sue, had 'been together ever since'. This would certainly confuse the issue of Bob's nervous breakdown and grief over his marital problems.

Sue had been given money at Bob's request, and got herself to Dar-es-Salaam, Tanzania, and then hitched all the way to Babananga, Zululand, an amazing journey of 2000 miles. It was not up to the producers to find accommodation for her, but they didn't need to. A mud hut would be fine, thank you very much. 'We had a choice of staying in a caravan, but we both thought it would be fun in the hut,' said Sue. 'It was a wonderful experience.'

'All the big journalists came down,' Jeff said, 'and Bob did his interviews in his *rondavle*, where his girlfriend had joined him. She was quite a free spirit.' And all those journalists, hanging out in Bob's mud hut, saw no reason not to report the romantic tale of a hitch through deepest Africa.

The only hitch being, of course, that they didn't know that Bob was still married, and that his wife, who knew about Sue and had quietly initiated divorce proceedings, would see the evidence of her husband's flagrant infidelity and happy-go-lucky escapades splashed across the newspapers. So would her friends and family. So would their children.

'I filed for divorce as soon as I knew there was another woman,' Jane told the *Daily Mail*. 'He's a brilliant actor but he used to live out his parts too fully. . . . He's a very unusual man and we have had a very unusual marriage. Our relationship has been stormy from time to time and there has come the time for a break.'

'Bob and I are in love,' twenty-seven-year-old Sue said. 'I know Bob is fond of [Jane], but they split up because they kept on fighting.'

'I am very hurt but I am not bitter towards him,' Jane also said, graciously under the circumstances. 'We have to put the children first and the divorce should be a civilized arrangement.' In fact it wasn't and Jane has no doubt who was to blame.

'Before they were married Bob would always bring Jane along with his mates in the pubs,' a friend said, 'but once they were hitched it was, "See if you can get rid of Jane." That's a real working-class mentality – it's okay to have the girlfriend but not the wife.'

'I decided I was actually going to find out what he was doing,' Jane explained. 'Once, for example, he told me was going to a press conference for *Pennies*, and the producer rang up wanting to speak to Bob. Where was he? Obviously not at a press conference. I knew he was with the woman he stayed with in London, and then all the other lies fell into place. All the time I said, "Probably . . . must be . . ." I never knew. So I confronted him and told him I wanted a divorce. It took from March to August to serve' – which is when the press pounced on the mud hut girlfriend story with glee – 'and the divorce was in the winter. It went through at the beginning of 1980. The reason it did not happen sooner was that although Bob had agreed to transfer the mortgage to me, this house [in Exeter] mattered more to me than life itself.' Jane could not risk losing possession of the house in case Bob changed his mind and decided to sell it. 'You are not mobile if you have a child with special problems, and I wouldn't allow the divorce to be finalized until I was certain I got the house.

'There are a lot of things Bob did that he wouldn't know I knew about. Six months after he moved out I received a phone call from a man saying what a nice week he'd had with us. Bob had registered in a hotel with another woman, using my name and giving my telephone number. I was terribly naive. Bob was around when he was around. We talked about scripts; we worked; there were the kids. I was perhaps being merely an audience. I think I was a very good audience. Bob only moves on when he has something more to gain, towards something that will get him somewhere. That to me is the way he is. "Hold it in your hand and cry – it'll get you anywhere," he used to say. And he was very good at crying. He would say one thing and do another. He has said many times, "You tell people what they want to hear and then you do what you want to do." It ends up very complicated and lots of people get hurt. And there's what all women say: "I indulged him because I didn't want him to be so humble." I know I've not stood up to him. He makes you feel responsible for him – so you write grotty letters, take the flak, pay the bills. You're willing to deny anything to protect him.

'He always calls his lady "missus" – he needs his servants and mothers. If you want to understand Bob, you only have to look at his parents. They are still parenting. They would do anything for him. They came from the back streets, and it's a tough world. I tried everything . . . his parents interfered. People say to you, "Why didn't you know. . . ." But you have children, you cease to believe you have any power or are worthwhile. And I was caught up.

'Bob has always been violent. He has a tendency to kick. He still kicks things if they get in his way. I don't like violence. I simply don't know what to do about things like that. But I have learned.'

She learned that her marriage was irreparable and her dreams were as unattainable as Arthur Parker's.

Bob, of course, suffered in his own way, and his grief at his irrevocable separation from the life he'd known for ten years, although he was used to long, regular separations, was not faked . . . even if he had the loving arms of Sue Carpenter to help him through.

'We were two people who just shouldn't have been together,' Bob once said of Jane in a moment of unusual candour. 'We did try but . . . it was a mistake right from the beginning, but when you've got kids, it's hard to say, "Right, let's finish."'

Ironically, Bob and Sue Carpenter broke up, not long after their return to England and during the divorce proceedings. 'We did each other a lot of good,' Sue said. 'I don't think Bob is as crazy as he was, but he still enjoys his fun.'

'It's all a bit of a caper to Bob,' said a friend. 'But he is pretty worried over how much his divorce is going to cost him. Having a good time is an expensive hobby.'

Bob didn't have to spend too much time worrying. First he had to take his clothes off at the National Theatre. Then he would become the leading man, Little Caesar in a crumbling empire, in a film that was going to show the world what Bob Hoskins could really do.

11

The Paddy Factor

'The thing I remember most clearly about the play was Bob's bum,' said Oliver Cotton, who'd previously worked with Bob at the Royal Court.

The World Turned Upside Down, written by Keith Dewhurst, was based on the acclaimed book by Christopher Hill, which chronicled the radical and revolutionary new beliefs that accompanied Oliver Cromwell's reshaping of English government. There were Diggers (precursors to kibbutzniks and hippies in communes), Levellers (grass-roots liberals), Muggletonians (stern Puritan disciplinarians), Ranters (believers in God without sin), twenty-four scenes, and forty-eight speaking parts played by twenty-one actors. Bob was William Everard, Captain Kirby, and Coppin. It all began on 2 November 1978.

'There were splinter groups of radicals put down by Cromwell,' Cotton said, 'and one such group was the Ranters. They believed that God was in everything, that heaven exists on earth and therefore there is no sin, so they would screw their asses off in orgies, shout dirty words and drink. 'We had a scene – based, actually, on a woodcut of two men smoking a pipe and a naked woman skipping with a rope – where a very innocent situation, with people dancing around and shouting dirty words, gets faster and faster, and then suddenly off come everyone's clothes, and they're rolling around on the floor in an orgy. Obviously unity was of the essence. There are a few times when nudity will benefit a play. When you take your clothes off, you realize just how powerful the taboo is. It's a very childish feeling, like you're being naughty. The actual day we did it for the first time, we were frightened. Bob was the only one who didn't care – he wanted to get to it! But we did it and it *did* work, because it was so fast . . . just a general melée of people rolling around on the stage, shouting Biblical phrases and doing . . . things!

'The audience couldn't believe their eyes. All of a sudden these people on stage had no clothes on at all. Women were lifting their skirts up. Bob is never backward in these types of scenes – he always put all his effort into every performance. Here he had to simulate sex. The joke was that he was getting this girl pregnant – and I don't think he was simulating.'

Sometimes there are perks to the acting profession – although, obviously, this scene was not one most critics chose to dwell upon at great length. 'It's exciting, then tantalizing, frustrating, and finally aggravating,' wrote David Self in *Plays and Players*. The problem was too many people and not enough focus. Yet the National Theatre troupe scored for 'its ensemble playing. In this respect, directors Bill Bryden and Sebastian Graham-Jones have certainly achieved success: here is a distinctive, trusting, and cooperative style of acting that works well in the intimate space of the Cottesloe.'

'Those of us who were in it remember with affection, and some astonishment, that Christopher Hill's stimulating book was even thought suitable for dramatisation; and that, in the event, it worked out so well,' said Norman Tyrrell, who played Mr Eyres and Stewer. 'It was a typical ensemble company piece where, if you were successful, you did not stand out from the others. We all played umpteen characters, including often very minor roles not worth putting in the programme, and only a few were central to the action. Bob was very conscientious and professional and a pleasure to have worked with.' Especially in the Ranters' scene.

After such an exhilarating on-stage episode, it can't have been too difficult for Bob to throw himself into another, only slightly more sedate production that opened on 29 November at the National's Cottesloe Theatre, especially since this one involved much fake blood-letting, special effects, film-world illusions . . . including the accidental bayoneting of the director. The author of *Has 'Washington' Legs?* was none other than Charles Woods, creator of *Veterans*, and once again his characters are making a film within the play, this time about the American Revolution (even if the cast is entirely English and Irish). Bob played an American named Joe Veriato, one of the producers of this Revolutionary epic. He is described by the playwright as being 'dapper', with 'very small feet which are encased in Gucci shoes'. Not normally how one would describe Bob Hoskins. He, and the rest of the principals, were intentionally upstaged by the larger-than-life figure of the self-absorbed and slightly insane director, John Bean, played with marvellous insouciance by Albert Finney.

Somehow, though, this production did not equal the magic of *Veterans*, which, in one sense, was a blessing: mailbags of hate-filled correspondence once in an actor's lifetime is quite enough. Neither could Bob have been too upset when his National stint ended, because he'd been plagued for some time with some rather weird rumblings in his gut. In January 1977 he was to become the donor of what seemed like the world's longest parasite. It was one of the less savoury souvenirs of the African bush.

'Bob was in the London Hospital for Tropical Diseases and I went to see him,' said Oliver Cotton. 'He was cheerful, sitting in a room, waiting for this twenty-seven-foot tapeworm to come out of his ass. "All they have to do," he told me, "is get the nice little head out."' If they didn't, the entire purging process would have to be repeated. Luckily, it worked the first time, although from looking at Bob's rotund-as-ever figure, you'd have thought the beast had gone on a hunger strike.

Bob also had a visit from another colleague, one from the old days of rep and 'gissa-job' in Hull: Barry Hanson. He arrived with scriptwriter Barrie Keeffe, and they had a little job in mind for Bob. It is highly improbable that any film can ever have been cast while waiting for a tapeworm to emerge. From such ignominious surroundings, however, a brilliant film emerged.

After his invigorating experience working with Bob at Hull and the BBC in Birmingham, Barry Hanson moved to Thames Television in 1974. He ran the play unit and produced some of their most acclaimed shows, like *The Naked Civil Servant*. One night in September 1976, in the Busabong Restaurant in Fulham Road, he met playwright Barrie Keeffe to talk about commissioning a new play for television, which would be the standard fifty-two minutes in length.

Hanson was doing another celebrated programme at the time – the mini-series *Out*. 'Series were the coming thing and there was more money in it, anyway,' Hanson explained. That night at dinner, inspired by a story about the Krays, he and Keeffe decided to do a thriller about gangsters. 'At first it had two different titles,' he said. 'One was *The Last Thriller*, then Barrie Keeffe renamed it *The Paddy Factor*. The police used to do vile things at that time. If a building blew up and they didn't know who'd done it, they would put it under a file called 'The Paddy Factor'. It was a wonderful title but given the nature of the film it couldn't actually be used.

'When the script came in, I tried to get Thames to do it and they wouldn't – one of the reasons was I was doing *Out* anyway. Then

John Mackenzie and I were supposed to be working together for Euston Films on a screenplay, which didn't work out, so I tried to get *them* interested in *The Paddy Factor*.' No luck. At this time, though, in 1977, Hanson signed to make three pictures – two for television and one as a feature for theatrical distribution with Black Lion Films, a production subsidiary of ITC Entertainment, run by Lord Grade. (This agreement was at the root of all the post-production problems which nearly killed the film stone dead.) The first television play, *Bloody Kids*, was written by Steven Poliakoff; the second, *Very Like a Whale*, by John Osborne; the third – the feature – was what became *The Long Good Friday*.

'It had been a television script about this guy Harold Shand, and the kernel of the fifty-two-minute original was good,' John Mackenzie said. He had made an enormous contribution to television with his direction of the Wednesday Plays and many others. 'Then Barry and Barrie decided to enlarge it to a film. I read *that* and thought it was bit twee. So when I was brought in I said, "Yeah, I like the television script. Let's start over and make a proper film script out of it. It's really just the business of having the time to get the script right."'

Getting the script of *The Long Good Friday* right became a joy. Hanson would secure £892,000 from Black Lion. Bob's intestinal visitor wormed its way out. And the quartet of highly talented men pooled their ideas.

'The important thing was that quite a lot of high–octane creativity produced what was then still called *The Paddy Factor*. It was kind of like passing hand grenades around,' said Hanson. 'Basically a lot of ideas and scenes came from the four of us being together. That was a happy time, and we were left alone to work on it. There was a very intelligent guy [at Black Lion] who allowed a lot when in actual fact . . . he couldn't *read* really; he was not big on continuous phrases and sentences. That actually is an asset in Hollywood!

'I don't think it's a repeatable experience at all. You can't. We set up an office in Carnaby Street and Bob would come in with a hunk of cheese and some bread and say, "Right, no more drinking, no more anything like that. . . ."'

'*The Long Good Friday* was great,' Mackenzie said. 'It was about the happiest film I've ever made. The producer and I were great friends because I'd known him quite a long time. Barrie was great. Bob was terrific; we were friends. And no one else could have played Harold Shand. Michael Caine said he could have, but that's not true. Bob was a natural. He was just right for it in every way.

And he was involved in the script too. The four of us did a lot of work together and then at the end I honed in just with Barry. I had the best sense of narrative; it's one of my few assets! And I knew how to deal with that and what was needed for this special kind of convoluted thriller. I hate thrillers that cheat, and rob the viewer of what you'd built up to.'

'John said he thought we ought to have a pub blowing up,' said Hanson. 'Barrie said, "No, that's not right – go away."' He was overruled and an exterior pub set was constructed and blown up. It was so realistic that a few passers-by nearly stepped in for a pint.

Another memorable scene is of a night watchman who is crucified on the floor of a warehouse. Contrary to the opinion of some critics, who objected to 'religious overtones', Barrie Keeffe included it because he remembered being told, when he was a reporter, that such punishment was a favourite among local villains.

It was Mackenzie who solved the dilemma of the film's title. 'It was one of those situation where everyone came in with a different title every day,' he says. '*The Paddy Factor* was the most terrible title on earth! The use of the world "factor" sounds so pseudo-smart. Apart from that, you're not sure *what* or *who's* involved in the beginning, and you learn the IRA's involved only as you go through the film. You can't give it away in the title. I came up with *The Long Good Friday* partly because it was an offshoot of *The Long Goodbye*, but also because I wanted to shoot it all over this very intense weekend, and give this feeling of the Feast of Easter. Most of the bloodshed took place on Good Friday; the crucifixion is on Holy Saturday. Some people didn't like the title, but it grew on you. Besides, we had to put *something* up on the clapper for the first shot, so I said, "Put up *Long Good Friday* as provisional." And it stayed. I quite liked it – it had *connotations*!'

There was one other person who would bring fresh ideas to the scirpt, and her input was to have a dramatic effect on many aspects of the film. Helen Mirren would play Victoria, Harold's classy mistress, who'd supposedly gone to public school with Princess Anne.

'Helen contributed a lot,' Mackenzie said, 'and she was a tremendous plus. She just gives it. Barrie had first written it as a gangster's moll, and there was one joke in it – this glamorous-looking girl named Viva who never said anything throughout the entire film, and in the end she smiled and had bad teeth. I said, "I can't sustain a film with that!" The most important thing is that Harold, who's so complex, should have a woman who's so complex as well. So I said we should make a gangster film *without* a moll, and, instead, with a woman who's got strength, power, influence, and all that. She loved Harold for what he was. Power is the aphrodisiac. And that was the only thing, really, restraining her from wanting to shoot the machine gun herself and take over.'

'I was sent a script,' Helen Mirren said, 'and I thought it was wonderful and clever – it was real *fun* to read; really good dialogue, witty, fast, interesting plot. Everything was great except I thought my part in it was pretty dull. So I said I'd do it but only on the condition that you rewrite my part. So we had a meeting and we all sat round in my little flat and discussed how to bring her into the story more as part of the actual action rather than as a sort of observer on the side, which is what she was originally. I didn't want to be the stereotype. I argued every line. I began to wonder if I wasn't just being egotistical and selfish – but I didn't think so, and in the end I think it made the film better.'

At the end of March 1979, during plans for *Long Good Friday*, Bob had accepted an invitation from Jonathan Lynn, director of the Cambridge Theatre Company and who'd already staged *Dog's Dinner*, to star with *Pennies* co-star Gemma Craven, Diane Langton, Anton Rodgers, and Andrew Wadsworth in the world première of a musical called *Songbook*. Written by Monty Norman and Julian More, who'd written *Irma La Douce* and *The Art of Living*, *Songbook* chronicles the musical output and highly improbable career of the fictitious songwriter Moony Shapiro. Because Moony's 'talents' spanned six decades, the authors were able to pen tunes in a pastiche of musical styles. It must have been Bob's fifteen-hour days on the set of *Pennies from Heaven* which gave him the courage to accept such a demanding song and dance role and attempt Gillian Lynne's choreography.

'We worked incredibly hard,' said Andrew Wadsworth, 'beginning at nine-fifteen in the morning. We did warmups for an hour, took a fifteen-minute break, then worked till six or sometimes nine in the evening. But after four weeks of rehearsals we were putting on the actual production, with only one week of rehearsal on Act Two.'

They opened to positive reviews on 2 May 1979 at the University of Warwick Arts Centre near Coventry, despite last-minute jitters. 'We were a very close bunch of people,' Wadsworth explained, 'and we were all terrified about the failure of this project, I more than most because it was the first time I'd pulled a plum, as they say. I did see Bob get very physically angry, once, at rehearsals, but I knew the frustration was directed at himself. There was a lot of pressure.

'At Darlington the CTC set it up so we could meet some of the friends of the theatre. Bob was surrounded by ladies from the ages of thirty to death, it seemed! He's every middle-class woman's ideal of a bit of rough trade. Although I've met his parents, and they're nice, middle-class people.'

Aside from adulation-craving, why Bob threw himself into such a physically demanding and exhausting musical at this time is a bit perplexing, as plans for *The Long Good Friday* were proceeding smoothly and Bob had committed himself to it fully. It can't have been a question of finances, since his contract stipulated that he was to receive £10,000, ten per cent of the net profits, star billing, and an additional £5000 fee for his work on the script. Perhaps he felt he owed the CTC a favour since they had staged *Dog's Dinner*. Perhaps workaholic Bob wanted a break from gangsters and bloodshed and thought he could squeeze *Songbook* in between *Friday* rewrites. Whatever his reasons, *Songbook* was a short-lived experience . . . for Bob, at least.

'While we were on the road, he was setting up *The Long Good Friday*,' says Wadsworth, 'and he was torn about what to do. When there are only five people you can get close quickly, and when he left he felt a bit guilty.' Although Bob should have anticipated this problem.

Songbook went on to major West End success with Bob's replacement, David Healy – 'Brilliant . . . *Songbook* is a musical to make Shaftesbury Avenue sing again and it's British through and through!' blared one review – and such a triumph without him must have assuaged any last remnants of Bob's guilt. Besides, he had his new role to worry about, and Harold Shand did not let anything get in his way.

'Bob was so happy with that part,' John Mackenzie explained. 'It was one of the best things he'd had. He was never off. He was in practically every scene and was there every day. So it was quite satisfying for us both to work together every day and our relationship grew very strong. I loved it!'

The storyline is simple. Harold Shand ruthlessly and efficiently rules his London manor – casinos, pubs, restaurants, and clubs – and is on the verge of clinching a major deal with the American Mafia to finance a gigantic leisure centre, the Las Vegas of London, in the then-rundown docklands. But over the long Easter weekend a perplexed and increasingly helpless and infuriated Harold watches his empire begin to crumble at his feet. Harold, on the rampage, hauls in – literally – his competition in an unforgettable sequence

95

where they are interrogated while hanging upside-down on meathooks in an abattoir. Only after Harold realizes that he has unwittingly been betrayed by his protégé, Jeff, and that through him his adversaries are not greedy London villains, but professional terrorists of the IRA, can he seek his revenge. But this time he has finally met his match.

The IRA element was based on fact. 'The thing with *The Long Good Friday* is the IRA,' said Hanson. 'You have that dialectic of the forces, plus you don't know what you're fighting. You *can* believe it – through Bob's extraordinary performance – when he doesn't accept it, rationalize it, or act in a way a sensible chap would. When Harold is told, in fact, "You can't wipe them out," is when he actually comes into his own and says, "You just watch me!" '

One of the reasons the story is so satisfying is that it works on so many levels: as a stomach-wrenching thriller with a convoluted yet convincing plot as Harold races to snare his unknown enemy; a scathing indictment of the upwardly mobile, Margaret Thatcher-inspired myth of success, a sort of Horatio Alger story gone astray; as well as a cynically subversive political statement. And it was all pulled together by Bob's portrayal of Harold Shand. As his empire erodes, so does the façade of normal, genteel behaviour, so that the swaggering Cockney braggart is reduced to a caged rat, teeth bared, desperation gleaming in his beady little eyes. Yet he had not ruled the manor by being a rat. He must have possessed the savvy of a boardroom executive, have watched his back better than any minion of MI5 and have expected the same of his employees. He is, as one critic put it, 'a miracle of vulnerable menace'. He also – and this is where Bob's innate skill at exuding grace and compassion under fire makes him so unforgettable – must love as fiercely as he despises the lower classes, any ethnic minority, and anyone who tries to grass him. He worships his woman and he mourns his friends.

'Conveying power in the type of villainous roles I've had,' Bob said, 'is merely a question of working out what the other person wants and what they will do to get it. If you know that, then you don't just play a stereotypical, tough gangster.'

A streak of trenchant, Hoskins-type black humour runs through the script as well. When the murdered body of Colin is secretly collected by an ice-cream van, Harold mutters, 'There's a lot of dignity in that, ain't there? Going out like a raspberry ripple.'

And Bob, of course, decided to do his inimitable brand of in-depth research. 'I grew up in a tough area and knew lots of gangsters,' he said. 'So when I wanted to study a gang boss I went around with some very heavy people I used to know. These guys were flattered that an actor wanted to be like them. They said, "Well, look at this little feller here, wants to be a gangster!" They were absolutely charming. The underworld loves show business.'

Learning from the Real Thing, as well as blabbing about the old days in Finsbury Park where he was or was not part of the criminal element, proved to be the inspiration for Bob. He has claimed he got on so well with his advisers that they gave him an Omega watch as a going-away present. 'They could be so gentle and quiet, but if anything went wrong – bang!, they exploded with terrifying violence. Then they'd go back to being quiet,' Bob said.

Bob's childlike glee at these lessons, however, was a bit exaggerated. 'Bob did his research in his own way,' Hanson says. 'Bob's like his *own* research! He knew quite a lot of the chaps from the East End, hanging around on the film unit.' And John Mackenzie had hired some of the real bad boys as extras; P. H. 'Blades' Moriarty, who played Harold's minder, Razors, and Brian Hall, Bob's co-star in *England, England*, were no strangers to that world either. American cult actor, Eddie Constantine, as the Yankee mobster, had played so many hoods he knew the genre inside out. If a movement or gesture seemed off, they quite easily knew how to maintain accuracy. 'They'd just hold up a hand and say quietly, "That ain't the way to do it,"' Bob explained. 'Nobody argued.'

'I remember when I was desperately trying to be a "believable" gangster, I was shouting and waving my arms around and doing that sort of thing.' One of the extras took him aside and said, 'Look, you don't have to shout. They know who you are, so why are you shouting?' It was simple yet effective advice. 'Since then,' Bob said, 'I've learned to do what a woman would do: show my intent on my face and just think about what I want to convey. That's what really works.'

This knowledge was put to absolutely riveting use by Bob and his director in the very last scene of the film, one of the best endings of a cinematic thriller ever, where the IRA drive Harold Shand off to his doom. He knows he's trapped, and every possible emotion – rage, fear, cunning, determination, and, finally, resignation, flicker across his face.

'That ending came early,' Mackenzie said. 'I knew from the moment we started to enlarge the script how it was going to end, and that doesn't often happen. I had this whole vision of Bob's face. I wanted to see *him*. All sorts of other things had been predicted for Harold, and I said, "Let's do none of that. Let's just have the face." And he's going somewhere. Will he get away . . . ?'

'We did it in two takes. I drove the car – if we'd had more money, we'd have had more elaborate rigs – and we only had room for me, the cameraman, and the sound man, who was in the boot. Not that we needed a lot of sound, but Bob said, "Here, hold up – where's Victoria" just as they take off, so we had to have a mike in there.

'I nearly killed them all. For the actual long take on Bob I drove and directed him in the rear-view mirror, and when we hit Trafalger Square I was watching in the mirrors so much that I drove along the Strand and looked up just in time.

'I had a whole order of emotion I wanted; eventually I wanted to arrive at acceptance, an almost ironic, Well, you've got me. Very few actors could do that . . . to respond. They start mugging. They say, "Uh-oh," but Bob doesn't. He just *thinks* it, and what his character *is* comes through.'

'I think there is a lesson in that sort of concentration,' says actor A Martinez, who would work with Bob and John Mackenzie in *The Honorary Consul*. 'A lot of actors would say, "Give me time to find myself emotionally." But a guy like Hoskins will just sit there in the back of a car with the director taking him through those moments as they occur, as the director conjures them, and play them with such effortlessness and concentration that you buy it. All those feelings compressed into a few minutes of film. It was remarkable.' Bob later confessed to an American journalist that he got stoned out of his brains to do it.

'Bob's great strength is as an inspirational, instinctive actor,' Mackenzie said. 'But at the same time he can let it go through; he *thinks* it in a way, he allows the brain *some* control, but it comes from the stomach. He's not a cerebral actor, he's a *stomach* actor.

'And I felt that he shouldn't be trammelled by moves and trying to remember things. He'd done a lot of acting but he hadn't done a lot of films, so I gave him a lot of freedom.' Whatever Mackenzie did, it worked, and the eight-week shoot flew by.

'It was such an enjoyable film,' said Mackenzie, 'rich in character and language and humour; and exciting and a thriller and all that. You don't often get that combination.' And if the Lord Grade organization was to get its way, that potent combination would be slashed, dubbed, and diced for easily digestible consumption on the television.

The real fight for *The Long Good Friday* was about to begin.

12

The Sweeps, the Silent Screen, and a Slave

'Oh, I just finished this gangster picture, Bob told me,' related Spencer Banks, who'd worked with him in *Pennies*. 'I think it's going to be rather good.'

Bob had every reason to be pleased with himself in the autumn of 1979. Shooting *The Long Good Friday* had been a fantastic collaborative effort and the post-production and editing were proceeding on schedule. He and his girlfriend, the actress Patti Love, were quite happy (she'd had a bit part in *The Long Good Friday*), and one of his plays was going to be staged in Paris in November. 'They sent me the script translated into French for me to approve,' Bob said. 'I can't read bleedin' French. I can't even pronounce the title.' And then BBC Television approached him in October with the lead in a 'Play of the Month': *Sheppey*, W. Somerset Maugham's last play, based on his own 1899 story, 'A Bad Example'.

Bob thought at first, before he read the script, that casting him would be as appropriate as Arthur Parker taking a lie-detector test. But he was mistaken. Casting him as another Depression Dreamer was quite clever, a near-perfect way to exorcise the rude boy-gangster mien he'd adopted for Harold Shand and a throwback to the more 'innocent', good-natured characters like Alf in *On the Move* and Colour Sergeant Williams in *Zulu Dawn*. (The mistaken assumption, typecasting Bob as a 'gangster', would come later in his career. At this stage he was still best known for *Pennies*, and Arthur Parker was certainly closer to Croydon than Kray territory.)

Sheppey is a barber who strikes it rich in the Irish sweeps. Uncomfortable in his new-found prosperity, and much to the bewilderment of his family, he gives everything away to those who have more need of it. Maugham's unsubtle point – that charity and

99

selflessness are tantamount to lunacy – was served by Bob's gentle portrayal. 'Sheppey is a lovely fellow,' Bob said. 'I wish I knew him. I read the play and fell in love with him.'

Sheppey was directed by Anthony Page and rehearsed at the familiar 'Acton Hilton' rooms. 'It's quite good to get out of there and have a roll and pint at lunchtime,' said Perry Benson, who played a young staff member in Bradley's barber shop. 'We were rehearsing on the set about three to four weeks, which is really good for a television play. And even though Anthony Page was a bit autocratic and rigid, I had great respect for the man because I knew *he* knew exactly what he was doing and it was going well. I remember in one scene saying, "No, I don't think this is right", and everyone stopping and turning round, looking at me as if I'd put my foot in it. That was after being in the pub for lunch when I'd had a pint for Dutch courage.

'Bob and I had a few drinks together. Working with him was like being with one of the lads. He was like the Godfather, put people at their ease, just like your mate. He's a fine example, because if you work with people like Bob, who you respect, you can learn so much.

'He had a lot of lines to learn, so he was doing a lot of walking around talking to himself, like you have to do when you've got a big part. He is also a guy that looks pretty fierce, you know, and I'm sure if it came out, he could knock you flat. But he's got a spark, a real spark. The funniest thing in *Sheppey* was that Bob had to shave someone and all the cut-throat razors had Sellotape on them so he wouldn't kill anyone.'

The critical reaction was mixed, but more because of the inherent flaws in the piece than the actual production or acting.

As a new decade started, however, Bob would find himself playing in another period piece, *Flickers*. This time the character was a sort of cross between Arthur Parker and the Boy Wonder in *Inserts*. His name was Arnie Cole, and all he wanted to do was make pictures.

Flickers was written by Roy Clarke, better known for *Last of the Summer Wine* and *Rosie*. It was more of a serial than a series: tracing the events in chronological order of the trials and tribulations of a brashy and determined movie pioneer in the very early, pre-World War I days of silent films – from his struggling days as a travelling bioscope moving picture salesman to creating his own studio and producing pictures. 'It was,' said Joan Brown, the producer, 'a fun series with serious elements.' Bob was the rogue and swindler showman, Arnie, and Frances de la Tour his wife, Maud, who persuades him to marry her even though she finds him 'uncouth' and 'utterly charmless', because she needs a father for her illegitimate baby and he needs a bankroll for his grandiose schemes. 'I'm not the type who sets men's pulses racing,' Maud says, 'and consequently not their feet.' But, she decides with a resigned shrug, 'with any luck I can always get him to change his tailor'. Their chemistry as a couple was one of the most satisfying elements in *Flickers*.

'He's [Arnie] a wonderful, flamboyant character,' said Bob, 'the sort most people would give their eye teeth to play. He's totally and utterly straight, he never changes, he never kids anyone, and yet there's so many conflicts there – he's a restless megalomaniac, a spiv, a man of vision and also of tenderness.' It was probably as close to an autobiographical statement as he has ever made.

'On paper, given the wrong character, that character would have been objectionable,' Clarke said, 'bumptious, often overtly crooked . . . but there was so much warmth that Arnie Cole could be as threatening as you like – yet you still like the guy. You can't pinpoint it, or select for that, but Bob has it in spades. He looks like he could choke you – and I'm sure he could – yet it's always down to Bob. I was very pleased with Frances and Bob. It was a marvellous combination.'

'I'm sure by the end they were fixing up each other's private lives,' said a colleague who worked on the production. 'There was a very strong personal attraction between them.'

The shooting lasted six months, and Bob, as usual, took charge on the set. 'By habit I tend not to go to shoots, because usually there's a time lapse and they're so far off anyway,' said Clarke. 'But I spent quite a bit of time on that one for sheer pleasure. It was Bob's energy that was so marvellous. I think for me he clicked first because he's more of an American than an English actor. It seems to me that British acting is a technical, intellectual thing. You go on and say, "Let's have a look at Laurence Olivier doing so-and-so", and it's often wonderful to watch. But it seems from way back that America has had this seemingly endless stream of guys who don't *look* like actors at all – Archie Armstrong, Ned Beatty, Alan Garfield, George Kennedy – and if you didn't know, you'd never for a minute figure they were actors. You can teach technique but not how to act,' he explained. 'There's a dual thing going there – the play itself, and then watching the actor *playing* the role, which is fascinating, and enjoyable, but as a writer you've got to say it's a bit like asking a guy to paint your portrait, and it's marvellous, but he's the one who got painted, not you. But when it's so instinctive, like it is with Bob, then there is no longer that duality, with the actor playing the role – it's for real. It's a rare commodity. And I can't think of a more pleasing one for a writer, and I certainly got that from the word go with Bob. I couldn't believe that this wasn't Arnie Cole. Bob's energy is phenomenal. It wasn't just in his part – it was strange in a way to see him sort of taking over the whole thing. It wasn't an obvious ploy or anything, but it was as if people are in a cold space and there's a heat source and they surround it instinctively. Like a heat source everyone is drawn to.'

'He's the most generous actor I've worked with in 30 years,' says Wilfred Grove, who played Sad Galloway. 'We only had one scene – a very funny short scene – where we were shot together, sitting in my kitchen drinking wine. They brought the camera over and the director said he wanted to see another shot – just fill the screen with a face. So Bob nudged me in the ribs and said: "It's all yours, boy, go with it" – and took himself out of the picture. There are not many times that this happens. With most other stars, if you put a close-up on, you're elbowed out – and if you don't move, you're elbowed out of the series! With actors like Bob, you can't go wrong.'

'He seemed to me the father confessor of the world, with this astonishing energy,' said Clarke, 'always on the go. He didn't have a flat of his own at the time' – he was living with Patti Love, and her dog Kipper was a frequent visitor to the set – 'though he'd got no concern about how or where he lived; his private life was chaotic. And everything went into the wind.'

Bob was often in a state because of the problems associated with his long drawn-out divorce. One *Daily Express* article (in 1979) had stated that 'the estranged wife of *Pennies* star Bob Hoskins is struggling to make ends meet . . . Jane manages to earn a few pennies from the sale of her homemade pottery.'

'At one point,' Jane also said of the situation that soon became laughably ludicrous, 'I got a letter from him signed R. W. Hoskins. Via a solicitor he put in an affidavit that I was making him take out the dog. The real reason was that he came in his Jeep to see the kids and I made him take them outside. So that meant I was making him "take out the dog".

'I also received a letter from a solicitor complaining that Sarah's hair had been plaited, and I was being extravagant. The truth was that Sarah had had her hair cut that one time that year, and Bob happened to see her soon after.

'Having left my relationship is a different matter,' she explained.

102

'It makes *him* so well-liked, so that if he's not behaving well to his wife, there must be something wrong with *her*. She is castigated and he has more freedom to do what he likes.'

'Bob would come in screaming with anger because of the rows at that time – his marriage and the quarrels and that – and he'd start kicking things about,' said Joan Brown. 'We had the usual things all through the filming of him not turning up, or sometimes late, and I used to get quite annoyed because when you're the producer you see it as wasted time.'

Yet Bob's personal dilemmas did not, in the long run, prevent him from performing to his usual high standards. He also joked about why he took on the role of Arnie: 'After *Pennies*, I had to face a lot of abuse from people who take television seriously.' At least you *hope* he was joking.

Yet because the series ambitiously tried to cover so much ground, several subplots were constantly vying for attention, and often upstaged the usually hilarious lines and situations. That's one of the reasons why reviews, when *Flickers* was shown from 16 September to 22 October 1980, were decidedly mixed, although some critics quite unfairly compared it to *Pennies*, with which it had little in common except Bob Hoskins.

'It didn't do so well here,' said Joan Brown, 'but in the States it was a huge success. Americans go very much for the chemistry between people; it's more of a Hollywood tradition. And these two characters touched something there. That sort of abrasiveness was much more Yankee, like Hepburn and Tracy [or Bogart, as a critic had remarked], which Bob and Frances had captured very well.'

Flickers was far more popular in the States than *Pennies*, and was shown repeatedly on public television. The *New York Times* called it 'marvellously wacky . . . one of the daffiest and most hilarious original screenplays written for television . . . Joan Brown and Cyril Coke have given the farce the pacing and ambiance of an old silent movie. At the center of all this Mr Hoskins . . . [who] clearly likes playing a character in a play of his own devising . . . Arnie Cole may be the ultimate loser, a bit of a clown, but Mr Hoskins makes sure that he demands attention.' And Miss de la Tour 'gives a comic performance that is a gem of tone and timing. Both performers seem to enjoy working together and their collaboration is a pure delight . . . *Flickers*, with all of its robust vulgarity intact, is perfect summer entertainment.'

Plans for a sequel were at first encouraging. 'There were all these characters to play with,' said Dickie Arnold, 'and we were all hoping to pick up on the threads of what happened to them. But Bob had other irons in the fire, so he wouldn't do it.'

Instead Bob went back to villainy.

'There are two kinds of films,' said Bob. 'High-grade films and Lew Grade films.' It was eighteen months before *The Long Good Friday* was eventually released. Its West End première was not until 26 February 1981. Hanson described the shock with which it was first greeted by its backers, and the almost obsessive struggle which followed to get it released.

'It was really curious, and basically not Lord Grade but Jack Gill, his henchman [Chairman of Black Lion Films] who saw the film and was horrified. It wasn't the kind of film they were making. They were also in deep financial trouble, but of course Lord Grade was out in the cosmos somewhere. And since it wasn't the kind of film they made, they didn't believe anybody else thought it was any good. To say they were neurotic about it was a little bit of an understatement.'

If the film were to be shown on television, two-thirds of its costs (and it ran over budget by about £300,000) could be recouped against advertising revenues. A cinema release was far less cost-effective: an advertising campaign was expensive, prints of the film were expensive, and, worse, it took ages for distributors to cough up the profits.

'Bob had done a deal with Black Lion to do three productions,' Mackenzie elaborated, 'which he did: two for television and one for theatrical distribution. I don't think this filtered through somehow to ITC. Black Lion had just been formed as a sort of little adjunct to the entire Lord Grade organization, and they had another branch designed to make feature films.' Like the £40 million abandon-ship *Raise The Titanic*. 'So they really didn't know what was going on. *We* were all contracted as a "film" film, so that's what it was from our point of view.'

Not only would half the length have to be cut for television – the film is 105 minutes – but all political references, the IRA, kickbacks, mob infiltration, Docklands development, and displacement of the locals would be lost as well, making the film no more than the meaningless mutterings of angry gangsters. Ironically, Harold's impassioned speech at the end, about the reviving glory of the British spirit, probably would have remained. The sarcasm would have been entirely lost.

'They were frightened about the Irish element,' Bob explained. 'They said, "You can't let the IRA win." I said, "You want a *gangster* to win?"'

'The IRA bit was all highly embarrassing,' said Mackenzie. "There's *still* one dubbed line in it, about the British soldiers running through Belfast. "With shit running down their legs" was the original line, meaning fear, *boys'* fear. It wasn't meant to denigrate soldiers. But they felt it denigrated the entire British army, so we had to change it to "with shit being *thrown* at them" or something. I said, "It's a sympathetic line. It's human! To have to go through those streets – anyone would be frightened."'

They didn't buy it. And while ITC was wringing its collective hands over what to slash first, *The Long Good Friday* made its first appearance in rough-cut form, with an incomplete soundtrack, at the Cannes Film Festival in May 1980. The response was enthusiastic, with both Bob and the writing singled out for praise in *Variety*, the American bible of the entertainment industry: 'Much more densely plotted and intelligently scripted by Barrie Keeffe than most such yarns. . . . Bob Hoskins, an already much-praised British TV actor, who here displays natural, and sizable, big-screen presence, works out first-rate in the anchor role.'

While plans were made to show *The Long Good Friday* at the Edinburgh Film Festival on 23 August 1983, Bob began rehearsing for a production of *The Duchess of Malfi* that was to open on 16 September at the Royal Exchange Theatre in Manchester. Co-starring as the Duchess was his *Long Good Friday* partner Helen Mirren, and the director was the 'Boy Wonder of the RSC', Adrian Noble.

It was a great test of his talent and skill to stage Webster's dark Jacobean 'revenge play', crammed full of dastardly deeds – incest, bloodlust, torture, strangling, poisoning (by a kiss on the Holy Book itself), stabbings, mummified bodies, lycanthropy, death, decay, and severed hands in the dark – which can so easily descend into ludicrous melodrama.

'I'd seen a production of the *Duchess* at Bristol when I was there,' said Noble, 'and it dehumanized the play by pulling out all the animal imagery so it was an overstressed animal show with people dressed like beetles. I've always thought it was the most amazing play. Contemporary audiences love the baroque sentiments. There's a great appreciation of style in the 1980s and there's quite a strong sense of classicism, well delivered, you see. It can really quite excite an audience, or turn it on. And that was certainly our experience with *Malfi*.'

Noble underscored the black baroque sentiments with a starkly simple set, designed by Bob Crowley: a floor of multicoloured tiles was overlaid with a carpet that changed from white to fur, from bloodstained to threadbare. Sound effects of clanking lunatics and off-stage screaming combined with George Fenton's eerie music; the lighting was strong and dramatic.

'I knew it needed a bit of surgery, because it gets a bit long, especially in the middle,' says Noble. 'I gave it a very strong structure by actually limiting certain scenes and transposing certain scenes and by giving extra value to certain things. The interest of the piece is the right to "dissent", the right to say no, to opt out, to lead your own life . . . and all that works. But that required very clever casting. You have to make "class" work in the play, which is why you start with the Duke and Duchess. Those people had a sense of received power and they had an individual, recognizable, emotional set that was very, very different. And then you have to cast the two outsiders – people from a different class. I went quite strongly to people with working-class roots. Pete Postlethwaite was absolutely against type; you have to do a bit of "Would you?" If you're going to marry out of your class, you're not going to do it with a gink who's a bit like you, are you? You're going to go for someone totally different. Likewise with Bob. I didn't cast him till towards the end. What Bob can bring to something like *Malfi* is a quality that's totally authentic and logical, because you can really quite easily wander off the path on Bosola – it's a very seductive role. You can get interested in the sensitive melancholia bullshit, but it's only bullshit in the sense of it being involved with the creation of something that's alive and happening and present. And of course it wouldn't occur to Bob to wander off the path. He approaches stuff from the actions of the character, *inwards*, which is quite proper for him. Let's say you get a basic credibility: here's a man who has been in the galleys for years, therefore *that* has to be visible, photographable, when he walks on stage. It's a *fact*. He is a man who is framed and notorious for his ability to execute. Bob is a great translator of experience, which is good. In rehearsals, we were talking about relating the play to an actual murder as opposed to *acting*, and then Bob pipes up – of course he's one of the few people who's witnessed a real murder in his life. So he starts to tell us about this astonishing scene that he witnessed as a kid in Finsbury Park, his manor – these gangland killings. You get this amazing sense of presence there that's rather alarming.'

'Bob sort of played it as himself,' says Postlethwaite. 'He played it from the heart. We were all cast because that's how we're seen, and we all came from very different angles. So Bob played Bosola like a man from that part of the world, trying to be himself, move himself up, and get going.'

Noble also told Steve Grant, 'Obviously, Bob hasn't *killed* anyone or anything like that, but he has seen a great deal of violence and he does know an awful amount of violent people, gangsters, the lot. Bob has an enormous immediacy, an immense gift as a vulgarian, in the real sense of the word, in that he can translate very complex emotions and language into intelligible experiences for the ordinary person.'

'We've got to cut the verbals,' Bob told Pete Postlethwaite during rehearsals. 'We'll never be able to make people fuckin' understand this – I can't understand it meself!'

'This is his drawback,' Noble remarked, 'in the sense that he'll read five lines of blank verse, and he'll say, "Does this mean, Come here, you cunt, or I'll smash you in the teeth?" and you'll say, "Yeah, sort of," and he'll deliver the five lines as if he's saying just that. To a degree you sort of have to finally wave goodbye to a perfectly spoken verse form anyway. He'll give you the *rhythm* of that, which is a distortion of Webster's rhythm, but the *intention* is so alive and dramatic that it's riveting, and therefore works as theatre.

'Bob got very into the language, because he's a great wordsmith, like a lot of Cockneys, a great lover of slang and *patois*, and little idioms that he used would creep into all our vocabularies. When you're in a sort of closed society of a rehearsal, after a period of time everyone would be picking up their Hoskinsisms, so juicy, like a little kind of *tapas*, you know, savouring those expressions. Like "Bosh."

'So Bob could say the words and savour the language but he would have to make the rhythm his own. He did very much get into the shape of the character. He understood something quite central to the Jacobean theatre, which is, those two hours and twenty minutes are a very particular, intense, all-embracing experience. It's not an intellectual experience so much as an *emotional* one. And some sort of journey has to be undergone, one in which all the actors must partake. Once Bob understood that concept of theatre, rather than as a sort of journalistic discourse, he went for it totally, which meant that when he would do a performance he would make his journey as long and as three-dimensional as he possibly could.

'That's the *sine qua non* of making any Jacobean theatre work – you have to grip the audience as you would in a *film noir*. It's verging on the melodramatic all the time, and that's fine – the *proper*

107

edge to be on. And we edited it like a thriller with brutal hard cuts.

'In one scene Bosola is disguised as a priest, and the Duchess can't recognize him. Either you express that with some sort of theatrical device or you say that she doesn't recognize him. So, you've got to do something about this situation . . . what do you do? As soon as you start discussing things like that people's imaginations come in. Bob would say, "Well, I'm pretty short and I can't get any taller, so I could get very very short." So he played twenty minutes practically on his knees, with a mask on. It was quite amazing. He nearly crippled himself inside this thing, and it was the most bizarre experience which came out of simply addressing the text. We didn't know if people would just scream with laughter. If they did, we'd had it.

'When we were organizing the deaths, Bob had this brilliant idea that when the Duke kills Bosola, he should tear Bosola's throat out, like a wolf would do. Mike [Gwilym] – whose Duke thinks he's become a wolf – accepted that as a wonderful idea.'

Others with conviction were the producer and director of *The Long Good Friday*. The film was scheduled to be screened at the Edinburgh Film Festival, and a tribute to John Mackenzie as well as a press conference were also organized.

'Bob and Helen were both rehearsing *Malfi* in Manchester,' said Barry Hanson, 'and they turned up halfway through this press conference, and Bob gave a speech which was pretty electric, and then Helen came out and absolutely everything stopped. She talked about why she did the film and what it meant to her, what it meant about England. Press conferences are always a bit naff, but she was extraordinary.'

'England isn't responsible,' Helen told a journalist later. 'It's lonely. It's the people who look at England from the outside, that persist in seeing it in this slightly Dickensian, quaint old way, still basically kind of Victorian that I really get angry about. England isn't like that. *The Long Good Friday* is much truer, accurate, grittier, violent, witty, active, aggressive – all those things. People from abroad love that upper-crust atmosphere and think that's what epitomizes England. And it's such a minority, so untrue to the population and the actual atmosphere in this country. My satisfaction in doing films has nothing to do with the people who come and watch me. It's a monetary reward, certainly, which is nice, but it's just the actual *doing* of it. Once I've done it, I lose interest. *The Long Good Friday* was an exception because I care about this one very

108

much; it represents something important to us in England. It symbolizes the rebirth, the reacceptance of the *potential*. Anything that makes English people feel that they *can* be successful, not just in films, is so important.'

Once again, critics loved the film, and Bob loved the adulation.

'Bob didn't want to go back to rehearsals,' Hanson related. 'I told him he's got to do all these interviews, so we would concoct a story for this guy Adrian Noble. I'd not yet heard of him and I thought he was some idiot from Manchester – until I saw his work. "He's got me sussed out," Bob said. "He can see me coming. I can't go back. I'll say there was a snowdrift." "But Bob," I said, "it's only August."' Bob went back.

A great deal of apprehension accompanied the first night of *The Duchess of Malfi*. 'Bob knew it was a big part and he knew he could do it,' said Pete Postlethwaite,' 'but he was struggling to a certain extent. It was a tough time. No one dominated the cast – we were all wondering if we would be laughed off the stage or do well.'

'I was nervous because we really went for it, you see,' Noble says. 'But the very first time we did it, it was wonderful. We had just an invited audience and they screamed and shrieked and reacted, because they were hearing the story for the very first time. It was an amazing experience. It did frightfully well.'

The critics raved in Manchester, and again when the production was brought down to London seven months later. John Wyver in *Time Out* was typical of many: 'Ultimately it is Bob Hoskins's brilliant Bosola, conspirator with all and respector of none save the Duchess, who makes the production so consummately credible.'

There were a few dissenters. Francis King in *The Sunday Telegraph* wrote: 'Mr Hoskins's Cockney inflections destroy much of the poetic beauty of his lines.'

'Bob came off really well if he hadn't had too much to drink before,' said one participant. 'He does like his liquor.'

Yet Bob had every reason to be pleased with his Bosola. Shakespeare, Webster, Shaw, Chekhov, O'Neill, Pinter, Bond, Woods – he'd taken them all on and succeeded. In mid-September 1980 he had a hit in the theatre, the well-publicized mini-series *Flickers* on the television, and a film that had whoever had seen it foaming at the mouth. The *Guardian*'s Derek Malcolm had written: '*The Long Good Friday* is apparently threatened with cauterisation for the television screen instead of a cinema showing. Lord Grade who put up the money will have to think again. . . . Come on, Lord Grade, this is one of the best you've been involved with, and you ought to be proud of it. If a man like John Mackenzie can't make a feature film, there really is no hope at all for what is laughably called the British film industry.'

The only problem, it seemed, was that Lord Grade and ITC didn't want to have to think again, despite another enthusiastic reception when the film was shown at the London Film Festival. Not only were plans to re-edit the film continuing, but a television screening was announced for March 1981. Far worse, Harold Shand was about to lose his voice.

'*The Long Good Friday*,' reported the *Guardian*, 'has run into trouble over the dubbing of a version for American television. Apparently the company involved, a subsidiary of Lord Grade's ITC, was worried that Bob Hoskins would not be intelligible to American viewers. So his voice has been replaced by another actor.'

Bob, still really an unknown in the States, had every reason to fear that Hollywood would have no interest in an actor who'd been dubbed. What could have been wrong with his voice? Or his acting? Of course he was not consulted about the dub, and to add insult to injury, the dub was in a Wolverhampton accent that would have been hardly more intelligible to American viewers who think 'sod' is what you turn over with a spade and 'grass' is what you walk on in parks.

'I saw the result for fifteen minutes,' Bob said to Steve Grant, 'and I said, "Right, you're fucking nicked!"'

Armed with affidavits from Helen Mirren, John Mackenzie, and Barrie Keeffe, Bob asked for a High Court injunction to prevent distribution of the dubbed version. On 17 November 1980, Mr Justice Vinelott was told that the dub was 'a prostitution of Bob's acting ability', as well as an alleged breach of contract, and a breach of the Performers' Protection Acts ('passing off' one actor for another). An application for a speedy trial was granted.

The press picked up the story and reported the impending battle as well as Bob and Helen's efforts to raise £1 million to buy the rights back from ITC. 'We made the film because we thought we were supporting the British film industry,' Bob said. 'If we'd known it was going to end up on television we would never have bothered. If it goes out on television, about twenty minutes of politically sensitive material will be cut and a great piece of work ruined.'

A spokesman for Black Lion said: 'It was always our right to decide how this film should be shown.'

'We hawked the film around,' said Barry Hanson, 'and the

110

people at ITC got so sick of us – they were used to far more worthwhile ventures – they said, "Look, Barry, if you've got £1 million you can have it," which I didn't happen to have handy at that time.'

'And then they decided not to sell it,' said Mackenzie. 'Instead, it was going as a sort of television package to the States. So I made an appointment to see Jack Gill. It was Christmas Eve, and I told him the case was proceeding and that Bob was saying we'd just have to sue them. I had gathered all these people, as many as I could, to come as character witnesses for Bob, to say how awful it was to do this to a leading man – including Alec Guinness, with whom I was working. So when I went to see that chap on Christmas Eve, I said, "You know, it's just ridiculous, if we can get you £700,000 [the original budget – they went over], why don't you just get out? You don't like the film, the court case is going to go ahead, you're now getting caught in this trap and you can still come out of it smelling so fabulous. Do you realise in the witness box we're going to have . . ." and when I got to Guinness his knees gave way. "I've got written confirmation that they're going to come," I said, "and they're going to say that you're damaging this man's career. This is a very bad odour for you to have." I'm sure that was the final straw. After Christmas they agreed to sell it.'

'Thus began,' wrote Barrie Keeffe, 'a last race against the clock to find a buyer who would release it theatrically as the 23 March transmission neared. [The] quoted reason to sell the film was that [it] was "uncommercial".'

Bob came to the rescue. At a party in January he met one of the Monty Pythons, Eric Idle, and decided to broach the subject of having Handmade Films, run by Idle, two other Pythons, and George Harrison, buy the film. After rescuing *The Life of Brian* (from Lord Grade's brother, ironically), Bob reckoned Handmade might have the necessary outlay. Fortunately they were indeed looking for somthing. And they found it.

ITC ate the budget overrun, selling the film to Handmade for £700,000. It opened on 26 February 1981 at four cinemas in London. Victory, at last. Even better was the news that the Ritz in Leicester Square took in the equivalent of their top box-office take in the film's first week of release.

'The acting is perfection,' wrote Alexander Walker in the *Evening Standard*. 'Its violence . . . almost fades in the shade of the monster Hoskins creates – a man who would be hilarious, if he weren't such a horror, because his hankering for the conservative virtues are so wildly at variance with his practice of the terrorist one.'

When Handmade's Denis O'Brien sold the film to Embassy Pictures, it opened a year later across America, and critics were flabbergasted that some British unknowns had created such a superb gangster film. Stephen Schaefer in *US* wrote: 'Bob Hoskins immediately joins the movies' most illustrious rogues gallery, a criminal roster that includes Edward G. Robinson's *Little Caesar,* James Cagney's *Public Enemy,* Rod Steiger's *Al Capone,* and Mickey Rooney's *Baby Face Nelson.*' Michael Sragow in *Rolling Stone* wrote: 'Bob Hoskins goes all the way with it. . . . [He] has a beefy, dark, intense physicality that in England has made him "Everyone's favorite Cockney actor". Hoskins is built like a bowling pin, and has a voice like a pin-setter's, a perpetual soft growl with a sandpaper roughness, even at its most tender. He can do more with his cheeks and jowls than Richard Nixon; he can make the curve of his teeth look as ominous as a crossbow, and he used his eyes as gun sights. Hoskins has the gift usually atributed to American, not English actors – of getting so far inside a character's skin that we seem to be witnessing vivid behavior rather than bravura performance.'

'Americans were kings at that genre of film,' said Mackenzie. 'British gangster films are awful. The praise I got from America pleased me a lot.'

If there was criticism – and there was, for violence and the underbelly of society always provoke strong sentiments, particularly if embodied by a reptilian Harold Shand-type; perhaps vociferous critics should have remembered E. M. Forster's words that 'England has always been disinclined to accept human nature.'

John Mackenzie defended the violence: 'You've got to see that Harold is likeable but he is not a nice lovable little pussycat. He's both those things, you see. Certainly what strikes people the most is when he kills the boy by the neck bleed. There was nothing gratuitous about that. I had to show that Harold, in one thoughtless blow from a bottle, killed the guy. He just hit him, and it so happened that he hit him in the most vital spot. So it wasn't premeditated or planned and Harold didn't think he was going to kill him. I wanted to show an action of uncontrolled fury and an accidental blow, and the jugular vein was the only way I could do it. Otherwise, you wouldn't believe the guy had died if Harold had just smashed him on the head, so I gave a very quick cut to see one spurt of blood. I kept it down a lot. But at the same time I don't believe in pussyfooting around and sort of playing it all with noises off or something. You've got to actually make people realize this is not a cowboy picture. And people *aren't* what they seem to be.

112

There are all these other layers – this likeable guy is at the same time a monster.'

And the man making him that monster would win the *Evening Standard*'s award for Best Actor of 1981, and be nominated for a BAFTA as Best Actor. For his first leading role in a film, that was quite an accomplishment.

Even with such glowing notices in the States, however, *The Long Good Friday* failed to break through to the larger audience it deserved. 'It ran for quite a long time in New York,' Mackenzie said, 'but it had no support. Embassy AVCO had decided to distribute the film and they started to build up a campaign for it, then AVCO folded and Embassy took over. Because it was a takeover they didn't do anything about it. Ironically Lord Grade was back in the picture again because he was the one who came in and bought Embassy! I'm sure he had forgotten about *The Long Good Friday*.'

'It's earned money for *somebody*,' said Hanson. 'What it should have grossed would have been nice for Handmade. You did deals on non-theatric then – we were excluded from the video rights, which were only a gleam in everybody's eye. It was also part of a film deal. So essentially Handmade did all right because they took over the Lord Grade contract, and we were only too glad. We would have paid just to have it out!'

There was even talk of a sequel.

'Barrie had this wonderful notion that the car ran out of petrol,' Hanson explained, 'so Harold apologized to them – "Sorry, lads, have to fill this up" – got a taxi, and went to see his mum to re-enact a scene, one we had to cut, where she was worried about all the violence and he was going to take her away to Greece.

'The scenario was that he had to get out of the country so he went to the States where he's turned into an American gangster. He worries about England being so washed up and sold lock, stock, and barrel and wants to know how much it is to buy the whole country. It's quite a nice story with essentially more humour.'

But Mackenzie, understandably, had his doubts. Sequels rarely work. And the beauty of that long, lingering, enigmatic ending most certainly would have been compromised. 'They asked me to do it,' said Mackenzie, 'and I said, "I've got to resurrect this man – what happens and how do we get out of it?" You don't see him being dead but in my mind he's not going to get out of it or get away. People came up with ideas where the car would go into a skid or into traffic and Harold could jump out . . . I wasn't really keen. I just couldn't see where I could take Harold Shand. Barrie said he

113

would go to America to escape from the IRA, and then get involved with the Mafia, but whereas in England he was a big fish in a small pond, in America he'd be a small fish in a big pond. In a way, you'd ruin it.'

The sequel was never made, yet Harold Shand lived on in the minds of those who'd seen him. As David Denby wrote in *New York* magazine: 'With a wolfish grin and a little boy's anxiety that sweats through the Mr Big exterior when things go out of control, Hoskins unleashes the kind of energy that the great short actors – Cagney, Robinson – were famous for. . . . By acting up a storm, Hoskins reminds us that the gangster has always been so popular in movies because he's a man experiencing his own wildly contradictory nature to the utmost.'

If anyone could be described as 'wildly contradictory', it was Bob Hoskins.

13

Bad Boys

'Acting sometimes unnerves me,' Bob once said. 'I mean, when you have to play a psychopath like Iago and you find you can do it, it's a bit worrying.'

If 1980 had been a year of two soft-hearted eccentrics – lovable Sheppey and rambunctious Arnie Cole – the next year would find Bob reaffirming his innate ability to step easily into Harold Shand's shoes . . . and be bad. Take Iago, for instance, that demon of, as Hazlitt put it, 'diseased intellectual activity with an almost perfect indifference to moral good and evil', that diabolically envious traitor who sets himself up as indispensable and systematically destroys everyone who has turned to him for help and consolation.

Auden said that there are as many Iagos as there are characters to deceive; he must pull out all the stops much as great actors do on stage. He succeeds in accomplishing everything he sets his mind to, even if it means his own destruction. And not a moment too soon.

In 1979, Jonathan Miller, physician, theatrical and opera director, television presenter, author, and pundit, was asked to produce the BBC's seven-year project to stage all thirty-seven of the Shakespeare plays. He was to do them 'straight'. It was reported that one TV executive said, 'I hope he's not going to do them underwater.' Instead he scaled down his vision of a stage production.

The topic of *Othello*, Jonathan Miller wrote in his book, *Subsequent Performances*, is not 'Othello's jealousy but the drama that results from the interaction of Iago's envy and Othello's jealousy'.

He also wrote, 'I took the sensible approach to Shakespeare, and I looked to cast realistic people in his plays. I always wanted to have Iago more like being a serf than a sinner. As a separate villain, a man with a class grudge much as an English army sergeant has his hatred for the commissioned officers.

'I'd seen Bob in *The Long Good Friday* and I'd seen *Veterans*. He was known to those of us in the business, and I knew he could be electric, with an animal vigour, as a performer. In casting Bob Hoskins as Iago there were two other important elements that I wanted to bring out. . . . One is the image of the Trickster, the person who conceals his identity like Rumpelstiltskin, and is destructively dangerous because he does not divulge his personal character. Apparently amiable and honest, he is a monstrous dwarf – and in that sense takes us back to the most ancient myths of the Trickster, the subversive, disruptive, anti-creative force that must constantly be resisted because it threatens to subvert the very fabric of the social universe. And, by making Iago into a working-class sergeant I wanted to stress the idea of social frustration, and to think again about the Puritan element in Shakespeare's plays.'

In Bob's usual quest for authenticity, he decided to do a bit of psychological delving as he prepared to immerse himself in Shakespeare's longest part. That meant taking temporary leave of absence from girlfriend Patti Love's flat in Ariel Road in West Hampstead and spending time with Dr Miller and his family in Primrose Hill.

'Imagine studying a part like that, the perfect study of a psychopath, written *then*,' Bob said. 'And there's Dr Miller, sitting downstairs, and you say, "'Ere, I've got an idea" and 'e says, "Right, what have you got? Ah, yeah, hang on, a friar in the thirteenth century said this" . . . and out came all these books. We used to sit up all night sometimes.'

'[Iago's] emotions are grey, he feels no kindness, he wants to create chaos just for a laugh,' Bob also said. 'I found it a very frightening thing to do. So did Jonathan's family. He told them, "We've got a psychopath coming to stay for a while." The temptation was there to cause all sorts of trouble for them. But I'm glad to say I didn't.' Well, not quite.

'We rehearsed for about a month and Bob stayed with me for tuition – every day we would scan his lines properly, to teach him the music – for about three weeks,' Miller said. 'He was living up on the top floor, and I felt I was his keeper rather than his host. Because I banned him from the pubs, sometimes I would come in and he would be sitting on the sofa giving enormous joints to my kids.

'He was rather overexcited about the forthcoming release of *The Long Good Friday*. And he did spend a lot of time in my house in endless escapes from his creditors. To me he was a working-class boy who was always in debt. He was also having terrible trouble with his ex-wife. I do hope he learns to save his money!'

If Bob was 'frightened' by Iago, he did manage a good job of hiding those fears.

'Anthony Hopkins [Othello] was much less confident,' said Miller. 'He was a juddering mass of nerves and misgivings. Bob had a tough native confidence – not trying to pass himself off as a gentleman – and with his help we tried to cajole Tony into doing what I wanted. Yet Hopkins's speech rather alarmed Bob. Rather than forcefully, Hopkins spoke with great passion and power. "Oh, that's great," Hopkins would say, invigoratedly. "Oh, that's all right, guv," Bob would say.'

'I had peculiar delusions that I was God,' Hopkins said about this phase of his life. 'I was oversensitive and twitching about every-thing and was looking for emotional peace of mind. I gave up seeking the truth the minute I stopped drinking.'

Penelope Wilton, who played Desdemona, had appeared with Bob ages ago in Bond's *Passion*. She also understood why Bob needed extra tutoring on what he'd call 'the verbals'.

'Saying the text is not easy,' she explained, 'but it's also not a great mystery. Once you have a great understanding of how Shakespeare wrote, it helps to illuminate how to play it, to your advantage. And it's a tricky piece if you've not done it before, especially for television. It's one of the few Shakespeare plays without a subplot, which is why it's so wonderful if it *does* work – the poison goes on and on and on. There's also the great humour between Roderigo and Iago.

'Iago is a tricky part as well. Bob's Iago was *bent*. He has a quality of *stillness*. His great strength as an actor is his very strong natural emotion, his ease and familiarity and warmth. He can create a feeling for the common man and is then so able to touch people, to feel *with* the character he's playing.'

In the cerebral Iago, Bob had finally found a character *without* a heart, *without* that soft marshmallow centre that had been at the core of nearly all his villains, and it is no small measure of Bob's talent that his brute, conscienceless little man was so compulsively watchable. In this sense, and for the first time in his career, Bob was playing a leading role completely against type. And, as ever, he took it over and succeeded.

Bob quickly recuperated from his curfew at the Millers, and, when *Othello* was screened on BBC2 on 4 October 1981, he claimed he rang up all his friends and acquaintances (which must have meant most of North London) to encourage them to watch it.

'I was very proud of it,' he said. 'I enjoyed every minute of working with Jonathan. He is one of those rare people who is brilliant and yet a thoroughly nice man with it. In addition he's such a funny man that the whole production was a joy to work on. Sometimes when work has been so enjoyable it's a bit of a letdown when you see it on screen. But this wasn't. . . .'

Most critics were not as enthusiastic. The response was fair to middling, especially to Hopkins's subdued Moor.

Times critic Dennis Hackett commented: 'One thing I will say about Bob Hoskins's Iago . . . is that it was difficult to take one's eyes off him . . . moving with such frantic energy that he made Anthony Hopkins in full roar of ravening jealousy seem an almost-muted Moor. Hoskins's voice, sibilant and insistent as a second-hand car salesman trying to sell someone a pup, hissed away in a manner that quite distracted my ear from the language . . . I found it difficult to believe that anyone could ever have been deceived by him . . . Iago here was not the cunning dog of war but the con man with a card around his neck.'

'Bob was all right as Iago, not *bad*, but I didn't think the *concept* worked,' John Mackenzie offered. 'Jonathan Miller gets very clever ideas, but the whole conception of Iago was off. Something about the logic of the way they'd conceived Iago went totally through me – the way he was plotting or pre-plotting or not plotting. Bob as a practical joker doesn't hang together as a characterization. Iago must be aware that by ruining Othello he ruins himself.'

'It's odd that Bob rarely talks about playing Iago,' Miller commented. 'And that he should exclude what was some of his best work. Bob was interested in making his way as an important actor, and he grabbed it with both hands. There are hundreds of actors who can play feisty little mobsters as he does.'

In April 1981, *The Duchess of Malfi* opened at the Roundhouse to rave notices and Bob shrugged off Iago's skin to inhabit what was now the comfortable role of Bosola once again.

By the summer, though, he was between jobs – 'resting', as he put it, although he was never one to fret. He actually relished the little amounts of time he had off – for he'd been working nonstop, since before *Pennies from Heaven* began shooting in 1977.

So on a lazy summer day – 29 July to be exact – a very famous lazy summer day as far as the succession to the throne is concerned – Bob had a close encounter of the Hoskins kind that was to change his life.

'I was intrumental in how Bob met Linda,' said Ken Campbell. 'Richard Eyre [director at the National Theatre] was away and his wife Susan rang me up and asked if I wanted to go on the river with

Bob Hoskins. (*Richard Young/Rex Features*)

Right: in Ken Campbell's play *Christopher Pea*, in 1968. (*Victoria Theatre*)

Below: An early publicity shot. (*Rex Features*)

Opposite above: Jane, Hoskins' first wife, with their two sons. (*Rex Features*)

Opposite below: After his marriage to Linda Banwell in 1982. (*London News Service*)

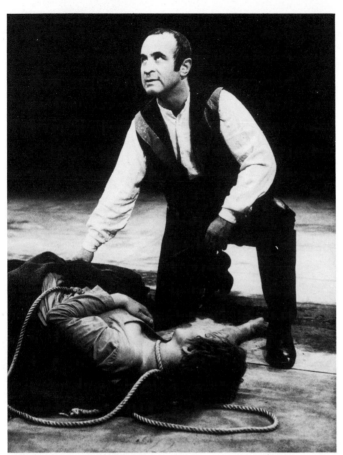

With Helen Mirren in *The Duchess of Malfi* . . . (*Kevin Cummins*)

. . . and in *The Long Good Friday.* (*Aquarius*)

Hoskins on the set of
The Long Good Friday.
(Rex Features)

*Below: The Cotton
Club. (Kobal Collection)*

Above: With Cathy Tyson in *Mona Lisa*, 1986. (*Hand Made Films/Aquarius*)

Right: That certain smile. Bob Hoskins, Cathy Tyson and a famous picture. (*Rex Features*)

Above: With Alan Alda in *Sweet Liberty.* (*Universal/Aquarius*)

Below: With Richard Gere in *The Honorary Consul.* (*World Film Services/Aquarius*)

Above right: With Julia MacKenzie in *Guys and Dolls.* (*Zoë Dominic*)

Below right: With a wax model in Madame Tussauds. (*Peter Brooker/Rex Features*)

The family man. (*Express Newspapers*)

her and a bunch of others, up the Thames, to celebrate Charles and Diana's marriage. The nation would be watching the telly and we'd be getting a cheap boat instead. I said sure. So that was that. And then Bob was round that very night, and he stayed, and I said, "Would you like to come on a boat, I'm sure it's all right." So he said, "Right." So we all went on the boat and had a nice day on the Thames, during the Royal Wedding. Then we got back and went to Haverstock Hill, and the Load of Hay pub. It was very crowded in there since it was a special day and everything. Bob said, "I'll have a pee", and went off to the toilet, while I went to get a drink. I spoke to the girl next to me at the bar to ask if it was her turn next or mine, just that sort of conversation. Bob arrived back and assumed I knew her. He said, "Well, are you gonna introduce me?" in his burly voice. I hadn't met her myself, really. So I said, "Bob, this is Linda." Introducing a second wife is a wee bit chancey, but that's how it came about. She was a schoolteacher named Linda Banwell. And she didn't know who he was.'

'When I spotted Linda, I thought, "That'll do me",' Bob said. It was a situation not unlike the meeting with Jane – in a pub, love at first sight. 'When I first met Linda, we just started talking, and when it was time to go home, she turned round and found this fella on her arm.'

'Aha, I thought,' Bob also said. 'That's exactly what I want. I pursued her. She knew who I was – though Ken said she didn't – but that didn't impress her. I didn't buy her any flowers or chocolates. I was skint.'

'For years and years and years,' Bob would later say, 'my life seemed to be a total and utter waste of time. And then – I met Linda. . . . Everything became sensible. All the things that I'd felt and thought for years suddenly made sense.' And his life would not be the same, as he said with complete candour: 'Everything broke, all the old patterns. Up until then, my career was all right . . . but as far as getting my life together – it didn't come about. I'd made too many mistakes to catch up . . . I went through an awful period and because of that I knew pretty well everything I didn't want in my life. Everybody goes for something they're told they want and by the time they get it, they realize they don't want it. I went through all that. When I met Linda I knew exactly what I did want. She didn't have much say in it. She thinks she did.'

In that fortuitous meeting – proving that opposites do attract – Bob found the woman who would calm him down, provide the stability he'd been craving, and soon become his soulmate. His off-and-on relationship with Patti Love had evidently not provided that sort of satisfaction, and it was now off, permanently. On 7 August, the *Daily Mirror* reported that Patti and Bob had split up. 'Bob is, and always will be, a very special person in my life,' Patti said. 'I don't think I ever want to get married. Having been through a very long relationship, I am not keen to start another.'

Bob *was* keen, however, and he soon moved in with Linda, at what he called a 'teachers' commune' in Hampstead. Linda was teaching sociology as well as being head of house at Haverstock Comprehensive School.

'I think we both decided that was it,' he remarked. 'Not straightaway, but it was like, "Yes, we'll have some of this."'

And while he had some, it was time to go west.

'I wanted to write a play about double nature,' said Sam Shepard, previous director of Bob in *Geography of a Horse Dreamer* and Pulitzer Prize winner for his play *Buried Child*, 'one that wouldn't be symbolic or metaphorical or any of that stuff. I just wanted to give a taste of what it feels like to be two-sided. It's a real thing, double nature. I think we're split in a much more devastating way than psychology can ever reveal. It's not so cute. Not some little thing we can get over. It's something we've got to live with.' Bob Hoskins could understand that philosophy.

True West is the Cain and Abel, *East of Eden* story of two brothers, Austin (Anthony Sher), an aspiring script writer, and Lee (Bob Hoskins), accomplished bum, drunk, and drifter, who sells his idea for a movie 'about two lamebrains chasing each other across Texas' to the producer who was going to buy a script from Austin. Lee must then switch roles with his loved/hated straight and narrow brother, to try and write. And when mom shows up unexpectedly to find the kitchen of her suburban Los Angeles bungalow trashed, she sensibly retreats to a motel, leaving Lee and Austin primed for the classic (and Shepard staple) western show-down.

'It's the classic confrontation of good guy and bad guy,' wrote Shepard biographer Don Shewey. 'They might as well be one guy, just good and bad tussling on metaphysical territory, wrestling with the modern day mystery of identity. The true west is in the mind. No, the true west is in the soul.'

Although it covered the familiar territory of myths, western culture, artistic sellouts, the disintegration of the family, and personal experiences, *True West* was by the far the most accessible and conventionally straightforward of all the Shepard plays, and he had rewritten it thirteen times before declaring himself satisfied with the result. 'This is the first one of my plays I've been able to sit through night after night and not have my stomach ball up in knots of embarrassment,' he said.

'People keep saying *True West* is so commercial,' said John Malkovitch, the definitive American Lee, 'but I think it's a more personal play than most of his. Shepard, like Lee, defies all the things we're told we have to do to be successful. He spent years in a loft picking his nose [one of Lee's more savoury on-stage gestures] and writing really punk stuff with Patti Smith, and then he wins a Pulitzer. He's like Austin when he shrugs off his writing to go make all these movies . . . Lee is the side of Shepard that's always been strangled but never quite killed.'

And Bob, naturally, recognized Lee as one close to his own experience as well, besides being an actor's dream. He began lobbying for the part.

'The National told me they wanted to do Sam Shepard, and presented me with his latest,' the director John Schlesinger related. 'I had seen *True West* in San Francisco and it didn't work for me at all, frankly, but I was convinced we could make it work. I also wanted to work on a production that was not too big, to work with actors in the purest form – theatre – which is what I love.

'First and foremost I couldn't see Bob as Lee. I had first really noticed him in *Pygmalion*. I knew that Bob's external appearance belies how sensitive he is, and I, too, work on instinct, not cerebrally, but Bob really had to convince me he could be an American. And he said he was not going to audition – he wouldn't test because he was afraid he wouldn't read well. So I had dinner with him and his girlfriend Linda, and we got together with Tony Sher – two more unlikely people to play brothers will never be found; they were unalike in every conceivable way – but bit by bit the Cockney disappeared and the Oklahoma came out.

'We made so much noise rehearsing – *The Oresteia* was also in rep at the time and we were disrupting their performances – that the National gave us an outside rehearsal room upstairs at Her Majesty's Theatre. So we went up to the Haymarket every day and sat and gossiped about Hollywood, in this marvellous room. There was lots to talk about!

'I do take everything with a pinch of salt – those standards by which we are judged in Hollywood are extremely questionable. And I don't ever listen to agents – they have ruined more careers by saying that so-and-so's price is now so many dollars. People have such overinflated views of themselves. It's very important to keep one's feet firmly planted, and the great thing about the British tradition as opposed to the Hollywood system is that there are no rules; nobody is going to suddenly question you if you work in all sorts of media. And actors are constantly working even for no money at all, which can be quite a problem. And it's just as well that we're not down on our knees to success, because then it's not so bad when you're no longer successful!'

Bob, of course, who had yet to shoot a film in America, lapped it up. The gifted Schlesinger in his way is as much a maverick as Bob is in his.

'Knowing the States and the people – those certain types – of Hollywood as well as I did helped me very much with *True West,*' Schlesinger continued. 'Naturally a British film critic couldn't resist the temptation at the time to say the play was a "jaundiced view of Hollywood", although my feelings and feuds there had nothing to do with how I staged this play.'

Since Shepard never flies, there was no question of his getting on a plane for the English première of his play, but Schlesinger did manage to talk to him about it. 'He has much more of a sense of humour than I expected.'

Bob described Sam Shepard as 'a smashing fella, but he's keener on being a film star now than writing plays. He would be more interested in Schlesinger offering him a part in a film.'

'Our rehearsals were like taking a Rolls-Royce out of the garage and driving it well,' Schlesinger said. 'But after four or five weeks, by the time we got to previews, we needed the feedback of the audience. It's the most followable of Sam's plays, an excellently structured plot, and I loved doing it. We all enjoyed it enormously. Bob used to say, "We *did* do it well. . . ."'

Fans and critics raved when the play opened on 10 December 1981 at the Cottesloe.

The Spectator's Mark Amory wrote: 'Hoskins, swinging his brawny tattooed arms and gnawing the ends of most words, takes the first act by storm. Perhaps Hoskins inhabits his role more firmly, while Sher explains his, but this is quibbling about some of the best acting in London; and they are very funny, too.'

Bob found he had some rather unexpected and unusual fans. 'The audience was packed with skinheads every night,' he said. 'It's because of the haircut. They'd come up to me after the show and say, "I liked the way you smashed up the room."'

He also found that three assignments were awaiting him. The first was taping an appearance on *Omnibus*, that would be transmitted on BBC1 on 9 May 1982, about the proposed development, by Greycoat Commercial Estates, of the South Bank's derelict Coin

Street, near the National Theatre. The local Lambeth Council preferred that the land be used for housing/public space, and an outraged public agreed. Bob, no stranger to extemporaneous speaking, was pleased to put his big mouth to good use.

'The Thames is being ruined for working people,' he said. 'I went to a public meeting about the redevelopment of Coin Street and said quite a lot. As a result I was asked to do this programme for *Omnibus*.'

Speaking with passionate fervour, he told a Department of the Environment inspector in April 1981 that he had 'just made a gangster film about a land carve-up in London. It is a piece of fiction about police and political corruption. When I made the film I thought it was over the top, but from what I have heard today it makes the film look like Winnie the Pooh.'

His pleas for the community fell on deaf ears, and a few days later the sale of ten acres to Greycoat was permitted. *Omnibus* had made a worthy documentary, and Bob had done what he could for the working class of South London.

The second job was a cameo in *Pink Floyd The Wall*, written by Roger Waters and directed by Alan Parker. He'd played 'The Manager' of a rock star named Pink (Bob Geldof), who is losing his mind in a hotel room in Los Angeles (a phenomenon not unknown to many who have stayed in hotel rooms in Los Angeles).

Third and most important was the offer of the part of the smooth-talking, crap-shooting Nathan Detroit in the National Theatre's major revival of *Guys and Dolls*.

These appearances were ignominiously interrupted in January 1982 by, as one headline blared, 'A Blow for Bob's Nose'. While returning on a plane from America after the release there of *The Long Good Friday*, his nose began to bleed uncontrollably from a burst vein, necessitating a stay in a London hospital.

Blood also featured prominently in *The Wall*. Based on the massively selling album and sell-out tour by the Floyd, *The Wall*, shot over a period of sixteen weeks, contained 977 shots, 4885 takes, and 350,000 feet of film – 60 hours – which was edited down in 5400 cuts to 99 minutes of screen time in which Bob Hoskins appears in three scenes for approximately 3 ½ minutes. He was seen walking down an airport corridor, cajoling his reluctant star; pigging out at the obligatory post-concert-groupie-crash-the-party scene, most memorably chomping into half a ripe pineapple and swilling champagne from the bottle before spitting it out; and then, when his star has flipped, breaking into the tomb-like hotel room and alternating between pleading and arguing as he tries to get the zombie Pink to go on for the night. As poor Pink is hauled away, Bob picks up the phone, lips pursed in frustration, only to find it has been ripped out of the wall. Hey, it's only rock'n'roll!

'I was particularly happy to get Bob Hoskins for The Manager,' wrote Parker in his production notes. 'For the hotel-room scene I wrote dialogue for Bob to work with, but he soon abandoned it and improvised his own, giving the crew a few laughs and some welcome light relief they'd been denied through the rest of the filming. His ad-libbed lines as the paramedics tried to revive Pink succeeded in making the crew laugh as well as Bob Geldof, who was interrupted out of his catatonic state by Bob's one-liners.'

A box office, but not altogether a critical, success – 'For a condemnation of British society,' said *Films in Review*, 'one only has to read Page 1 of *Screen International* to see that *The Wall* is currently the top-selling film in London.' *The Wall* did please Pink Floyd fans. And whether the film was loved or hated did not much matter to Bob. *The Wall* was hardly riding on his performance. He came, he joked, he ate a pineapple, and he left . . . heading straight back to the familiar corridors of the National Theatre where, if he lingered too long in the toilet, his name would be paged on the loudspeakers and where he would astonish critics and fans alike as the tap-dancing, gambling, New York hood: Nathan Detroit.

The Bob Hoskins who lived his roles couldn't have picked a better role model than Nathan, who finally weds his 'well-known fiancée', Miss Adelaide, after fourteen years of delays. Bob set the date for his own wedding to Linda.

Yet the Bob Hoskins who lived his role as the philandering Arthur Parker would find himself faced with the most agonizing public humiliation of his life when his ex-wife Jane told her version of one of the songs from *Pennies,* 'I'll Be Glad When You're Dead, You Rascal You' to the avid readers of *The Sun*.

14

Get Me to the Church on Time

'It was a cast made in heaven,' said Richard Eyre, 'and I found it difficult to conceive of doing *Guys and Dolls* without Bob Hoskins. In fact, I would have thought of *not* doing it had we not got him. There certainly would have been a conflict had he wavered.'

Guys and Dolls had been a dream nearly as long in the making as Miss Adelaide's engagement. One of the then Managing Director of the National Theatre Laurence Olivier's preferred projects in 1970 – he'd play Nathan – it had been scrapped when an embolism in Olivier's leg prevented him from performing. When Richard Eyre joined the National as Associate Director in mid 1981 and was asked to think of staging a 'major popular classic', he remembered *Guys and Dolls*. It was only fitting that his £94,000 production would fill the theatre bearing Olivier's name. By the end of 1981 the musical was cast and by early January 1982 a lot of National Theatre actors were getting sore feet.

'I rarely do musicals,' Eyre explained, 'but I've always wanted to do *Guys and Dolls* because of Kenneth Tynan's assessment that this was the second best American play.' (The first was Arthur Miller's *Death of a Salesman*.) 'I had known the Damon Runyon stories for years, and I found them very very attractive. It was an irresistible combination: the best book of unusual stories and characters combined with the best words and wonderfully irresistible songs.'

Runyon's romanticized Broadway, where euphemisms abound and hoods are guys and hookers are dolls, led Jo Swelling and Abe Burrows to write a book that is true to Runyon, and songsmith Frank Loesser to pen some of the most witty and literate tunes ever written. The romantic comedy storyline, however, of gambler Sky Masterson (Ian Charleson), Sister Sarah of the Save-a-Soul Mission (Julie Covington), Nathan Detroit (Bob) and Miss Adelaide (Julia

125

McKenzie), as well as assorted gamblers and lovers, sinners and repenters, is really quite preposterous.

Bob, of course, fitted right in. In a way his brooding Bill Cracker and menacing 'Ronnie Kray' and miming Arthur Parker and all those characters in *Songbook* had prepared him for a six-month stint in a fully-staged musical. Besides, he'd always thought that Sinatra had been miscast in the Hollywood film, with Marlon Brando as Sky, Jean Simmons as Sarah, and Vivian Blaine – 'the definitive Adelaide', according to Julia McKenzie.

'Sinatra is very musical,' Bob explained, 'but he's a bit heavy-handed, a bit mump-headed. I can't wait to get stuck into it. The language is so rich. I've only got one song on my own and I might just manage it. You could do a sort of comic-strip character with it, completely surfacy, but I think we can get further than that. Anyway, I'm going to have a go.'

'On the first day of rehearsals,' said Kevin Williams, who played Rusty Charley, 'it was immediately apparent that Bob would be the leader. "Ooh, it's cold in this room," he said, so he marched over to the phone and said, "It's bleedin' freezin' in here, get some heat on." Half an hour later he went to the phone again. "What – it's too 'ot, turn it off for fuck's sake. Wot you tryin' to do – burn us up?" From then on we were all singing his praises. Everybody very quickly recognized his basic quality – his open warmth. He's not an *imposing* person, but Bob is just pure sensitivity and a humane human being. It's an East End type of quality – he's the common man who can adapt to any situation. Sophisticated people find him novel and the common man finds him an equal. And as an actor he works inside out. He's the nearest thing to the English 'Method'. He uses his own persona – it all comes out of him. Suddenly, the final stroke of a brush is what makes you an actor, and he finds it like Brando or De Niro found it. What he did was clever, instinctive, naturalistic; he adapted his style to the broadness of musical comedy, so he didn't appear a caricature. We all read the Runyon stories – Richard Eyre was a stickler for them. Before rehearsals actually began he told us, "This is the material you can glean from – find out who you want to be." We were lucky to have that to hang on to. But Richard's casting was brilliant and having Bob was inspired. There was not one person in the show who could be mistaken for anyone else, and that's very unusual.'

'We rehearsed like a play,' Eyre says. Most of the company, who were actors, not musical-comedy stars, was appearing in rep at the time as either ancient Greeks in *The Oresteia* (which had been disturbed by the rambunctious rehearsals for *True West*) or as

American Indians in *Hiawatha*. 'It really was an outstanding group of actors; their singing was quite musical and there was a real sense of energy. It wasn't regimented. What was also clear was that although Bob and Julia were clearly stars, there was no sense of hierarchy.'

'When I first started working with Bob his down-to-earth manner scared me a bit,' Julia McKenzie said. 'He was panicky and got cross with himself when he didn't master new things straight away. But he's doing fine now. He has a lovely, croaky voice. . . . It wasn't a technically demanding show – it was always a magical show, and you can't go far wrong with it,' she also said. 'We had dialect coaching and Bob had tap lessons every day. He has two left feet but he buckled down to it and smiled a lot, like I do.'

'To see Bob tap dancing . . .' Williams said. 'It *is* very hard to do, and I was lucky because I had studied from the ages of nine to seventeen. It's like riding a bike – you never lose the actual technique even if you get a bit rusty. Besides the Hat Box dancers, only Julia, Bernard Sharpe [Hot Horse Herbie] and myself had training. The basic problem is rhythm – I don't think Brits are born with it! There were workshops every morning and the choreographer, David Toguri, worked with the actors, keeping the rhythm basic and then alternating with more experienced dancers to create a nice ensemble effect. It does wonders to see twenty-six people doing the same steps at a time.'

'Every day,' Eyre remarked. 'I'm surprised and moved at the courage and commitment of these actors and the energy they give. Rehearsals were fun, although Bob broke a vein in his nose and was out of the picture for about a week. He got slightly behind in his tap. I always thought it was an exercise of will – the will doing the work of the imagination, with the will you can convince an audience that the feet are moving! Bob would look at me with that helplessly appealing "You know I'm dancing" look.'

'David made people who couldn't move, move,' said Sue Blane, designer of the wonderful clothes based on old American movies of the forties and tacky Frederick of Hollywood catalogues. 'He focused on the ones who could dance, and it's all to his credit that the finale was such a treat.

'The wonderful thing about *Guys and Dolls* is that you can vulgarize it, especially Miss Adelaide and her dancers. When you work with period clothes it's helpful for the *focus* of the character, to give people helpful information and pointers on how to feel. You can't use real clothes because they're too detailed and faded and don't fit perfectly. I talked to everybody about their costumes and showed them drawings first. For Bob, it was hard to get anything in a broad pin-stripe, so his suit was made of the inside-out-side of Italian suiting. You can't get wonderful broad pin-stripes like that on the outside any more! To see Bob's suit on a hanger . . . it was completely square! It was so sweet. Ironically you'd think someone of Bob's size wouldn't move as well as he did – he was quite stocky at the time – but as long as you're brave enough anything can work. I did have tremendous back up from the cast, although it was very hard to get people to wear hats. Bob wore his, with a great big wide brim, in the first two scenes, and he'd come off stage, swearing that he couldn't see. But he had to wear it, because we had to establish who he is early on.'

'Everyone, cast and crew, was very proud of the show,' Blane continued. 'It was a very close company. Julia worked so hard on her character it had to fall into place. And it was bloody hard work. The real fun didn't begin until the technical run-through. We all knew there was something exciting and the buzzing went on all week.' ITV's *South Bank Show* came and taped the rehearsal-in-progress for a teaser show to be seen on 7 March. 'The first run-through was devastating. We didn't stop laughing for an hour and a half.'

'We *were* a jolly bunch,' said Julia. And Bob was jolly with them, until 2 February 1982, when the headline 'My Long, Bad Years with Hard Man Hoskins' was splashed across two tell-all pages of the *Sun*.

'Bob is a very violent man,' Jane, as interviewed by Jean Ritchie, said. 'The parts he plays are usually violent and he admits he almost always plays himself. Very early in our marriage he broke my finger. And my rib cage will never be the same again. . . . He kicked the gearbox out of a car once because it was in his way and he would kick us if we were in his way. . . . He has thrown knives around and come into the room carrying a hangman's noose. We have holes in the plaster where he has hurled things in temper. Sarah, particularly, was terrified by him. Our son Alex certainly knows what it is like when Daddy is violent. . . .

'I think he probably always had other women on the side,' she went on. 'But I always believed him when he told me how everyone else was doing it, not him . . . Bob always lies. He is a compulsive liar. . . . He embroidered stories to make them sound better. Just fantasy, really, but there is a difference between that and the sort of lies you tell to keep out of trouble. I didn't know Bob told those till later. . . . He had a lot of problems. . . . Bob was sensitive, artistic, and very egocentric. Everything revolved around him. He had a great belief in his own talent. I do too and I still respect him as an actor . . . but I don't think he'll ever change.'

Furthermore, Bob had reneged on his promise to pay £11,000 a year in child support, and Jane had been forced to take him to court. As the marriage had disappeared, so had hopes of an amicable settlement. Bob quite regularly and publicly complained that he was broke, homeless, and reduced to living in a Jeep, surviving on £50 a week.

'Living on £50 a week lasted for six months when he was having matrimonial problems,' explained Sally Hope, who in essence had babysat Bob through his divorce. 'It was drawn from the bank on the advice of his solicitor.'

As Jonathan Miller remarked, Bob always did have a problem with his money. Whatever he had, he spent. And when he didn't have it, he still spent it. And as for the sob story about having no roof of his own, he always had a place to stay. The door to Sally Hope's house was always open and Bob was almost a part of her family. His parents kept a room for him. Various girlfriends let him move in. Claims of nights spent in a Jeep may make for good stories, but they weren't necessary.

Of course the Hoskins marriage had always been stormy and the divorce *had* been traumatic for Bob. Jane's pithy comment was that Bob didn't like being divorced because 'he doesn't believe anyone can fall out of love with him'.

The airing of his dirty laundry in public, however, left him thoroughly shocked, depressed, and embarrassed. For a man who does not believe in 'yesterday', it was particularly unbelievable that his old problems should yet again be brought up and discussed in detail. In that same *Sun* article, he said, 'Divorce is a very painful and personal subject and I do not wish to comment on mine in public, especially as the marriage has been over for at least five years.' At this point they had been divorced for eighteen months.

He also told Steve Grant: 'I think she was put up to it – I certainly hope she got well paid, though I hate to think of the effect it's having on the kids. They've had enough to put up with already. All that has happened is that I've stopped buying the *Sun* and a lot of people have told me that the wife was well out of order.'

'When the article came out,' Sally said, 'the solicitor wanted Bob to answer, which would have been very unwise. He made a "no comment" on the grounds that he didn't wish to upset the children and had no wish to drag it out.'

However bad the problems are between two adults, however justifiable the anger and frustration, the end result is always that it's the children who suffer the most. Jane Hoskins still has ambivalent feelings about the piece, but, as she explains, whatever impact or humiliation that article may have had for Alex and Sarah, it was, unfortunately, unavoidable . . . due to Bob's own insensitivity towards those same children he'd said 'had had enough to put up with already'.

'I took no money from the *Sun*,' Jane said with a rueful laugh. 'Maybe I should have. I couldn't accept their money. Bob had said I wasn't hypocritical enough. After poverty, homelessness for us, and a handicapped child, I couldn't give in. My son would have gone into care. We were being cut off, and these appalling games were being played in court. It wasn't just Bob's money. You can't organize anything with a man who hides and won't speak to you. Bob always insisted that he was going to find the best help for Alex, but I was the one who incorporated exercising him three to four times a day into my lifestyle. Bob's "help" never materialized; yet again nothing happened. Whenever he feels safe he can push anybody over to one side, but during adolescence the children needed to have somebody other than myself. I feel sorry that Bob picks the children up and drops them. When you have two children who are vulnerable, sitting shivering in Paddington Station because Daddy forgot he was supposed to pick them up . . . but of course that's not *his* fault. Bob has such problems with ordinary, simple matters of organization.

'For example, Alex had an operation, and he was on crutches afterward. Bob met us at the station, and he said, "What's the matter with Alex?" It's his way of denying that his son is handicapped. But if I say, "Take him for walks", he won't. He'll do the opposite. If he is forced to treat them as equals, he recognizes them as equals. I am not so much interested in what has happened as what *will* happen. It's up to a child to leave his parents, but I want my children to be able to go and visit their father. If the only way I can do it is through the law, then I will use it. If Bob feels he can chuck you around, he does so. There have been Christmases with no presents. He has let them down on holidays.'

It was the Christmas of 1981, though, that proved to be the last straw, when Bob's behaviour could have had a major, detrimental effect on his son's future and physical well-being. 'I didn't know where he was living,' Jane explained, 'and he cut me off again. Bob made an issue about Christmas access, but because I had made an appointment back in September for Alex to see a specialist at the end of December, Bob went straight to the High Courts, claiming I was impeding access. That I was denying his fatherhood.

'I simply couldn't fight this. So, at Christmas, Sarah went up three days early and I took Alex up on the bus after he had seen the specialist, who had told me that my son must see a neurologist immediately. Once I arrived in London Bob's father gave me £5 to "help" with the travelling expenses. Where was Bob? I always felt he wouldn't do that to his child. I just couldn't face it. Of all the things he'd done, nothing had the same cruelty.'

Whatever the reasons, it was done with. Bob's bitterness would be apparent in comments he'd make to journalists like, 'I had a terrible first marriage, a bleeding awful time. It didn't put me off women, though – just women like my first wife . . .' or . . . 'Marriage is definitely better the second time around. In the first one I found out all the things I *didn't* want.' Saying things like that are, of course, equally hurtful to Jane and his children.

Bob has been fortunate that most allegations made in the *Sun* tend not to be taken all that seriously – as if anyone admits to reading it anyway – and yesterday's edition is more likely to be tomorrow's fish and chips wrapping. Even more luckily, he had found a woman he was planning to marry as soon as he found proper space – making one wonder just how 'broke' he was if he was out house-hunting.

He was also planning to make Nathan Detroit come alive.

'*Guys and Dolls* was probably the biggest party ever held on stage,' Kevin Williams says. 'It was the ultimate fusion of a near-perfect company.'

'We *were* surprised at the fantastic reaction of the National Theatre – it was more like a pop concert,' said Julia McKenzie.

'Bob walked out and 1200 people were actually in the palm of his hand,' Richard Eyre says. 'To get that response and affection from the audience, to control them as he did takes an extraordinary ability.'

'Nathan Detroit has to come out at the beginning in a terrible blather,' said Norman Rossington, who would later perform the role 467 times. 'His big game is on in ten minutes, the law is after him, you've got to establish his relationship with Miss Adelaide and his sidekicks, his fear of the cops, deal with Sky, and the guys at the crap shoot . . . and pace the show. The piece itself dictates the speed – it's midtown Manhattan rat-a-tat-tat and the most marvellous musical.'

'Informing the audience of the entire plot – especially in the first minutes; you *can't* do it wrong – is the most difficult task for any actor,' Williams agreed. 'To do that pure exposition and still appeal as a character you must have a total hold of yourself and of who you are to do that. Bob was great – even his singing. The punters can forgive the singer even if he didn't do well – he gets the sympathy vote!'

The London critics were, for once, unanimous in their praise of the show when it opened on 9 March: the tight-knit ensemble, the distinctive personalities of the leads, the wonderful idiosyncrasies of the gamblers, Toguri's choreography, and especially John Gunter's magnificent neon evocation of the bright lights in the big, skyscrapered city. 'I doubt if in its career the National Theatre has given the audience such unalloyed pleasure as this production of *Guys and Dolls* did last night,' said Milton Shulman in the *Standard*. 'And Bob Hoskins has the anxious bewilderment of an accident looking for somewhere to happen. His frantic efforts to avoid the law and romance are a delight to behold.'

Mark Amory in *The Spectator* wrote: 'Bob Hoskins creates devious, vulnerably comic variations on his past gangster to endearing effect and Julia McKenzie earns the right to be hailed as a new star as usual.'

'It takes self-discipline to keep each show fresh,' Julia said, 'but as we weren't performing continuously – it was in rep – it wasn't too difficult.'

Guys and Dolls was an instant sell-out success. 'A lot of Yanks came to see it and didn't realize it was an English company,' says Norman Rossington. 'I'd hear, "Gee, I didn't know there were so many Americans acting in London." But Nathan Detroit suited Bob down to the ground.'

Far more astonishing, though, was the overwhelming response to the National's new Bargain Night at £2 per seat. Chris Voisey, manager of a film memorabilia shop in Soho, told the tale: 'Bob had been a favourite of mine since *Thick as Thieves* and he evokes a fanatical following among ordinary people. He became a conduit for getting me into the theatre, which had a rather snob status, something rich people did, or those who used the theatre as if it were a planet – to look at the stars, not the production. Besides, tickets for *Guys and Dolls* were impossible to get. So when I read about Bargain Night I knew there was nothing to stop me. And I also knew that a lot of people would be queuing up when the box office opened at nine that morning for that evening's tickets, so I decided to get there at 5 am. Even so, I must have been about 130th in the queue.

'It was really a great atmosphere, waiting. The National served us coffee and croissants. Jim Carter [Big Jule] did a magic act. By the time the doors opened there was a queue all the way down to Big Ben – about 1000 people and ninety-nine per cent of them were there for *Guys and Dolls*. When it was my turn, I very fearfully asked for two front row seats. They still had them because no one thought it was a very good seat. Later, on *London Reports*, a helicopter shot showed the queue all the way down to the Houses of Parliament.

'A lot of the cast said that night was the best ever. Bernard Sharpe said it was like performing at Wembley. Everyone put themselves out because they knew the audience that was there *really* wanted to see the show, so it affected the cast like magic. "Rocking the Boat" got six encores. Bob is supposed to say, "Well, Brother Brannigan, what can we do for you?" and he couldn't say it. Everyone was screaming so much.

'Well, that was it for me. I slept out at the National, in a sleeping bag in the cold. I got to know a lot of the people and made quite a few friends. We knew what we'd be seeing the next night so it didn't matter. One girl lost her job and when the box office heard about it, the National hired her as a dresser. We became the front-row regulars, and the cast got to like us. Bob used to say that line after "Rocking the Boat", pause, then look at us to see if we liked it. If we did, he'd slap David Healy [Nicely-Nicely Johnson, and the man who'd replaced Bob in *Songbook*] on the back and wait for another encore.'

'"Rocking the Boat" was a show-stopper,' said Eyre. 'Bob would kind of conduct the scene; the orchestration of the audience was in his hands, and he would provoke encore after encore.'

'I've never seen a more crowded stage door,' Voisey said. 'The actors were such a nice bunch and they were always so concerned if we were cold from sleeping out. The reason I went back so many times was that I was trying to get a night as good as the first one. The chemistry was sheer magic. The big thing was to grab a "petal" from a showgirl in "A Bushel and a Peck". Once I got Julia's garter. The unfair thing about Bob was that he never threw anything into the audience.'

'We did things the right way, the proper, pukka way,' Bob said. And he wasn't talking about Nathan's long-overdue hitch to Miss Adelaide. He was talking about his second marriage.

Bob and Linda had been engaged for several months and invitations were sent out for the wedding on 12 June at Islington

Central Methodist Church. The guys and dolls of the National Theatre decided to throw a party in a rehearsal room to celebrate it, since most of them would be on a much-deserved week-long holiday during the week of the wedding. It was only fitting that Julia McKenzie should lustily sing 'Making Whoopie'.

'We gave Bob and Linda a wonderful party before their wedding,' she said, 'with bagpipes and a cabaret and poached salmon and champagne. He was very moved and so were we.'

Bob was even more moved on his wedding day, despite gloomy wet weather and an erroneous report a few days earlier in the *Daily Mail*. It read, 'Sorry, Bob, heaven must wait' and quoted him as saying 'I wish I'd never said anything about it. It's not definite now.'

Linda wore a lovely flapper-style dress and headpiece, designed by Ossie Clarke, and Bob a dapper suit from *The Long Good Friday*; daughter Sarah was a bridesmaid; best friend Gawn Grainger, who had acted with him at the National Theatre, was best man; and the Albion Band, featuring Maddy Prior, provided the music. Over 300 guests eagerly retired to Bob's £50,000 brick semi-detached house within walking distance of his mum and dad – they were pleased as punch about *this* marriage – for vast quantities of barbecued beef spit-roasted in the large garden. Bob timed the wedding cleverly to coincide with extensive renovations in his new home so guests could stub out their cigarettes on the concrete floors, scrawl graffiti on soon-to-be-painted walls, at their host's suggestion, and happily make a mess.

There was only one discordant note for some of the guests. Of all the publications in the world, the only one lucky enough to have a journalist at the wedding – she was a personal friend of Bob's – was the high-society magazine *Harper's & Queen*. As unlikely a magazine to be associated with left-wing Bob as *Gourmet* would be with the kitchens of Pentonville Prison. 'For a guy who was obsessed with the press not knowing anything about his wedding, that woman from *Harper's* was appalling,' a guest said. 'Everybody was upset; they were harassed by this woman with a tape recorder as soon as they arrived.'

But that was soon forgotten. Bob said the wedding was just wonderful and Linda said it was the best day of her life. And then both of them went back to work.

' "Usually, when you get a cast, there's one person who buggers it up and makes it hell," Bob told me,' said Chris Voisey. ' "Not so with this one. There was no one! The cast used to hurry on to do it." '

Guys and Dolls did it for the dough and the dolls, the etiquette of the crap game. It did it for the players. 'We recorded the soundtrack album in three days, live in the studio,' said Kevin Williams. 'We were all riding high. And Bob led us again. No one makes money out of cast albums, and the stars usually split the nonexistent royalties down the middle. "No, everybody gets the same," Bob insisted.'

Bob *has* always said that if he stays too long in any one production he begins to look longingly at the exit signs, and *Guys and Dolls* was no exception, resounding success or not.

'It was never the same again once the ensemble changed, although Julia was still there,' Voisey said. Trevor Peacock took over as Nathan. 'You could tell.'

Guys and Dolls swept most of the top honours at the Society of West End Theatre Awards for 1982. The *Plays and Players* 1982 Awards, voted by the London theatre critics, honoured Richard Eyre as 'Best Director' and John Gunter as 'Best Designer'.

'Bob wears his talent very lightly – he's serious but not ostentatious about it,' Richard Eyre said. '*Guys and Dolls* marked the beginning of his ascension, his moving into the stratosphere. He's become a phenomenon.'

The phenomenon was about to travel as far as he could from the chilly back corridors of the National Theatre and discover the joys of a three-month location shoot in steamy Coatzacoalcos and even steamier Veracruz, Mexico.

15

Honorary Coppers

'What a waste!' Bob said. 'It could have been the first Graham Greene film that's been done properly since *Brighton Rock*.'

The Honorary Consul could have been subtitled, 'Don't Cry for Gere, Argentina'. Richard Gere played Eduardo Plarr, the doctor son of a *desaparecido* father and a Paraguayan mother, whose detachment from his emotions is worn as slickly as his clothes. He becomes entangled with the young prostitute wife, Clara (Elipedia Carrillo), of the 'pitiably small beer' alcoholic Consul, Charlie Fortnum (Michael Caine), and drawn into the terrorist plans of boyhood–chum–turned–priest (Joaquim de Almeida) who gave it up for the love of a good woman, and his friend (A Martinez) who's been tortured in prison and might know the whereabouts of Plarr's father. When the guerilla group botch their kidnap attempt of the American ambassador and snatch Charlie instead, Plarr finds himself in over his head, with predictably fatal consequences. All this action is overseen by the shrewd and ever-suspicious Colonel Perez (Bob Hoskins).

Welcome to Graham Greene territory, where the morals and passions of disillusioned British expatriates in the hot climes of the third world are explored with subtle complexity. Unfortunately, Hollywood hocus-pocus territory tends to be a bit more trashy and money orientated. The making of *The Honorary Consul* became nearly as much of a tangled web, with its late-night machinations and tropical diseases, as any plot ever conceived by Greene.

'The producer, Norma Heyman, came to me and said she had Richard Gere,' John Mackenzie explained. He had by now recuperated from the ordeal of getting *The Long Good Friday* into theatres. 'And I was not too keen on that . . . but I'd always wanted to do Graham Greene. Norma insisted that Paramount would only put up the money if Gere was in it, so I went to see him. When I met him, I was agreeably surprised. I liked him and found him very intelligent. He talked about the book, its implications and philosophy. I thought he was great; he knew what he was talking about and wasn't just a Hollywood fool with a pretty face. So I said I'd do it.'

Yet the film was problematic from the outset – making *The Honorary Consul* into a feature film proved an ambitious task. Conveying the emotional resonances of the book would have been easier perhaps in a mini-series, not a 103-minute movie. Playwright and adaptor Christopher Hampton had to wrestle with the script from day one.

'It was trying to compress too big a thing into too short a time and in the meantime simplify it to the extent that it degraded the novel,' Mackenzie said. 'If I were to do the film over again, I could make it much better, working with Christopher from the beginning, without a script. He had done three versions so we worked on that basis. I did certain things to it, but it wasn't like the collaborative effort of *The Long Good Friday*.

'There were areas of it I thought were fine, but in the end [the film company] took out anything that gave it any depth. There was this whole thing about "We don't want any of your religious claptrap philosophy." We tried to keep it to a minimum in the original script, but it was filleted out anyway. But I mean some of that *is* Graham Greene, who's a deep writer. If you take all that out you're left with a rather melodramatic, slightly boring narrative. The weakness was not the acting, but what wasn't there to begin with. And what they really wanted was a love story with Richard Gere.

'The other thing is, I would have hesitated longer about making the film if I'd known that Richard is *such* a sex symbol, like a male Marilyn Monroe, in America. Once you're in that category it's very difficult to get out; certain audiences and critics don't want to see you do or be anything else. That's why Richard wanted to do it, to *break* it, you see. But when you try to do something like this, it's dismissed. Richard suffered from that a lot. He got a raw deal. He's an intelligent, hard-working actor who was very good and worked hard. What more do you want?'

Paramount, evidently, wanted a whole lot more. They wanted Richard Gere to take off his clothes and flex his pecs. And they were going to make sure that the steam on screen was more than what was rising from the virgin jungles of Coatzacoalcos. But the reason Gere wanted to do this film was exactly the same reason Paramount was so unhappy about it.

Principal shooting began in Veracruz on 12 October 1982. Three days before, Richard Gere had finished shooting the remake of *Breathless* in Los Angeles. Three days before in London Bob Hoskins had had his last crap shoot in *Guys and Dolls*. And very soon after that, *An Officer and a Gentleman*, starring Gere and Debra Winger, went over the $100 million mark, bringing the film completely unforeseen megabuck glory.

So where was the studio's prodigal son? Stuck being a disaffected and detached Catholic doctor who falls in love with a hooker in Veracruz, Mexico.

'Suddenly, Paramount has a star,' Mackenzie said. 'Then I started to film, and after I sent the first set of rushes the phone calls came. "What do you think Richard Gere is doing – is he trying to *act!?* What *is* this? No, he must – he's trying to speak with a *British* accent? What is this British accent he's putting on? *He's an international star and no international stars have ever changed their accent!!!*" ' I said, "Oh really?" And the battle began. I argued that the audience might expect a hero, but that I didn't think the accent mattered. Paramount couldn't stand that Plarr wasn't a very sympathetic character. But Richard insisted.'

Bob must have wondered why he'd insisted on doing this film, though any actor who'd had as much success with a character and film as he'd had with Harold Shand and working with John Mackenzie would certainly have wanted to work with that director again, even in a supporting role.

'I wasn't going to cast Bob,' Mackenzie explained, 'because I didn't think it was a big enough part. It was substantial, but small, and I thought he was too big for it. But Sally Hope said it would put him in the American scene, and reveal to Hollywood that he wasn't just a Cockney actor. They'd never seen him in anything else. "Look," she said, "it's not a big part but it's quite showy. It's got two key scenes in it. I would certainly want him to be in it, if you'll have him." So I asked Bob if he really wanted to be in this and he said he did. I said, "I'm going to have to hear you doing a South American accent and I'm going to have to have some idea of how authentic you can be." And he did it, in my house, just the two of us. He'd been practising because he knew he was coming up for a little audition. He was great. I'd seen him in *Inserts* and knew he could *do* American – because all British actors *say* they can – but he did the Hispanic accent well. He can do Irish too – anything but straight English. True Cockneys never can!'

So there Bob was, where he'd wanted to be, ensconced in the wilds of Veracruz for three months, playing 'not a bad man, as policemen go,' according to Plarr, one who possesses a gruff charm and an extrovert belief in his own invincibility and power, yet who would nonetheless shoot his own grandmother if it proved expedient.

Luckily, Bob found a soul mate when Michael Caine reported for duty.

Caine's first words to Bob on the set were, according to Bob, 'Come 'ere, my son. You're gonna earn a lotta money and you've gotter learn 'ow to look after your money. Come to your Uncle Michael and I'll tell yer.'

It was a stroke of genius on Mackenzie's part that he asked Caine, the true professional, to play the old lush Consul, a despicably pathetic man if he weren't so charmingly self-effacing. 'It was a real departure for me,' Caine said. 'I've always played strong, young men – now I was playing an older, weaker one. But it's a very funny part as well, and in the end – like a lot of weak men – they look weak until they're under pressure and then the one you thought was going to collapse stands up to it marvellously.'

'Bob and Caine would let rip in Cockney,' said A Martinez, who played the hot-headed Aquino. 'It was like you were transported to another planet. It just goes to show that it's basically humans rapping about humans. For my money Richard's accent was a lot more consistent than Bob's was and yet Bob got nothing but praise and Richard was castigated for his evil attempts at an Englishman. If people have a bug up their asses about you they're going to get you. And there are a lot of bugs up a lot of asses about Richard Gere.

'He did a great job in a thankless part, and I think he knew what was happening when he was in it. One night by the hotel pool, Michael Caine came down after we'd done the first scene, and Richard turned to him and said, "You sonofabitch, you come down here and I've been busting my ass in this horrid slime-bog backwater. You're going to come waltzing in here for a few weeks and steal this movie." And that was the case.

'But it was a wonderful atmosphere, especially for me because I hadn't had the opportunity to work with such good people. I thought *The Long Good Friday* was an amazing film on all levels and then to get a chance to work with Mackenzie – I was pretty happy. Almost everyone involved was from England and a lot had worked together previously and the fact that they all got on was a great way of breaking the ice.

'I was amazed by how ferociously everyone drank after work. I mean every single day. Of course it was a lot easier to talk to everybody when we were mutually shit-faced than when you're on the set and your ass is on the line! One night, Bob, Joaquim, and I went out drinking in some little place outside of Veracruz. And I was moanin' and bitchin' about the fact that my character, who like all of them in the book, was so well-rounded, had been cut to shreds.

'We all got pretty loaded, and then Bob said, "That's all bullshit. If you're in front of a camera, you have the opportunity to tell the whole story. What you need to do is break out of it and take some chances. Don't be predictable. *Scare* people – scared people are going to watch. They don't know what the hell you're going to do next . . . it's probably going to be unpleasant and it's probably going to be something strong and the next time they see you they're going to be worried. So they'll be waiting for it." He went on for a long time about the need to put danger in your work, and be dangerous . . . to take those kinds of chances and risks. He was like really loud and intense and bug-eyed about it, and he made me remember an American Indian I had worked with one time who said, after a night of drinking, "I'm going to show you how to break a guy's nose." It was an insane thing to experience because this Indian was huge and extremely drunk and had a look on his face like he wasn't quite sure who I was any more, and I found it really challenging to be calm in this situation – which was definitely the best course of action. Bob reminded me of that guy, that night. On the edge. He was giving me the "message", as it were, not to be safe, to try and find more. To look for the animal in the character as opposed to the intellect. It was brilliant advice.'

Yet as the shoot progressed the relentless 100-degree heat and tropical humidity began to affect even the most energetic, and nearly everyone fell ill with Montezuma's revenge.

'I was so sick,' Gere said. 'They had to take me to the hospital after a day of shooting; they hooked me up to an IV. I'd fall asleep, and at four in the morning they'd wake me up, unhook the IV, and carry me to the set. It's like being in the trenches, especially being on location like that. But you just have to keep going . . . you *have* to get up at four in the morning and do a love scene and you're so exhausted you don't want to. You think, Oh, leave me alone!'

'It was really ferocious,' Martinez said. 'It just gutted you. We were shooting a scene where Aquino went outside to relieve a guard, and from the moment when I walked out to the door to when I arrived at his side I had lost eleven pounds.'

Of course iron-gut Hoskins, the one actor who could always stand to drop a few ounces, came through relatively unscathed.

'Mackenzie was always on Bob to lose some weight, but Bob

was more interested in ways to sneak around that than deal with it,' said Martinez.

'Even Bob became a bit subdued,' Mackenzie said. 'He was left hanging around an awful lot because it was quite a small part, and the way the schedule plotted out he had to be there for two days, and then nothing for a week, and so on, so he couldn't really go anywhere. He kept people lively because he's good fun, but after you've done *The Long Good Friday*, which you're in every day, well, even Bob got a bit dejected. But Bob's a worker – he's got to keep working. He can't just sit around the hotel all day and enjoy it. Although Bob likes the good life and a drink, he doesn't like doing that all the time. I would see him going off with Joaquim – they'd become very good friends. I came across them one day and they said, "We've come up with a new way to do this scene." "But", I said, "it's weeks till we shoot. Stop! I strictly forbid you to do it. By the time we get on the set, every inspiration, every sort of nuance or freshness will be gone." It's all right to do a vague rehearsal – then it really happens when the camera starts rolling. But to rehearse yourself sick is death to do on films. For someone of Bob's energy, he killed half his performance and lost the spirit. It was just too long hanging about.'

By mid-January 1983, the weary cast and crew welcomed the sodden skies of London for one more month of interior shots. 'They took the shack where we hid the Consul board by board and reassembled it in the studio at Shepperton,' said Martinez. 'I thought it was fantastic that there was a pub in the commissary and that it was considered perfectly civilized behaviour to belly-up and get a buzz on at lunchtime.

'Bob invited me and my wife and some of the cast and crew to his house one night for dinner, and I was feeling poorly and didn't want to go, but Bob called me up and insisted so strongly that I gave in! He has a wonderful dining room, filled with books, and he was a charming host and a lot of laughs. Linda was quiet and seemed really devoted to him' – she was pregnant with their daughter Rosa – 'and there was a really warm feeling in the place.'

There was a warm feeling in everyone to be away from the bacteria of Mexico. There was, however, one man in the hot seat when Paramount, in its infinite wisdom, decided that *The Honorary Consul* was perhaps not such a great title for dumb Yanks who might not know what an 'honorary consul' is. Paramount insisted on the title *Beyond the Limit*, which could have led audiences to think it was either another ageing alcoholic saga or a documentary about the hazards of speeding on the highway.

141

'The title change was totally out of my hands,' Mackenzie said. 'Maybe some ignoramuses don't know who Graham Greene is, but a lot of the world does. It was an insult to him. Apart from that, *Beyond the Limit* is beyond the limit! It's unutterably awful, and it doesn't say *anything*. I think it was one of those titles that got arrived at by market research.'

Still worse, after months of late-night phone calls and harassment from know-it-all studio executives, Paramount did absolutely *nothing* to promote the film and film star they'd been so interested in controlling just a few short months before.

'They showed the trailer at Cannes in May,' Martinez said, 'and all the foreign distributors thought it was amazing, that all the elements were there for it to be something special.' And then . . . nothing, although the film was scheduled for release in the States at the end of September 1983. Perhaps it was fear of what bad word-of-mouth might do to superstar Gere. Better to keep mum and let the film die a quiet, undeserved death. Reviews were decidedly mixed, although most praised Bob and Michael Caine.

When the film opened in England in May 1984, the *Evening Standard*'s Alexander Walker had a balanced comment to make: 'People who want more worldly entertainment from screenwriter Christopher Hampton's attempt to cross a political thriller with a theological message – each of which refuses to combine with the other – can take heart from John Mackenzie's direction of the players. . . . Bob Hoskins sinks the East End gangster he played in *The Long Good Friday* untraceably into a cynical policeman. Richard Gere is an even greater surprise . . . and best of all is Michael Caine.' Just like Gere said he would be.

'At least I had control of the title in England!' Mackenzie said. 'It had a lot of good ingredients, but the parts didn't add up and so the puzzle didn't quite fit. It was an honorary failure.'

Yet Sally Hope's canny perception that *The Honorary Consul* would be a good showcase for Bob's versatility as well as crack the American market was spot on. Bob was hired to play another policeman. This time in England. And this time with an even huger hunk – physically, at least – of American beefcake.

London, 1939. There's only one man who can intercept $50 million-worth of stolen uncut diamonds that are being routed through the German Embassy. His name: Lassiter (Tom Selleck). His occupation: jewel thief. His girlfriend: dancer Sara (Jane Seymour). The woman he must seduce, whose idea of fun in bed can best be described as kinky: Kari von Fursten (Lauren Hutton).

And his nemesis, the hard-nosed copper with no sympathy for criminals – he'd probably give himself a ticket for jaywalking – Inspector Becker of Scotland Yard (Bob Hoskins).

Becker frames Lassiter for a robbery he didn't commit, and offers him a Hobson's choice: get himself into the heavily fortified Nazi Embassy in London and help himself to the safe, wherever it is; or go to prison for twenty years, maybe life. Our hero, being the kind of man he is, opts for the sparklers.

Tom Selleck had become America's latest pin-up when his weekly detective series, 'Magnum P.I.', hit the TV. Its picture-postcard Hawaiian locations gave six-foot-four Selleck every opportunity to show off his physique, and the scripts every opportunity to focus his blue eyes and 3-D dimples on another escapade. No wonder he's been compared to Gable, Newman, Reynolds, and even a Viking sea-lord by American women's magazines.

Inspector Becker, however, is one of Bob Hoskins's rare one-dimensional characters.

'I'm a copper,' he states as if in explanation for his Javert-like implacability. 'I don't forgive and I don't forget. Not 'ere, not on my patch.'

Becker is even further outraged when Lassiter has the cheek to show up for a little tête-à-tête. 'My 'ome! You don't come to my bloody 'ome! Don't chu talk to *me* about the law!' Becker shouts as he somehow manages to push back the six-foot-four Lassiter. And he is even more accommodating when sending Lassiter into the German viper's nest: 'If you're messing me about you're looking at your last day on the street. . . . If you don't find those diamonds, don't come out!!'

Somehow the blustering was more convincing when Harold Shand said it. Still, *Lassiter* was not intended to be much more than a show-off vehicle for Selleck and an antidote for Bob's spate of bad guys and Montezuma's revenge. Bob had a good time playing, as he put it, a 'bloody fanatic copper' in the streets of London. At one point it rained for thirty-seven days straight; naturally, on the one day that they really needed the rain it was sunny and beautiful. Enter the rainmakers, courtesy of the City of London Fire Brigade.

'I enjoy working with American actors,' Bob said. 'The difference in technique is remarkable. Take a fight scene. A British actor will work himself slowly, gradually into a frenzy. But Americans plunge right in . . . WHAM . . . and you'd better be ready.'

Bob was also impressed by smoothie Selleck. 'I've always envied that kind of nerveless charm,' Bob said. 'In one scene, when I corner Lassiter on the Orient Express' – he's trying to escape – 'to blackmail him into completing the embassy job, he's as cool and witty as if we were old school chums. If I tried to do that bit, I'd trip on the stairs or smoke the wrong end of the cigarette and burn my lips. Fortunately, there's not much call for someone like me, five-foot six and built like the back of a bus, to play suave sophisticated types.'

Lassiter opened in the States at the end of 1983 (and in England nearly a year later) to lacklustre reviews. 'Even by the standards of escapist entertainment, little of *Lassiter* seems to matter,' said the *New York Times*.

British critic Tom Milne was rather more opinionated: 'Tom Selleck miming a desperately shallow vein of laconic charm, Bob Hoskins doing another of his tediously forceful heavies, and Lauren Hutton stuck with stereotype as she licks crimson lips to indicate perverted bloodlust, are devoid of life and interest.'

It wasn't so much that the film was bad, it was just . . . another thriller about as exciting as a kiddie-land roller coaster. See it, enjoy it, forget about it five minutes later.

Playing a hard-boiled Cockney cop was something Bob could do in his sleep, but working with an American director (Roger Young) and crew, on a decently budgeted film that was bound to receive a lot of attention – good, bad or indifferent – thanks to Selleck, was still an invaluable experience for an actor who'd only had important roles in two other films, both helmed by the same director.

Besides, a late-night phone call that summer of 1983 was going to provide Bob with a big-time Tinseltown experience Harold Shand couldn't have invented in his wildest dreams of power and glory.

16

Hoskins Goes to Harlem

'Gangsters, music, and pussy,' said producer Robert Evans. 'How could I lose?'

For a start, you can spend $12 million over five years and still not have a script. Then you can hire Francis Ford Coppola to rewrite Mario (*Godfather*) Puzo's rejected script, and spend $140,000 per week on pre-production costs with neither story nor financial support. Next you can spend another $2.5 million to hire Coppola as director, with a script that only meets with the tentative approval of star Richard Gere and the investors. Then you can keep spending money as if your budget is $47 million – which it isn't but it will be – while bringing in Pulitzer-Prize-winning author William Kennedy to help with the dialogue and script, and let him begin the actual writing with Coppola five days before rehearsals are scheduled to start, on 26 July. Finally, you can have your director encourage the cast to improvise throughout rehearsals and keep rewriting the script – twelve versions in a month – so that when you are ready to begin filming on 22 August your leading man is so unhappy with all the changes he refuses to work, and renegotiates his contract to double his $1.5 million and add $25,000 for each *week* of work he might have to do beyond 29 October. That was the saga of *The Cotton Club*.

As if all these costly blunders weren't enough, the cost of production was $1.2 million each week – that's $300 per minute, and the script changed so often (there were, in Kennedy's opinion, 'somewhere between thirty and forty rewrites') that cast and crew often had no idea what would happen next or what had happened already, and when. Or why. They also wondered if their pay cheques would bounce.

'What we created,' said Kennedy, 'was a gangster story about race and subjugation, about rising in the world through show

145

business, all this pervaded by music and dancing. What we also had was 600 people building sets, creating costumes, arranging music, rehearsing dancers, or just waiting for the script . . . a throbbing condition that can put a certain stress on a writer.'

'I don't want to make a gangster picture and I don't want to make a musical,' said Francis Ford Coppola. 'I want to make something nobody's seen before.' That he did. Too bad the making of it was far more dramatic than the end result. It took nearly as long to read *The Cotton Club*'s production notes as it did to see the thing.

The story of the real Cotton Club had 'film me' written all over it, and was based on the combination of fact and fiction found in Jim Haskins's book, *The Cotton Club*, first published in 1977. It had been optioned by a business executive who had also sold the rights to *Godfather*, *Chinatown*, and *Urban Cowboy* producer Robert Evans.

The club on 142nd Street and Lenox Avenue, in the heart of Harlem, opened in 1923. During Prohibition, a stylish speakeasy with a revue act would bring in the monied downtown crowd who wanted a drink – illicit booze was suddenly big business – and a show. A certain mobster named Owney Madden needed an East Coast outlet for his Madden's No. 1 Beer, so he orchestrated the details from his deluxe cell in Sing-Sing prison, where he was serving a manslaughter sentence, and formed a syndicate to buy a pre-existing space, renaming it the Cotton Club.

According to Haskins's book, Owney was 'one of the most notorious of the pre-Prohibition gang leaders'. He 'did not look like a hood; he had the gentlest smile in New York's underworld. But he possessed great cunning and was capable of extreme cruelty.' He also had a flair for settling gangland rivalries, especially once he was out of jail, and settling differences with the cops and corrupt politicians with his own brand of savoir-faire – cold, hard cash.

Word spread of the Cotton Club's spectacular shows, jungle decor, discreet staff, and late hours, for stars, socialites, and sophisticates – as long as they were white. The blacks might have been sensational on stage . . . but only on stage. They were banned from the Club itself.

'Only the tops of the tops in terms of name or influence could get a reservation,' said Cab Calloway, who succeeded Duke Ellington as the house bandleader. 'But even on an ordinary Sunday night it was difficult to get in. Negroes from the Harlem community would line up outside to watch the limousines drive up – Cadillacs and Rolls-Royces and Dusenbergs long enough to make you choke.'

The music and shows featured the talents of Calloway and Ellington, Lena Horne, Louis Armstrong, Bessie Smith, the

Nicholas Brothers, and Ethel Waters; the ambiance was one of raw sensuality with undercurrents of power. Up to 700 guests sat at tiny tables in tiers where they could rub elbows with real gangsters like Big Frenchy Demange, a large, jovial, poker-playing hood hired by the canny Madden so that slumming rich bitches could live vicariously for the evening. Madden also knew that any violence in the club could threaten his truce with the coppers, despite all the payola. Any crimes plotted there were behind locked doors, while impeccable behaviour was demanded from both guests and staff. No wonder Lady Mountbatten called the Cotton Club 'the Aristocrat of Harlem'. Madden was so chuffed he had the phrase emblazoned on the club's matchbooks and etched on its swizzle sticks.

What better setting for a film? *The Cotton Club* would be Coppola's twenty-fourth film in an erratic yet influential career, and with it he was trying to dig out from the enormous debt he'd incurred from the utter flop of *One From the Heart*.

While all the intricate machinations of creating *Cotton Club* the film as opposed to *Cotton Club* the albatross continued, Bob Hoskins was quite happily ensconced in his Islington home, celebrating the birth of daughter Rosa. He'd been geting the usual pile of scripts, so the story goes – one he's related many a time, although colleagues have said it's probably apocryphal – and since most were no more than pipe dreams sandwiched between glossy covers, he paid little attention to whatever version of *The Cotton Club* arrived on his doorstep. Late one night, however, the phone rang. 'The voice said, "This is Francis Ford Coppola. I want you to do a movie of mine," ' Bob told Steve Grant. 'I said, "Oh really. Well I'm Henry the VIII and you've just woken up my kid, you cunt," so that started out well. But he rang back.'

Coppola. *The Godfather*. New York City. Working again with Richard Gere. The whole lavish Hollywood spectacle. What a great experience. His first film in America.

It was a clever casting choice. Ten weeks shooting, Bob was told. He was in New York for eight months.

Bob was also thrown straight into *The Cotton Club* loony bin. He'd been told on a Friday that he was to be at rehearsals at the refurbished Astoria Studios in Queens, New York, on Monday morning. His Concorde was late. A jet-lagged Bob was handed four pages of dialogue he'd never seen before for his first scene, and was told to do a run-through in front of *all* the American actors assembled there. Bob told *The Face* that Coppola gleefully said, 'Okay, we're gonna break the ice.' Bob's reply: 'You're breaking the ice on my fucking back!' Coppola's reply to that: 'Nah, nah, nah, *nah*. Believe me. It's gonna be fine.'

'Some of the actors there were really heavy numbers,' Bob told the *Evening Standard*. 'One or two of them were into this Method business . . . practically chewing up the furniture. So I had to go and sort them out. Yeah, I walloped them. One guy lost a tooth. Anyway, I got the scene together and when it was over they actually applauded me. We were okay then.'

A little nervous energy, a little display of anger was certainly understandable under the circumstances. Linda and Rosa had come with Bob, but he had realized with a jolt that *The Cotton Club* was perhaps not going to be quite the film he thought he'd be shooting with master craftsman Coppola.

'I didn't know what the fuck was going on,' he said. 'Nobody had a script except Francis, so the crew had to have every single scene set up every morning. Then Coppola'd walk in and say, "I wanna do *that* scene" – so nobody could take over the film because only he had the script. There was a lot of insanity going on.'

For an actor used to discipline and rehearsals and research, such a method was anathema. At least the studio delays and shenanigans meant Bob was able to cross the East River into Manhattan where he would check out the notorious neighbourhood, to the west of Times Square, where Madden had shot his first victim.

'I spent a lot of time in Hell's Kitchen,' Bob told John Powers, 'in the bars where Owney grew up, talking to people who knew him [who must have been a bit on the old side]. There was far more to Madden than just a gangster and a killer. Given the poverty of that society, a lot of people would have starved if it hadn't been for him. He had a whole industry going. For one thing, he made the best beer in America – Madden's No. 1. I met one guy whose mother was run over by one of Owney's beer trucks, and Owney himself turned up at the house, where they lived in terrible poverty. He gave the father a job, paid for the funeral, and got the two kids through college. And one of those kids is now an architect – *because* of Owney Madden. Although he was a heavy gangster, although he was a killer, there was a certain amount of humanity in him. He was a part of society, and felt responsible for it. That's why I played him as a kind of father figure.'

'He was a fine, intelligent man,' Bob told Steve Grant, 'a villain but a great humanitarian. Lots of people didn't starve in the Depression because of his kindness. An artist, an immensely clever businessman. Another common hero. Someone who comes out of the pack who's a bit special.'

148

Owney's greatest display of love, though, was with his brotherly relationship with Big Frenchy, enhanced no doubt by the friendship Bob had struck with the actor who played the role, Fred Gwynne, who impressed him more than meeting Marlon Brando ever would. Fred had made his name as Herman Munster in *The Munsters*.

'I felt out of my depth making my first movie in America,' Bob said. Even though he'd spent four months making *The Honorary Consul* with Gere, his co-star was under severe pressure during *The Cotton Club* shoot, nor is he known for being the most accessible of colleagues; his reclusive behaviour is said to stem more from shyness than condescension, however. 'Then Francis came to me and said, "Here's Fred Gwynne. He'll play your partner." Well, Herman Munster was my idol. I'm standing there stagestruck, and Fred comes over and puts me at ease right off. "Do you know Richard Burton?" he asks. I don't. "Have you ever noticed his eyes?" he asks. "They look right through you! I met him once and he looked into my eyes, right down inside me, looked around, and there was no one there, so he walked away." Well, me and Fred were mates after that.'

Encouraged, as was all the cast (except Gere, who refused), to improvise scenes, Bob and his American friend twice his size, with whom he'd commiserate during the interminable delays on the set, began to throw ideas at each other. It was a long way from the outskirts of Veracruz, where Bob had been told by his director not to over-prepare. In Astoria Studios they could prepare all they wanted. They had no idea what they'd be shooting anyway.

'He would just toss things in the air,' Bob said. 'I could never figure Francis out at all. I just did what he told me. It's into Aladdin's cave with him.'

'I bring to my life a certain amount of mess,' said Coppola. 'But it is an Italian-American mess, *al dente* productive.'

So Bob and Fred kept at it, writing one scene around the two of them having a pee. But the most memorable and to many the single most successful moment in the entire film is the wholly improvised watch scene, when Frenchy has been kidnapped by Dixie's crazed brother and is ransomed by what he thinks is a pitiably small figure.

'Francis said, "I've got this scene where you two come back together, and I really don't know what to do with it,"' Bob told John Powers. 'We'd been writing our own stuff all along, so Fred said, "Get a watch and follow me." So I followed him in the scene, and if you look, it's all in one shot. We only did it once.' They had no choice. '[Frenchy] smashed the watch I have because he thinks I

149

only paid $500 for him,' Bob told Steve Grant, 'and then he gives me a platinum watch when I tell him the ransom was fifty grand.'

'Fifty grand! Fifty grand I paid for you,' Owney shouts. 'They only wanted thirty-five! I gave him fifty not to hurt you!

'I would have given $500,000. I'm worried sick about you! Look whatcha done to my fuckin' watch.'

When they hug, that simple gesture carried more emotional weight than any love scene, dance scene, or death scene in the film.

Writing and performing scenes like this, though, could not compensate for what was becoming a long-drawn-out job. Midway through the filming Coppola left town, explaining in a letter to the cast that the producers (Las Vegas casino operators Edward and Fred Doumani were bankrolling what Evans had started) had reneged on certain pre-production commitments and he hadn't yet been paid any of his $2.5 million fee. When that dilemma was finally sorted out, he came back only to find that the payroll for the week hadn't been delivered and the union had ordered all work to cease. The money then arrived in an armoured car. It was not a relaxed set. It was also a disappointment for anyone expecting collaborative Hollywood magic. Instead of discovering another *Godfather*, Bob and Fred discovered the joys of junk food, hamburgers, and cold American beer.

'I gained around twenty pounds waiting around for something to happen,' Bob said. 'You sort of sit around and eat and drink and philosophise, and suddenly you've forgotten what you do for a living. Then somebody says, "You're on the set," and you say, "What do you mean I'm on?" '; 'Fred kept me together through the whole thing or I'd have gone off my chump.'

'I was shooting *The Razor's Edge* and wanted Bob to play the pivotal part of the coalminer who sends this guy on a spiritual odyssey to India,' said *Inserts* director John Byrum. 'I only needed Bob for two days and he wanted to do it. One day in northern France in a coal mine and the next day on a stage in London. He *could* have done it. But Francis wouldn't let him out for months and months.'

'I spent eight months in New York, which was way too much, even though I liked the city,' Bob told Steve Grant. 'I couldn't live there and Linda and the kid were with me in this part of the Village where we were getting worried . . . and this guy said that I shouldn't worry because everyone knew where they were at any one time.' So even if the film was not to be as brilliant as *The Godfather*, at least real life could emulate certain aspects of it. 'Actually, the Mafia were very easy to deal with because they're totally straight,' Bob said. 'The ground rules are that they're there to do the business and they'll give you a fair deal, they'll pay you well, and they'll look after you. But fuck 'em up and they'll fuck *you* up, obviously.'

Bob learned *that* lesson well. Principal filming was completed on 23 December 1983 – Coppola had shot 400,000 feet of film in eighty-four days – and the Hoskins family was heaving a sigh of relief back in Islington when the phone rang once again. Bob, and everyone else, was needed for 'two more weeks' (which meant 'two more months') in New York. Bob said no. He'd done his bit and he'd had enough. He was going to be playing Benito Mussolini for an Italian television production and he'd already shaved his head. Eight weeks had stretched into more than six months by then. . . .

Doumani associate and line producer Joey Cusumano was dispatched to London to take Bob out to dinner. So Bob would have to wear a wig. Big deal. Bob still said no. Cusumano said yes. Bob came back.

One of the reasons Bob would have preferred to stay in London was that a short work of his, the scathing black comedy *All for the Nation*, was to be staged as a platform play at the National Theatre in February 1984. It is an indictment of government and bureaucracy. The central character, Tom, wants to claim a paltry £10 National Assistance and is locked in a room with a strange man named Cyril, who likes to 'tinker', and a Frankenstein-like monster named Bloke. Cyril creates 'blokes' from spare parts on behest of the government, and his creations are now everywhere – the Foreign Office, the police force, the army, at university. 'They're like my own sons,' Cyril says. 'I get really pleased when they do well for themselves.' Guess who is going to become the first Superior Bloke? Not to worry, Tom, it's all for the nation.

The play is in the Ken Campbell vein, but its hilarity helps enhance its Big Brother message and proves that Bob does have a knack for social comedy.

All filming for *The Cotton Club* was completed on 31 March 1984. Bob even more gratefully went home and Coppola began editing. Problems continued. Evans sued Doumani. Coppola went for Evans. A judge ruled that Evans was 'controlling partner' and Coppola was allowed to maintain 'creative control'. 'He was a disaster,' Evans said of Coppola. 'It was a nightmare to end all nightmares.' 'How could I have gone over budget? There was no budget!' said Coppola. 'I was called in long after Evans had put together all his deals. He lied to everyone.' 'The biggest mistake I made was calling the company Totally Independent Productions,' said Doumani. 'I should have called it Totally Dependent on Amateurs.'

'You make a suggestion to Coppola,' Bob said, 'and he says, "Who made you the director"?' Supposedly, Bob had told Coppola that he couldn't 'direct his piss into a bucket'. Given the circumstances . . . Bob later denied it. 'I liked Coppola,' he also said. 'He's a mixture between Santa Claus and Stalin.'

Several years later, when the memory of endless fattening hours on the set had faded to yet another showbiz memory, Bob would tell Steve Grant: 'I know there were rumours that we didn't hit it off, but I liked working with Francis. If he'd been left alone it would have been a classic movie, but he got fucked up by Robert Evans, who brought in a lot of weird gangsterish people and interfered too much.'

It is without doubt to Coppola's credit that the film was completed and released on schedule on 14 December 1984 in America. It was also to his credit that he coordinated the logistical nightmare of shooting such a convoluted story under fire, with no proper script or real time to write one . . . and with the focus of the film centred ironically on a white cornet player in a black club in a black neighbourhood.

'I think I always wanted to do a character who on some level wanted to be black,' Richard Gere said. 'And this character is generally in that mould.'

Of course, without the pulling power of a white Hollywood star, a romantic film about the blacks in the Cotton Club would never have been financed. Whatever the problems in the film, Coppola did provide a showcase and an unprecedented opportunity for black talent: 65 dancers and a total of 170 black performers.

'The film celebrates black beauty, black talent, black private life, and black love,' said Kennedy, 'the likes of which hadn't been seen on-screen in recent memory, if ever.'

Coppola called it a 'night club epic': 'I'm glad *The Cotton Club* has a few laughs, slick production numbers, and drama. . . . It's like cooking spaghetti. It's Spaghetti *à la* Cotton Club.' He also said that *The Cotton Club* is 'about, literally, that *theatricality*, which allows me to act with the action.' Yet not one production number was seen in its entirety; chronic crosscuts interrupted every dance or song.

Gere decided $3 million wasn't enough to justify his going on the road to promote the film. There had been such extensive pre-release press that it became almost *de rigueur* to slag it off sight unseen. And viewing the film itself was disappointingly frustrating because the emotional resonance needed to pull the pieces togather simply didn't exist. Despite all the talent, sensational dancing, jazz soundtrack, and gangland shootouts; despite the genius of Coppola and Kennedy; the relentless nagging by Evans; the atmospheric cinematography and lavish period detail; despite the *blitzkrieg* of Christmas-release publicity, Bob Hoskins ran away with it.

New York magazine film critic David Denby wrote: '*The Cotton Club* is certainly not the mess that some feared it might be. . . . The trouble is, the movie is *all* atmosphere and flux; the moods never settle in and reach for anything deeper. . . . The performer who preserves his individuality best in this flashing mosaic is the powerful English actor Bob Hoskins . . . who plays Madden as a courtly, shrewd, rational man. . . . If Coppola had centered the movie on Madden, a man we could love, a man who keeps getting drawn back into the gangster world against his will, he might have done something with emotional force. As it is, *The Cotton Club* touches on everything and nothing.'

The film wasn't a total flop. A lot of viewers liked it; it took in a respectable $2.9 million on its first weekend of release, although it eventually needed to take in $100 million to break even. And Coppola at his least effective was still in many ways more interesting, visually at least, than most other Hollywood fodder.

'Coming to New York from the muted mistiness of London is like travelling from a monochrome antique shop to a technicolour bazaar,' critic Kenneth Tynan once said.

Bob Hoskins of Islington, London, in his first appearance in a major Hollywood production, came to the bizarre bazaar of *The Cotton Club* and stole the film.

17

A Plumber, a Fishmonger,
and the Fascist Salute

'Who fixed *your* ducts?' the heating engineer hisses. Never has a repairman attached such an air of menace to a simple sentence. Nothing, it seems, is simple, somewhere in the twentieth century, in the mindless paper-pushing metropolis in *Brazil*.

'My taste runs to grotesque scatology and I like things to be a bit crude,' said *Brazil*'s creator/director/maverick Terry Gilliam, formerly with *Monty Python*, director of *Jabberwocky* and surprise hit *Time Bandits*. 'My mind works the way a kid's mind works, and that's not a pretty sight. Everything I do is done to please myself. That may sound egocentric, but it's all I know how to do.'

Bob Hoskins would understand that sentiment, and when he was offered a cameo in the futuristic/black political comedy *Brazil* he quickly agreed, despite his exhaustion from an enforced hitch in New York and his preparations for his forthcoming role in the Italian *Mussolini and I*.

'The size of the part isn't important to me,' Bob told John Powers, 'it's whether I'd enjoy it. I look at *Brazil* and I think, "I'd give *anything* to be in that." It's a wonderful show. So when [Gilliam] asked Robert De Niro and me to play plumbers, we both leapt at it: "That sounds great!"'

The nearly unrecognizable De Niro played Tuttle, the freelance Robin Hood of a heating engineer who is pursued in his illegal repair jobs across the intestinal ducts coiled around the faceless apartment blocks by two government-sanctioned repairmen: the take-charge Spoor (Hoskins) and the babbling Dowser (Derrick O'Connor). *Brazil* the film has nothing in common with Brazil the country – the title stems from a 1930s' hit that Dennis Potter could have used in *Pennies from Heaven*. It's set in a bureaucratic state where computers can get botched and paperwork rules with nightmare consequences and where every submissively grateful home has a surfeit of ducts for plumbed-in Central Services provided by Big Brother government. When one man, daydreaming functionary Sam Lowry (Jonathan Pryce), discovers the girl of his dreams (Kim Greist), he finds himself on the wrong side of the system he worked for and destroyed by it as he pursues his dream.

Gilliam, with his penchant for combining elements of cruelty and humour with a perverse sense of fun, saw *Brazil* as a 'light-hearted nightmare . . . a very funny film about a young, unambitious man and the girl he falls for faced with situations entirely beyond their control. I didn't want to make a grim story. I am making entertainment. If you're going to say something, say it in an entertaining manner, so people will catch themselves laughing and suddenly realize, "I shouldn't be laughing at that." *Brazil* is funnier than most comedies and more nightmarish than most horror films, so it demands a lot more from the audience.'

Brazil's Walter-Mitty-meets-Franz-Kafka story provided astonishingly imaginative conceits and was a production designer's (Norman Garwood) dream. Not since *Bladerunner* had the future or people (like Sam's mother, played by Katherine Helmond, with a penchant for shoe-shaped headwear and plastic surgery) been depicted with such terrifying lunacy.

Bob's Spoor, clad in a cheery red and yellow baseball jacket, the kind rock bands give their roadies, with a Central Services badge sewn on the back, and a large red cap with an oversized peak perched on top of his head, was every apartment dweller's nightmare of an incompetent, unctuous and then thoroughly nasty repairman who enjoys destroying property. If that duct's broken, he'll fix it. If only he can find it. It was a savage comic portrait.

'If it shows anything,' said Gilliam, 'it is that people carry on. . . . The human spirit is not that easily extinguishable, so this could never have been a solemn story of depersonalization and victimization. People hang on to their individuality no matter what.'

And in an all-too-familiar twist for Bob Hoskins, who, like so many actors not afraid to take risks, often found himself involved in controversial projects, *Brazil* came up against the powers-that-be at Universal who'd decided they'd wasted their money on this film, despite it being delivered on time, under the $15 million budget, and already quite popular in Europe. *Brazil* became Gilliam's *Long Good Friday*; and his Jack Gill was Sidney Jay Sheinberg, president of Universal's parent company, MCA Inc.

They said the film was too long. Gilliam cut it. It was too much of a downer. Gilliam refused to change the ending. The battle for

Brazil was on. Universal refused to release it. Gilliam ran a full-page ad in *Variety* that read: 'Dear Sid Sheinberg. When are you going to release my film *Brazil*?'

By December 1985, a sneak preview for the 'wildly enthusiastic' Los Angeles Film Critics Association had a result to vindicate all Gilliam's effort: prizes for Best Film, Best Director, and Best Screenplay of the Year. Tuttle would have loved it.

Days later, Universal opened it in an 'emergency run' to qualify the film for the Academy Awards – and it was nominated for two Oscars (for Best Screenplay and Art Direction). After little more than a month in general release, *Brazil* had already grossed $10 million and received rave reviews. Even those who agreed with Sid and found the ending too negative could not dispute the film's mind-boggling creativity.

'[Gilliam] had the script. I only put in a few jokes,' one of the co-writers, Tom Stoppard, said. 'The resulting film was a bit bleak, a bit relentless for my taste. I was speaking at Harvard [University] and I happened to mention that I thought that it was too black and about fifty minutes too long. I guess I was being too flip. The audience nearly hissed me off the stage.'

The successful release of *Brazil* had also elevated Bob Hoskins to cult status. He had joined the ranks of those sufficiently popular to be considered a 'draw', even in a cameo. And even if the intended audience – like Pink Floyd fans – had no idea of who he was exactly, his characterizations left indelible impressions.

Playing Spoor was more of a lark, an exorcism of Owney Madden and a practice session for the evils he was about to release on the world as Il Duce. It was also as much a social statement for the anarchist in Hoskins, who protested the encroaching Thatcherism, as it was a catharsis for Gilliam.

'There were a lot of frustrations that had been building up about the world we live in, and I just wanted to get them out of my system,' Terry Gilliam said. 'I couldn't distinguish my dreams from the dreams that had been processed for me. Walking down a beach at sunset, I couldn't tell whether I was enjoying it because it was enjoyable, or because I'd seen it on too many commercials.'

His nightmare, at least, had a happy ending.

'Mussolini was a little, shortsighted, bald-headed cube with a big mouth,' Bob Hoskins explained. 'That's me exactly – except that to play a short fat dictator I had to diet and wear lifts. That's the shape I'm in. But I don't mind. It's my figure that earns my living.'

Springtime in Italy is glorious, unless you're up at 5 am for a three-hour torture session with a head shaver (for Bob, that was the easy part) and make-up people who'd rearrange your face into Benito-like form. Hired by Radio Televisione Italiana (RAI) to star in an international production of *Mussolini: The Decline and Fall of Il Duce* (the American title) or *Mussolini and I* (the English video title) that was written and directed by Alberto Negrin, Bob's co-stars included in an international cast Anthony Hopkins as his pacifist-orientated son-in-law, Count Galeazzo Ciano; Susan Sarandon as his daughter, Edda; Annie Girardot as his jealous wife; Barbara De Rossi as his blindly devoted mistress, Claretta; and Kurt Raab as Hitler. The art direction and mounting of the production was sumptuous and it was gorgeously shot, with camera angles designed to sweep over lavish interiors. Mussolini's homes, Villa Torlonia and Villa Feltrinelli at Lake Garda, where he spent his last days under German guard, had been shut for forty years; they were reopened for historical verisimilitude. Such was the power of television that the doors could be flung open and the ghosts dusted to oblivion so that a man from Finsbury Park could don his jackboots and assume the role of its former owner.

But why should an Englishman play Mussolini? After several weeks of low-key filming, at the end of May 1984, Bob attended a press conference. He managed enough menace – he certainly *looked* the part – to assuage the Italians' fears . . . for the moment.

'I was very worried about that,' Bob said. 'What would happen at home if an Italian played Churchill? They'd go bananas. But so far, it's been okay. The Italians have been so friendly and welcoming. I've fallen in love with the lot of them.'

As usual he had prepared diligently for the part and he was reassured that he had succeeded by the locals' horror at seeing him in full Fascist regalia, sauntering unconcerned into the neighbourhood *trattoria*. He was soon accepted, but Bob has often told the tale of driving to a location, uniform starched and stiff, and offering the Fascist salute to an old peasant by the side of the road. Supposedly, the shocked farmer fell into a ditch. Of course it was only a practical joke, but perhaps not quite so funny to anyone who had lived through Mussolini's reign of terror.

'Well, you've got to have a laugh, haven't you?' Bob told the *Evening Standard*'s Michael Owen. 'But I've been doing the business. I've watched twenty-five hours of documentary film on Mussolini. I've read up on the politics, the philosophies, the art, even the agriculture of the period . . . I'm playing him when he was sixty. As far as I can see, I've got three main responsibilities. First he was Italian so I've got to get that, get the essence of it. He is old so I have got to look

157

right and we are going to a lot of trouble over that, and third he was a beaten and defeated man. He was a monster, of course he was. A right vicious bastard and the atrocitities were horrendous. He was a world leader but he was still a bloke. I'm trying to learn the little things about him. Don't forget he ruled Italy for twenty years and before him the place was an even bigger shambles. There are some people who look back on him almost with fondness.'

Linda and Rosa kept Bob company, although Bob was slightly peeved when Linda arrived with copious amounts of luggage and kept 'borrowing' his driver for short expeditions. But it was a relaxed time on the set, and Bob taught ribald songs to the non-English-speaking Italian crew. Luckily the shoot did not turn into a modern Tower of Babel.

'I found the film quite interesting when I was doing it,' Anthony Hopkins said. 'It was good to be on location in Rome and in Verona. Mussolini's office and an execution in the film were shot on the field where the events actually happened. We had interpreters on the set so we could communicate. We got along fine. The film is engrossing, a complicated story.'

The angle of the story – the pitiful end to a once raging bull – is told from the increasingly crabby and mistrustful family's point of view. It is narrated by Edda, who finally feels the tiniest pinpricks of conscience once she realizes Daddy is no sweetheart and that his loyalty to her husband is less mighty than his fealty to his Führer. By focusing on petty squabbles while the bombs dropped, the realization of who Mussolini was, his rise to power and what he'd done for his country before the war is missed entirely. This Mussolini is no more a dictator than Hitler was a friend of the Jews. Spoor, *Brazil*'s heating engineer, had more fury in his, 'Who fixed your ducts?' than this Fascist did. Aiming for a benevolent dictator may work for an Owney Madden, but not with a man who brought his country to war in alliance with one of the most despicable humans in history.

Bob was not, of course, helped by the quality of the dialogue, especially in cosy scenes of the Mussolinis at home. During riots, when Mussolini's head is burned in effigy, one of the *bambini* asks, 'Why are they burning Grandpa?'

'We'll go on fighting – to the last bullet, to the last Eye-talian,' Mussolini announces several years before he tries to escape over the border with a caravan of German soldiers, but is instead caught by the partisans and hung ignominiously, by the heels, like a captured shark.

'Spare me the daily scene,' 'Ben' had told his now-dead Claretta.

'Don't you realize I have more important problems on my mind?' Like the war, perhaps?

The most successful actors were Hopkins, who kept his dignity and oil-slick hair intact; and Sarandon, who fought a losing battle and ended up bereft of both husband and father. The usually splendid Girardot was a nagging shrew of a wife and Barbara de Rossi a nagging wimp of a mistress who keeps telling her Ben to 'listen to your heart'. No wonder they were defeated.

'As Mussolini,' wrote *New York Times* critic John J. O'Connor, 'Bob Hoskins is all done up in elaborate makeup with no place to go except look terribly unhappy.'

He was savaged in Monica Collins's review in *USA Today*: 'Il Duce. In this treatment, better call him Ill Duce. . . . Bob Hoskins's portrayal of Big (as in rotund) Benito lends no subtlety or perspective. [He] looks like Bluto and acts like blotto. He's a mumbler and a bumbler, the type who can't remember his own phone number, much less the war plan . . . *Mussolini* could easily be called "Musholini".'

Bob, obviously, was not pleased with the end result either, and was aware of the problems in his portrayal. For one thing, he looked more like Telly Savalas as Kojak or Nikita Khruschev debating with Richard Nixon than a man of immense *puissance*. For another, he brought the wrong kind of energy to his preparation of Il Duce as Daddy. His Ben was too soft; he had no *cojones*.

'If people remember the heavies,' Bob said, 'it's because what I try to do is make the audience understand them. If you just show a bad man, that's rubbish, that's cartoon time. . . . That's the great thing about film as opposed to stage: You can show someone thinking. You can take the audience into your mind and your bloodstream so they are not just observing you, they're feeling with you. Mind you, it doesn't always work. I was heartbroken when I saw the Mussolini film. It was flat as a pancake because the Italians dub sound very badly, so there was this great bald thing on the screen and a voice that seemed to come from somewhere else. I realized what they were doing and should have compensated by acting with the facial muscles more than the voice.'

Too late. It was his only failure to date in a starring role. However the mini-series made no impact whatsoever except on those enthralled with Italian design, property houses, costume houses, purveyors of fine vintage automobiles, and furs by Fendi.

Bob had taken a break from heavies, dictators, and coppers to play a role more akin to Sheppey than anything else in *You Don't Have to*

Walk to Fly, the first of seven hour-long plays made by LWT's *Weekend Playhouse* and aired on Sunday, 8 July 1984. It was a project especially dear to his heart because it was written by his friend, colleague, and best man at his wedding – Gawn Grainger. He played Eddie Reed, life and soul of the local hang-gliding club, and indispensable whether out on the hills or back in the pub. However this avid flier is confined to a wheelchair, we are led to assume, due to an unfortunate prang while practising his favourite sport. The twist is that he'd actually fallen off a roof while drunkenly singing 'Land of Hope and Glory'. His wife Anne (Janet Key) is left to support them both, while growing ever more bitter at her exclusion from his Boys' Own adventures, and knowing that he is living a lie.

This low-key project proved an invaluable lesson for avid learner Bob, who was confined all day to a wheelchair during rehearsals. 'You feel trapped,' he said, 'because you can't use anything below the shoulders and suddenly you realize that you have not got the same kind of body language you might otherwise have. By the end of the week I really began to understand the problems of people angered at being stuck in wheelchairs.'

He was soon to find out about the problems of another sort of confinement: in an internment camp in the Australian Outback. Next stop: Oz.

In an ironic twist, Bob went from playing a man who killed Jews to an irascible Cockney fishmonger named Morrie Mendellsohn, German Jew by birth and assimilated Briton by profession, who was rounded up in the panic after France fell to the Germans, along with 2541 other 'friendly enemy aliens' and shipped out of Liverpool on 10 July 1941 aboard the troop ship *Dunera* for internment far, far away. In Australia. That nearly all of those forcibly rounded up and expelled were refugees from Nazi atrocities – many had already been in concentration camps – didn't faze the British officers on board. 'They're not human beings,' one of them says. 'They're scum.' The prisoners were treated so abysmally that many died and several officers were later court-martialled.

When the bewildered Jews reached the Promised Land, they were treated more like slaves in Egypt and shipped off to a hastily arranged camp in the middle of nowhere by the equally bewildered Australians who had no idea what to do with them. They at least treated the group with kindly good humour instead of contempt, until their release about a year later. Churchill called it a 'deplorable and regrettable mistake'.

From this poignantly true tale of confusion, prejudice, and displacement came an altogether astonishing result: the re-creation of Viennese café society in the heat of the Outback, for the Dunera Boys included some of the cream of exiled Eastern European intelligentsia – musicians, writers, artists, professors, scientists, lawyers, doctors, and scholars. They gave lectures, painted murals, performed concerts, and even printed their own currency – the "Goodonya" – named after a comic misinterpretation of the Aussie 'Good on yer'. The Jews thought 'Good on yer' was a Polish town near Bratislava.

It would have been easy to have made a simple news story out of this, but writer/director Ben Lewin, a post-war refugee from Poland, decided to 'view it basically as a kind of theatre of the absurd, a comedy of errors. . . . The whole thing was so grotesque that you didn't feel you could reproduce it in a documentary.' In this manner, he could be inspired by the 'spirit of the events' while creating fictional characters to move the plot along.

'I think that the one area where I feel I worked very hard and it paid off is the casting,' Lewin said. 'If as a writer I've learned about the art of characterization, which is for me the most crucial thing in story-telling, then the other half of that is to learn about casting.'

There was concert violinist Alexander Engelhardt (Joseph Spano); Mr Baum (Warren Mitchell), who loses his mind; the long-suffering Rabbi (Moshe Kedem); the quickly sympathetic camp commandant Colonel Berry (Simon Chilvers); and the unforgettable Morrie, as East End as jellied eels and deported by bureaucratic error. He eases his frustration at the confinement ('No one's gonna sit on my face and not expect to get teef marks on his ass,' he states) by venturing into the local town and befriending the locals.

'I thought Bob was perfect for the part,' Lewin explained. 'I'd been really enamoured of him since *Pennies from Heaven*, which was a remarkable piece of characterization, quite vivid and different. And then I bumped into him in London and we became friends. He's always been very generous-spirited to me.

'We tried to make *Dunera* as a feature film in 1981, but it became a bit touchy when the financiers found out it was about Jews. Of course I wanted Bob for it then. And when the first incarnation collapsed Bob wrote me a very, very touching letter saying that if there was anything he could do to help resuscitate this project – including sitting on a jar of Vaseline or some colourful expression like that. Well, it was very comforting, a sort of special gesture on his part to indicate to me that whenever we got the film up again he'd be there. I don't think that is typical of a lot of actors, who are more like "If you've got the money, I've got the time." To add a touch of personal commitment makes quite a difference.' Bob had described the script as 'tasty, a real beauty'.

'And because Bob fell into acting by accident, mostly, on the strength of a personality that he didn't have to cultivate,' the Australian Lewin continued, '*it* was already there. He's got such enthusiasm; he hasn't got a calm or detached handle. He's all exuberance and he was a lot of fun. What was so evident in Australia was how generous Bob was with other actors. He'd stay on the set even if he had nothing to do if someone seemed insecure about an accent. He'd wear headphones, and make everyone more confident. He really endeared himself to the rest of the cast.

'Bob is the sort of actor – as opposed to Warren Mitchell who is incredibly disciplined and possesses a demanding professionalism – who shows up the first thing in the morning, a bit bleary-eyed perhaps, and when you shove a sheaf of script at him, he says, "What the hell is this – are there any verbals?" "Yes, Bob, about three or four pages." "Oh, fucking hell," he says, as if he's not sure what he's filming or when or where. And he goes away and comes back and in the first run-through it's word-perfect. I think it's because he reads a script so thoroughly to begin with, and if it's his cup of tea then that's enough. He hasn't worked out his technique consciously – what he does works fine for him. I could do very long takes with him, with complicated moves and cues and he'd hold it with no difficulty.'

'Bob is not the type of actor who takes things terribly seriously,' Lewin continued. 'I was happily surprised by him – we'd do takes without much relying on discussion or run-throughs and then, afterwards, talk about doing it another way or modifying it. On the last day of filming, we were stuck on a box-line set – the recreation of East End London – and I remember correcting Bob on one line. He said, "I've lived in London all my life." I said, "No, can you say *nearly* all my life?" Bob looked at me. "I wasn't born there?" he asked. "You mean to tell me that after working in fucking England all my life for this shoot *now* you tell me I wasn't?"

'"Well," I said, "you weren't. You were born in Germany."

'"I was born in fucking Germany," he said. "Oh. Well, that's all right, then."

That was the end of the discussion. He did it perfectly.

'It's better for a director to use Bob's quality of spontaneity rather than dampening it by too much preparation,' Levin said. 'We also

162

felt secure about making things happen. I discovered as I got to know Bob better that he has a strong sentimental streak, and we'd sometimes talk about the text of various scenes. On the ship, he sits on the steps and says, with tears in his eyes, "I'm not 'appy 'ere. I'm not 'appy 'ere at all. Do you know that, Mum?" He made that up on the spot. You can do that with actors who are using their own personalities and not a set of acquired disciplines.'

Nor was there any need to invent scenes for the Dunera Boys. History had provided enough bizarre moments. 'I've not even gone half-way in the film to showing the complexity of social and political life there,' said Lewin. One scene had the British officers throwing the prisoners' suitcases overboard from the troop ship. Several, with German labels inside, were picked up by a nearby German U-boat. Convinced that captured Nazis were aboard, the U-boat provided an unseen escort instead of a swift jab with a torpedo. 'That was true,' said Lewin. 'The truest things in the film are the most farfetched.'

To help in his research, Bob went with Lewin, Warren Mitchell, and Joseph Furst to a real Dunera Boys reunion in Melbourne. 'Everyone was pleased to see us,' Lewin said. 'But it was an odd evening. It was like being on the set but everyone was forty years older.' Bob enjoyed that opportunity to meet a living incarnation of what he was trying to portray.

'Bob likes being recognized, too,' Lewin said with a chuckle, 'especially by very ordinary people. On our first day in Australia we were wandering around one of the local markets and one of the stallholders looked at him and said, "Aren't you da-da-da?" To go over to the other side of the world and some grubby little guy in a market stall recognizes you – it was a big thrill for Bob. It kind of suggests to me that he's more like a bloke than an actor. He's a *real* person.'

Filming was completed by Christmas 1984, and when the two-part, four-hour mini-series was shown in Australia in September 1985, the response was phenomenal. 'It is arguably the finest Australian production to date,' said one critic. 'Without doubt, it is the most innovative.' Just about everyone else agreed.

When, however, *Dunera* hit Channel Four several weeks later, the response was vehemently mixed. 'This is quite the best television drama yet made for commercial screening in Australia,' wrote one critic.

'I'm worried about the Australians,' James Murray of the *Daily Express* wrote. 'They seem to think that *The Dunera Boys* is the best mini-series ever to come out of the southern hemisphere. All it proves is that they are capable of taking a true story with all the makings of a rich drama and turning it into a load of wallaby waffle.'

Although the beginning of the programme, set in fake London and populated by Australians trying out their Cockney accents, was laid on with rather a thick trowel – Morrie more worried about his sister's virginity than his fish stall or the war, for example – viewers had more deeply rooted and strenuous objections.

'There are several messages to be gleaned from *The Dunera Boys*,' wrote Australian critic Alan Gill, 'not least of which is the evil of giving power in stressful times to the corrupt, cowardly, and incompetent. For many of the Dunera internees the Nazis and British might have been cousins.' This did not sit well with the British, who refused to believe their boys were capable of being brutes.

'The British,' said the *Sunday Times*'s Byron Rogers,' as you've come to expect now from anything Australian, were sadists and nutters.'

Ironically, Lewin had toned the real story down.

'I have understated the degree of mistreatment on board the ship,' he said, 'because I didn't want to set a tone of this as a story about suffering.'

One Dunera veteran claimed that 'Our guards used to smash whisky glasses on the deck and make us walk through the glass with bare feet. The food was riddled with maggots . . . I will never forget that voyage. A lot of very good people died.'

'I think Bob was thrilled with the result,' Lewin said. '*The Dunera Boys* was a challenge, a chance to display his range in something that was not a gangster role. It was more interesting for him, a bit more like *Sheppey*, which was lovely. And what is also important is how well he carried it off as part of an ensemble.'

Goodonya, mate!

18

A Moustache and a Loud Plaid Jacket

'It appears to me,' said the priest to loyal parishioner Mary, 'that, theologically speaking, always provided that you keep the great end in view at any time – I see no objection to your deciding that you are living with this Mr Clark Gable.'

Except she wasn't. Mary, living in working-class Dublin with her English husband George, who works in a candle-making factory, has a rather active fantasy life. After repeated viewings of *San Francisco*, starring Clark Gable as Blackie and Jeanette MacDonald as Mary, she becomes obsessed with the similarity between her sweet innocuous George – who is trying to grow a moustache – and the rapscallion Blackie. So when she reads film magazine gossip about Gable's infidelities, she can only accuse George of deceiving her as well. Poor George has no idea what he's done, and eventually shaves off his moustache in frustration. *Bringing Up Baby* begins playing at the local cinema, and Mary goes back to her normal self. Such was the 'plot' of a thoroughly delightful, evocatively monochrome, twenty-eight-minute short film called *The Woman Who Married Clark Gable*, directed by Thaddeus O'Sullivan and written by Andrew Pattman (based on a short story by Sean O'Faolain). That Bob Hoskins as George looked as much like Clark Gable as Mary (Brenda Fricker) looked like Greta Garbo only added to the film's charm.

One of the reasons Bob was cast, apart from his dissimilarity to Clark Gable, was because his agent, Sally Hope, was one of the film's producers.

'Like every movie,' Thaddeus O'Sullivan, director and camera-man-by-training, says, 'it was simply a question of money coming together. We had a budget of £125,000 – people thought that was a lot for a ten-day shoot in black and white, but the financing came at a time when the Irish Film Board was going to put up a lot of money

165

for a feature which collapsed so it just got shifted. And about one-third of the money was from television, although the whole look of the film was ostensibly designed and shot for the cinema. When I couldn't get a feature off the ground, I wasn't just going to turn around and make a half-hour television show – the idea was to make something that could work theatrically.

'Very early on we decided who was going to be in it, but I didn't really think Bob would do it. Sally did have a great influence on him at that time. He got a Sony television system as payment because the money couldn't be in cash, for some reason.' Bob evidently need a new TV. He also liked the scipt.

Clark Gable was set in the thirties, but O'Sullivan was able to imbue the story with his experience of working-class Ireland in the fifties, when, he said, 'It was rather a gloomy place, a cultural backwater, really, and an emotional vacuum as well.' Mary was emblematic of their emotionally restrained upbringings. She is forced into a fantasy life for satisfaction, which as O'Sullivan is the first to admit, is not a new idea. But, he explained, 'It was my memory of the cinema in the fifties as well, when there was no TV.

'This is why in a way Bob was quite brave to take this role. At the time we talked about it before he took the job he would say things like he was to "play a foil to this woman". But when we got to Dublin I found that he had drastically underestimated it and it wasn't a sleepwalking part at all. One of the other reasons he took it was because it *wasn't* a gangster part. He was also pretty disenchanted with *The Cotton Club* [which had been released in America shortly before he went to Dublin]. As far as Bob registers on a scale of what we would call regularly upset, he was *upset*. The Irish crews, on the other hand, are very good and nice to be around. They all know each other well and it's quite a relaxed atmosphere. The project was simple and he enjoyed the breathing space. He probably just thought it would be a nice thing to do and he didn't see any particular depth to it. It was only when he began to try and appreciate what his character was through this rather unusual situation – this woman, Mary, who had such a limited experience of life, and that it was Ireland – that he was really caught by surprise and had difficulty understanding it.

'Bob's an only child and there was no way his upbringing could have prepared for that – not that it should have. I've found that English people haven't a clue what Ireland is like! Many English don't even go because they think it's very similar, or because of the IRA and all that. Most just shrug and think it's pretty much the same as England and then they're flabbergasted when they go there.

'We had two or three days of rehearsal before we started shooting. Bob didn't want to do *any*, which was a reflection of how he saw George, as such a simple thing. "I walk on, Brenda reacts to me, and I walk off again. . . ." So I had to steer him. And because he is an ebullient character it's easy to be a little awed by him when you start being insistent! He was also a little bit nervous.

'So we started rehearsing in this room and had a very enjoyable, funny couple of days. We had a couple of dinners out because Bob is a very generous character and is a great one for inviting the crew out, although in the Irish pubs they don't like you to hang around too much. His grasp of why a woman should react like Mary does was extremely funny. When we started telling him about religion and all the basic stuff – what the Church is like in Ireland – he saw it as something tribal, like a sociological study of an American Indian tribe. He thought the Irish and all their attitudes and rituals were pretty weird. Most English people do!'

Once the film was completed, it was shown to five distributors in London and received offers from two of them. 'It was amazing, for a short,' said O'Sullivan. 'Steve Woolley [of Palace Productions] saw it and made us an offer on the spot and I was really knocked out about it. So many shorts get made for the cinema and are never shown. We were very pleased because we felt we'd made something that wasn't kowtowing to the classic notion of a support film, which has to be light in tone. We were also lucky that it went out with *Letter to Brezhnev*, that was very popular, so it had quite a lot of exposure before it was on Channel Four. It also went round to festivals and won prizes in San Francisco, Moscow, and Vienna, as well as a BAFTA nomination for best short.'

'*Cotton Club* was a great experience, but of the two I actually prefer the short film,' Bob said after the British première of Coppola's extravaganza in May 1985. 'It was exactly the opposite sort of exercise, where we all got involved and made that film together. I enjoyed that.'

'It was a monochrome gem,' wrote the *Daily Mail* critic Alan Coren after a late-night screening on Channel Four in 1986, 'and those responsible for sticking it on at midnight should be turned slowly over a peat fire.'

Once again Bob had proven his versatility. In the last few years he'd shot Richard Gere in Veracruz and had his son-in-law shot in Italy. He'd frustratedly eaten too many hamburgers in New York and got a suntan in New South Wales. He'd accepted starring roles in two international mini-series as eagerly as he'd taken cameos in projects he'd liked. He'd tapped and sung his way to fame at the

National and stayed in a wheelchair on LWT. Even workaholic, enthusiastic Bob was worn out. His son Jack had just been born. So he decided to take some time off and putter around, fixing up the house in Islington, avoiding any new projects and certainly not dreaming of going back to any place remotely near New York City. Until Alan Alda made him an offer he couldn't refuse.

Stanley Gould has a smile nearly as wide as the plaid checks on his ill-fitting sports jacket and a maniacal laugh of pure childlike pleasure. He'll fib to anybody if it will convince them he's got integrity. He is a man of sophisticated tastes. 'I need pears, bananas, the works,' he demands in a seedy hotel. 'And grapes, plenty of grapes. I'm a writer. I need to *chew* on things.' He is a brash bigmouth who has spent twenty years writing questions for television game shows – until he decides to adapt a book about the American revolution, written by college professor Michael Burgess, and bowdlerizes it into Hollywood pap.

Bob described his part in *Sweet Liberty* as a screenwriter 'who's written a kind of *Carry On Up the Revolution*. An obsequious individual with a dress sense to rival Rupert the Bear's and a talent only for manipulating the outsized egos around him. He persuades the academic to defy the director and reinstate some dialogue from the original book in the hope of basking in a little reflected glory.'

Burgess, after all, had said, 'I wanted to make history readable – not obliterate it!' Stanley of course counters with: 'Work on me, step on me, curse me, tell me I have no talent, but just let a little of you rub off on me . . . I love ya.'

Welcome to Tinseltown. The director, who has invaded this sleepy university town with cast and crew, is making a film for the white male ticket-buyers of America. There are, according to him, three reasons why they go to the cimena: to see people defying authority, destroying property, or taking their clothes off. Preferably all three.

Alan Alda wrote, directed, and starred as Professor Burgess in this light-hearted spoof about a film within a film and its effect – the differences between illusion and reality – on all those involved.

Bob actually needed little convincing to be reunited with his *Honorary Consul* co-star Michael Caine, who played the swashbuckling, skirt-chasing daredevil roué Elliot James, opposite the lovely Michelle Pfeiffer as Faith Healy, who will do just about anything to prepare for her role.

For one thing, Bob would be quartered in sumptuous digs in Sag Harbor, in the Hamptons, the Ibiza of Long Island, where well-heeled New Yorkers spend upwards of $25,000 to rent a house by pristine Atlantic beaches for the sweltering summer months, and then make sure everyone knows exactly how much they've paid. Bob, Linda, toddler Rosa, and teething Jack were happily set up in a huge house with a sweeping lawn, large patio, and obligatory pool. Producer Martin Bregman made sure his cast was comfortable, to say the least. 'We all had luxury homes and our wives spent all day lounging by the pools,' Bob explained. 'Michael Caine said that he'd been in fifty-three films and this was the best treatment he'd ever received.'

For another, it would be a treat to play a broad character in an American comedy. 'This is an entertainment movie,' said Alda. 'And if the audience takes it as just that, it's fine with me. But I like to tickle my brain a little as well as my funny bone.' And as he told reporter Bob Darden, he'd always been interested in the American colonial period, too. 'I'm not critical of Hollywood. What I'm doing is having fun with conflicting visions. I just thought people would find it amusing to see the impact of a typical Hollywood film on a small town. They end up having as much trouble getting along as the British and the patriots in the real Revolution.'

The cast had no such problems. 'It's a wonderful part,' Michael Caine told *Film 86*'s Barry Norman. 'The only thing that worried me about it [was that] Alda said he'd written it for me, and it was this dreadfully conceited movie star. I mean, he could do anything – he was one of those guys who could fly a helicopter, save a fight, drive stunt cars, ride horses, anything. I spent more time learning to do that than doing the picture!'

He was a bit riled, though, at his redcoat gear: 'Real, tropical-weight uniform,' he moaned. 'No wonder we lost the war.' And four-hooved friends were a pain, too. 'If there's anything I hate it's acting on a horse!' he also said. 'You have a scene worked out with the skill of a brain surgeon! You're right in the middle and the damn horse backs right out of the picture.'

He and Bob also played a trick on the unfortunate crew member who informed Caine he'd need to strap on a sword. 'Michael looked at this geezer,' Bob said, 'and said, "I have reached a point in my life where I can do anything I want. What I don't want to do is be Errol Flynn." Then he pointed to his head and said, "You can have this bit and stick in an understudy for the bodywork." Of course he didn't mean it; he was winding 'em up. But I was falling about.'

Bob also found making *Sweet Liberty* an unusual experience, because contrary to his usual custom of learning as much as possible about the character (which meant he would have had to spend time in L.A. hanging out with neurotic Jewish screenwriters), Alda insisted that he invent a family history for Stanley, so he gave Bob tapes of 'real people' with broad Brooklyn accents to listen to. Bob, ever the dedicated pro, ended up hanging out not in L.A., but in a local deli. 'I figured Stanley would spend most of his time there,' Bob said, 'so I found this delicatessen near the location in Southampton, hung around it for days talking to this woman who was a real Jewish mother – not as myself, Bob Hoskins, but as Stanley, pretending I was a screenwriter. It grew out of that. I became everything this woman expected of me. I felt rather guilty in the end.'

It was, of course, amazing that of all the available American actors who could play a Stanley while sleepwalking, Alan Alda still chose Bob. Alda simply thought he was the best choice for the part. And he was right. When the film was released – in May 1986 in America and September 1986 in England – to lukewarm reviews and box office, Bob, acting his heart out and popping his eyes in wonder, once again stole the film . . . even from the divine eighty-seven-year-old Lillian Gish, who played Burgess's loopy mum in her 104th film. But the film had an inherent problem. It tried to combine the story of the film within a film, which worked well, with that of Burgess's endless procrastination over commit- ting himself to his girlfriend, which quickly wore thin. *Sweet Liberty* fell flat. If only Burgess had shut up and stopped being so earnest, we could have watched Michael Caine seduce anything that twitched in his direction.

'*Sweet Liberty* rambles on amiably and pointlessly until it runs out of pleasant, second-rate ideas and just stops,' wrote David Denby in *New York*.

New Yorker critic Pauline Kael referred to Stanley as a 'loveable vulgarian', an apt description of Bob himself. 'His American accent may not be altogether convincing (at times he might be a gay Cockney cowboy), but he's better than convincing – he's hugely funny. (And his role is a well-written broad caricature of an amiable hack.)'

Sometimes it pays to hang out in delis. If you have to earn a living, making *Sweet Liberty* had certainly been an enjoyable way to go about it, surrounded by leisure and luxury, family and friends. It was a well-organized, amiable filming directed by an efficient, affable man.

In that sense it was a rather pointed contrast to Bob's previous film experience in New York. Yet Bob, the true son of Finsbury

Park, was not swayed by the opulent lifestyle and Hollywood mystique, which he discovered to be nothing more than media hype. 'I won't come to America just to make films,' Bob said. 'I'll come to America to make *good* films. America doesn't automatically mean quality, it means money. There's far too much concentration on the wealth of life and not the quality of life.'

So Bob, far more relaxed after a poolside summer than he'd been in years, went with his family back to Islington. He had signed in May to do a film about a small-time crook that was to be the culmination of every role he'd ever played – though he'd deny this – every criminal or comic, every hard-boiled bastard or vulnerable softie. The character's name was George, and the film's name was *Mona Lisa*.

19

For the Love of Mona Lisa

'With *Mona Lisa*,' said Bob Hoskins, 'there was a chance to work with Neil Jordan, a great script, and a fuckin' amazing part.'

'I wanted to make a personal film,' explained director Jordan, 'a film about the emotions men feel for women. The Bob Hoskins character is a man who always gets things wrong about women. He has this idealised image about the female – whose ideas of women will always be hopelessly inadequate, whose naivete is as irritating as it is appealing – and the film is about the woman he meets, on to whom he transfers all his obsessions.'

Mona Lisa was about much more than that as well, for the already much-accomplished Neil Jordan was no stranger to creating his own poetic vision in the telling of slightly skewed, brilliantly imagined tales. Founder of the Irish Writers' Cooperative in 1974, he won the *Guardian* Fiction Prize for his short story collection *Nights in Tunisia* in 1979 and the novel *The Dream of the Breast*, and was creative consultant on John Boorman's *Excalibur*. His first film, *Angel*, won him accolades as 'Most Promising Newcomer' in the 1982 London *Evening Standard* Awards. His second, *The Company of Wolves*, based on a short story by Angela Carter, was a bizarre, fanciful, often surreal reworking of the 'Little Red Riding Hood' myth, heavily influenced by Jordan's mentors Buñuel, Rossellini, Visconti, and Fellini. *Mona Lisa*, like Bob's *The Bystander*, was based on a few column inches in a newspaper, about a thug who was in court on a charge of 'grievous bodily harm'. 'He claimed,' Jordan said, 'he was protecting these young girls, who were prostitutes, from their pimps. And he had this wonderful vision of himself as a knight in shining armour. He was obviously a totally inarticulate man and probably a very dangerous criminal, too. I just thought what a wonderful situation you could have from that, and I just made up the story.'

As Thaddeus O'Sullivan pointed out, Ireland *is* a foreign country. Jordan, who was born in Sligo and raised in Dublin, would look upon London much as an American might Liverpool: although the basic language may be the same, the cultural differences become more glaringly apparent with each successive visit and the tourist's veneer is stripped away to the raw fibre of the city itself. Jordan's London is a James Ensor nightmare sprung to life. His streetwalkers disappear in gaudy, colour-saturated mists in the dark byways of Kings Cross. It is a vision of hell as well as one of mystery and seduction.

His film intertwines, in its story of romantic love obsessed and thwarted, three separate myths. Hoskins's St George, off to slay the dragon, is as much an Orpheus who seeks his Eurydice as he is a Frog Prince desperately awaiting the kiss to set him free.

In this descent into vice and perversion has stepped squat, balding George, who looks more like a bull in heat than a traditional romantic figure. He is gullible, pathetic, not particularly intelligent, so obviously vulnerable and poignant, yet in the blink of an eye he can smash a pimp's face or head-butt a thug and knock him cold. If he has to fight, he fights, but his heart can bleed as much as the arm he has slashed to protect the tart he adores from the vindictiveness of her pimp, Anderson.

George is newly sprung from seven years in jail, after taking the rap for his unscrupulous boss, Dinny Mortwell (Michael Caine). To reward such loyalty, Mortwell sets George up as the chauffeur/minder for a 'tall, thin black tart' named Simone (Cathy Tyson). By degrees he falls in love, and she snookers his devotion by treating him the only way she knows how to treat a man: by using him. She sends him off to find her lost love and fellow tart, Cathy, who is strung out on heroin and in Anderson's clutches. In his quest, the naive and humbly romantic George discovers that fairy tales don't come true, and that the enigmatic Mona Lisa of Nat King Cole's song was not real, but just a 'cold and lonely, lovely work of art'.

'I wanted to do a film that was just about characters,' Jordan said. 'A film in which I could get some really wonderful actors and construct a story and shoot it in a way that would allow me to explore the characters and acting as far as I possibly could. And besides that, I wanted to do a love story. I wanted *Mona Lisa* to be an anti-erotic story. If you release the possibility of sex from the two characters, you're left with great tension and real passion.' The script contained a love scene, but that was edited out.

He also wanted it to sound real. 'One thing I wanted to get into this film was people talking to each other in language that was rich and witty and meaningful.' Thus was created George's best mate, Thomas (Robbie Coltrane), who spins his own tales with George throughout the film, when he is not mass-producing plastic spaghetti for the Japanese market. He also provides a cryptic commentary on George's deepening immersion in things sordid.

'People were perplexed that I wanted to something *realistic* after the last film,' Jordan said. 'It should be like an operatic melodrama. There's a lot of sex and death. It's soaked in blood, really, in the way that Jacobean drama was.'

Jordan had begun writing his unlikely love story in collaboration with Englishman David Leland. He then sent a draft to the man who could best embody an unlikely hero. Hoskins rejected the first script he received. It was too bleak, cynical, heavily *noir*. Jordan, he decided, didn't need a 'little, short, fat version of Rambo. . . . It just had me running around bashing everyone up, like Superted.'

'When Neil first brought the script – he sent it actually – I said that it was okay but not for me,' Bob told Steve Grant. 'Then this scruffy Irishman turns up on my doorstep one day and says, "What didn't you like about my script then?" So I said, "Come in and have a drink and I'll tell you."'

That, however, is not quite the whole story. 'It wasn't only offered to Bob,' Sally Hope explained. 'He was given a script to read and he didn't like it. But there was something in it, and Neil thought he'd be interested. So an appointment was made and Neil went to see Bob because it was more convenient; he wasn't like some Irish poet who came in off the street. Neil is a highly talented writer/director. He had a concept, and once he met with Bob he saw how the character could be interpreted. It was a mutual reworking. Once he was in the film, Bob's input was huge.'

'When he wrote it originally, it was too much of a thriller, and it had too much violence in it,' Bob said. 'I wanted the relationship between the driver and the girl to be developed more. And the relationship between George and his daughter who is growing up and optimistic [and the same age as the prostitutes in Kings Cross], the contrast between his relationship with a whore and with his kid, who he really cares for. That's important. . . . If you don't care for anyone it's worse, far worse, than not having anyone who cares for you. What really appealed to me about George is that the guy *is* a mug. I think he's the ultimate hero because he's not invincible. He wears his heart on his sleeve, he's totally emotional, and he cannot help getting involved. The interest for me is the loser learning. George is a loser, but he learns very painfully.

'What I had about George was this bloke who's an ordinary

geezer, but who'd got a deep sense of decency, a bloke who's there when he is needed, who doesn't welch, who reveals that sense of right and wrong that is there in most of us when it comes down to it. I see myself as a cheerleader for the common man because people like George may not have any style, may not have so much sophistication or intellect, but they are the kind of people who built London, built New York. George is a hero, a lonely guy with a great light that is waiting to burst out.'

Bob kept his trademark preparation to a minimum for *Mona Lisa*. 'The point was,' he explained, 'the fella had to be naive. So I couldn't get involved in [trawling around Soho peep shows and strip clubs]. So when I get there, the shock that registered on film is the shock I was feeling, and it is quite an awful sort of situation.' What he did do was take three-year-old Rosa to London Zoo. 'To look at all those caged, trapped beasts, all those birds, the birds in particular, waiting to fly. Wanting to fly.

'Neil and I thought the guy had a wonderful spirit inside him; there was something very beautiful inside the man. Trapped within prison life, *trapped* within his own environment, *trapped* within his own naivete. And that was the sort of study I did with those birds. Trapped in cages. They couldn't fly and expend, and become part of the sky. George is such an ordinary fella, but in being ordinary, so *ex*traordinary. He's no different from anybody, really. Any chance you have to put an ordinary man in the cinema and turn him into a hero is wonderful. . . . Ordinary men, man on the street . . . we sort of pooh-pooh them, but . . . these are the people you should be proud of.'

What made George a hero was not his descent into darkness as a favour for a friend – it was love, a love unhampered with self-pity and transfigured by forgiveness.

'I fell in love with George, the man fresh out of prison,' Bob said. 'He's a loser, a naive mug who finds himself back on the roller coaster of life and not coping at all well. . . . He's the sort of noble hero played for a sucker. There are so many solid people out there who have got morality, who do care, but who are *total* mugs. George is one of them. George is closer to me than anybody I have ever played – which is why I wanted to do it so much.

Making *Mona Lisa* was a 'total, utter joy,' Bob also said. 'It offered me a chance to act, which is quite rare in films. And Neil let me be part of the actual film-making, instead of just turning up, doing my performance, copping my money, and going home.'

And Bob had come a long way from the breezy days of regarding his profession as a mere lark. This was his first proper starring role since *The Long Good Friday*, his first proper role shooting on home turf as well . . . and he was not about to blow it. In *The Long Good Friday* he'd been in nearly every scene. In *Mona Lisa* he'd be in *every* scene.

'It wasn't easy to do, actually,' he said. 'I had to bring about a man who is strong, vulnerable, serious, funny, sympathetic, hateful, ridiculous, dignified. You know, all those paradoxes. You couldn't present him in just one aspect.'

Filming began late in October 1985 after Handmade Films came to the rescue of a Bob Hoskins film once more. Steve Woolley – who had distributed *Clark Gable* – and his colleagues at Palace Pictures put up the development money and ITC had at first planned to make the film, but they eventually pulled out and Denis O'Brien and George Harrison stepped in with £2 million.

Jordan decided that *Mona Lisa* would be as distinctive visually as it would become emotionally. By hiring the talented Roger Pratt, who as lighting cameraman on *Brazil* had lit Bob's Spoor in lurid red and yellow, he would undoubtedly capture the 'hyper-realism in the images; a strong, dramatic use of colour; and quite melodramatic lighting style' he required, especially in the cold harsh light of the winter sun.

Jordan and co-producer Patrick Cassavetti (who'd also worked on *Brazil*) researched the Soho milieu by taking a punter's tour of low-life nightlife, and found it totally depressing. They encouraged feedback from the actors and then did improvisations based on these suggestions while on the set, so Jordan could have his script 'shaped around the characters'. Such close-knit collaboration had worked wonders for Bob and John Mackenzie on *The Long Good Friday* and even in the few scenes he'd invented with Fred Gwynne in *The Cotton Club*.

'It was a very emotional shoot,' Jordan said. 'Some scenes were so draining that it would take the actors an hour to retreat out of them.'

Cathy Tyson has remarked that, for her, this big break was 'a happy time, not like work. Bob and I were like twins – " 'Ere, Bob; 'Ere, Cath." For me it's a job. You make believe with the camera.'

George was less easily shaken off, especially for Bob, who tends to 'become' his roles. 'I think the film affected Bob profoundly,' Jordan said. 'I think he began to dream about George – I don't think he actually *became* him, but George became like a kind of guiding spirit to him, a friend he could always ask questions of.'

'I felt,' Bob said, 'if people didn't like George, fuck 'em! He's

176

okay. He would be a person I would make a friend of.' And because George was so close to Bob and so instinctively sentimental and desperate for love, when he tells Simone that he needs someone 'all the time', he brings tears to the audience's eyes, giving this film, at times, that inexplicable and ineffable experience that can only be called 'magical'.

'You're with someone and suddenly you're into something and you're away,' Bob said. 'You can't explain it, that *is* magic and anyone who's experienced it knows what I'm talking about. With Cathy, with Michael Caine and Robbie Coltrane, everyone in *Mona Lisa*, that magic was there. A lot of it was down to Neil, I think; he's got a great way of opening the floodgates and letting it all in. Even the catering lady wound up in the film; she had all kinds of suggestions, some of them really valid. It was that kind of set.

'It's the seedy side of London seen through the eyes of an Irish poet. I think Neil is a magician. And I believe in magic.'

What he also believed in was bloody hard work. One of his co-stars – who gave new meaning to the word 'workaholic' – was Michael Caine, who'd first heard of *Mona Lisa* when Bob passed him the script during the lovely *Sweet Liberty* summer that now seemed very far away. Playing the heartless personification of evil, Mortwell, was a courageous risk for Caine, even as a small cameo. It was a man of his own age, hair slicked back with snake oil and a viper's soul, and it was a terrifying, brutal, stiletto-edged perform-ance, done for, as Bob put it, 'two bob and a lollipop'.

'He turned up on the first day and said to me, "I bet you never thought I'd do it, you cunt!"' Bob told Steve Grant. All Caine's scenes were crammed into four days of shooting. 'He loves being in the game, he loves being in films, and he lives a wonderful life,' Bob said of the man who's starred with him in three films in as many years. 'You offer him the money, give him the part, a good location, and he's there.

'He has incredible screen knowledge,' Bob also told John Powers. 'He knows where his light is, he knows where to stand, and he doesn't want to think about it until everybody's ready. When he did *Mona Lisa*, he just came in, smarmed his hair down and *bam!*: he was the seediest man I've ever met in my life.'

Freezing your bum on a dirty street in Kings Cross does not fall into the 'good location' category. The loveless Mortwell could be looked at as a labour of love for Michael Caine. Bob hadn't played on their friendship at all to convince Caine to take the part. It was actually the sort of role Bob might have been offered and played had he not been the lead. What in retrospect seems faintly ludicrous is that Sean Connery had initially been offered George and had turned it down.

The script was not devoid of problems, like most scripts. At times George's naivete seems unwarranted. He is, after all, an East End crook and part of the criminal underworld who'd most likely grown up with girls on the game if not availing himself of their services. 'A lot of people that came up from a tough patch have done a bit of villainy,' Bob said, 'but you wouldn't say they were actual villains. George is just trying to earn a living. If he could have earned an honest living he probably would have done.' That he would have been so astonished at Simone and Cathy's lesbian relationship – which also seems a little far-fetched; these are hard ladies – is also stretching the 'love is blind' point; viewers had caught on ages before George. And the convoluted ending, with Simone blowing Mortwell and his henchmen to oblivion, was predictable yet uncomfortably gratuitous.

Jordan did have problems with the ending – several different versions were shot. 'I wanted to build a character that was inherently good and hopeful and it developed towards a climax of such savagery and emotional intensity that it was difficult to get out of,' he said. 'I didn't want to bring the audience on this journey and then just leave them.'

Still, as Bob said with completely deserved conviction, '*Mona Lisa* is the best thing I've ever done.' His performance transcended whatever limitations there were to the plot and left audiences stunned with his flawless incarnation. As sentimental as Arthur Parker, as determined as Harold Shand, as loud-mouthed as Nathan Detroit, as vulnerable as Morrie Mendellsohn, as cocky as Arnie Cole, embittered by prison and as hopelessly in love with the wrong woman as Bosola, George was completely compelling and the synthesis of every disparate role Bob Hoskins has ever played. He understood the yearnings.

When *Mona Lisa* was entered into competition at Cannes, the jury evidently agreed. For the first time in twenty-one years, in fact since Terence Stamp won for *The Collector*, an Englishman would receive the Best Actor Award.

The sandy beach strewn with bronzing topless bodies is a long way from Finsbury Park. The Cannes Film Festival, first held in September 1946, is a two-week media circus and PR factory.

'It's such a bizarre mixture of art and hype,' said film-maker Henry Jaglom. 'In one location, you have the people who crank out fantasies for the whole world, but for two weeks out of the year they're living a fantasy of their own. The illusion of films that will probably never get made, actors accepting upfront money for parts they will probably never play, people signing contracts on paper napkins. I've seen people out on yachts with Arab sheiks, people who I know don't have a penny to their name. Still, there they are. Hustlers hustling hustlers.'

Into this madhouse of pushy paparazzi and perpetual publicity parties came Bob Hoskins, wife Linda, agent Sally Hope, and director Neil Jordan. The Thirty-ninth Annual Cannes Film Festival was marred only by the non-appearance of famous Americans wary of Mediterranean proximity to Libyan terrorists. Even that self-inflated Rambo doll, Sylvester Stallone, stayed at home. Despite this cowardice, the festival was the largest ever – about 14,500 particpants saw more than 600 films at 1500 screenings in twelve days.

'I'm having a ball,' an undeterred and champagne-swilling Bob told *Film 86*'s Barry Norman. 'I'm having a wonderful time. It's so exciting. You know what's amazing about this place, because everyone has to dress up to go to the cinema, it's got a sort of timeless thing – it seems to go on forever, 'cos there's people walking about first thing in the morning dressed as penguins.'

Mona Lisa was extremely well received, and Bob did not at first realize that the lengthy post-screening standing ovation on 11 May was a visceral, unpremeditated response to his performance. Yet Bob and Linda had to get back to the children in London. Barry Norman had teased Bob about not being there should he win the prize for Best Actor. 'Listen,' Bob replied, laughing. 'If I win, I shall be here. You're kidding! I'll swim!'

He flew instead. He wasn't in Cannes when the phone rang on 19 May. No, it wasn't Francis Ford Coppola. Bob was in the garden with the children and the roses, when it was breathlessly announced that he'd won. And he had to get down there on the double. 'Wot d'ya think I am, a bleedin' pigeon?' was Bob's response. No, a private jet was waiting. There wasn't even time to panic. They had four hours, door-to-door, to fly 700 miles and then drive from the airport in Nice to the Festival Palace in Cannes. 'We got on that private jet,' Bob told Terry Wogan, 'Linda and meself, and we changed into the dicky bow and all the business, you know, and we got there, and there's a racing driver with two policemen [as an escort], right, and we got from Nice to Cannes in twelve minutes, and it usually takes an hour. I was sort of hanging on to Linda's leg in the car.'

'It took a lot longer than twelve minutes,' said a producer who often goes to Cannes. 'The more he tells that story the shorter the amount of time it gets. Once he even said nine minutes. It takes about nine minutes just to get out of the airport!'

However long or short the drive, Bob arrived just a little too late. He'd just missed the ceremony. Reportedly he was handed his prize as if it were a can of baked beans. But they'd spent all that money to fly him down – shouldn't he do something? 'They said, "Go through there,"' Bob explained. 'I walk through, and there I am, in front of 2000 people.' He naturally worried that he was 'mucking up the show'. Not to worry. The crowd was thrilled to see him, and he deservedly hogged the spotlight until jury member and director Sidney Pollack gestured to him to get down in front. 'It was amazing,' Bob said. 'I felt like I had robbed a bank.'

Bob shared his award with French actor Michel Blanc, who'd won for his confused homosexual in *Tenue de Soirée*. 'They picked these two little bald fellas!' Bob laughed. 'And he's even balder than I am – and shorter! It was great.'

For the first time in thirteen years an English film won top honours as *The Mission* took home the Palme D'Or. A scheduled flight took Bob and Linda home, where Bob prepared for a whirlwind publicity tour of the States to coincide with the early June release of *Mona Lisa*. Not even the honour bestowed by the eleven-person Cannes jury could have prepared him for the outstanding notices he would receive there.

John Powers of *L.A. Weekly* wrote: 'He gives the performance of the year. Funny, driven, and finally quite moving, he shows us a not-so-bright guy who finds spiritual resources that neither he nor we could have imagined at the beginning.' David Ansen wrote in *Newsweek*: 'Bob Hoskins is ferociously good. George is both a comic figure and a tragic one, and Hoskins never overplays either hand.' David Denby wrote in *New York*: 'Hoskins's characters are men of action who have resources of feeling denied most of us. Utterly decisive in action, Hoskins becomes not merely the hero of his movies but an actor who is loved by the camera – loved, that is, the way Humphrey Bogart and James Cagney were loved – as a possibility of honour and courage.'

Bob found the number and staggering pace of the scheduled media appearances on both coasts exhausting yet amazing. 'In Los Angeles the press was great,' Sally Hope said. 'They kept saying it was so refreshing to meet someone so honest. We did interviews from ten to six, going all the time. No one does that in England. But that only works for a week – you can only be new once, and then you are judged against that.'

When the film was released in England – it made its debut at the Cambridge Film Festival in July – the press went wild. First was the charity première on 4 September at the Haymarket Odeon; proceeds went to associations for the blind. The party for 600 was held at the National Portrait Gallery.

The next night Bob caused a near-riot after his taping of the *Wogan* show at the BBC Studio in Shepherd's Bush. 'I was waiting at the stage door beforehand,' said fan Lynne Robinson, who had tickets for the show, 'and with all the publicity at that time Bob must have been sick of it. Some people were shouting for autographs and Bob said he wasn't signing anything right now. He was very nervous, although he didn't mind having his photo taken in the green room. But then when he left, everybody flocked all over him and he started swearing. He's got a lot more fans now and they're a lot more aggressive.'

'Bob was mobbed like something from *Day of the Locust*,' said Chris Voisey, who'd remembered more genteel fans from the *Guys and Dolls* days. 'A huge phalanx of people – not the regular fans – pushed Bob up against the door and wouldn't let him pass. Little plebs and kids getting him to sign their bus tickets, shoving anything in his face. It was ridiculous. He finally made it to his car. "Don't you fucking threaten me, right!" he shouted. Then he jumped in a car. The crowd tried to pull his sun-hood off. "Leave the fucking thing alone!" he yelled and the car sped away.'

It was obviously not quite the same *frisson* of delight Bob had experienced when recognized by a stallholder Down Under. He had made the big league now, and this was Hollywood style. 'Once you get successful you have to deal with everybody wanting stardom second-hand,' Sally Hope says. 'And you've got to deal with other people's concepts of you. After *Wogan*, that was other people creating the reality – if they touched Bob they could go home and say, "I touched him" and be changed.'

British reviewers pounced with pleasure on the film, and many called it the best British film of that year.

'Hoskins is simply sensational,' wrote Pauline McLeod in the *Daily Mirror*. 'Only Bob Hoskins could have risen to the task of authenticating an old lag with the ingenuousness of a child,' wrote Neil Norman in *The Face*. *Sunday Express*'s Clive Hirschhorn said: 'It is a performance of remarkable subtlety, observation, and compassion, and it puts him in the forefront of contemporary British actors.' 'George may be something of a self-parodying Cockney sentimentalist,' said critic John Pym, 'but he has, too, that plain old-fashioned likeability which wins audience hearts and fills cinemas.' Perhaps because Bob Hoskins possesses that old-fashioned likeability himself.

The awards for Bob began flooding in. In November he won Best Actor at the Valladolid Film Festival in Spain. A month later he was voted Best Actor by the Los Angeles Film Critics, the same reviewers who'd saved *Brazil* from distribution purgatory the year before. The National Society of Film Critics in New York as well as Boston critics also chose him as Best Actor.

On 26 January 1987, however, he was surprisingly snubbed by the London *Evening Standard* Film Awards, although Ray McAnally, who won for *The Mission* and *No Surrender*, was a deserving recipient of the accolades. Even more surprisingly, *Mona Lisa* did not pull in one award that night.

That slight was overlooked just a few days later when the Hollywood Foreign Press Corps gave Bob the Best Actor trophy, this time a Golden Globe. It was a particularly important triumph since Golden Globe winners are usually top-rated for Oscars. The London Critics' Circle also gave Bob a Best Actor award.

'I honestly don't know what they're all about, but they look wonderful on my shelf above the fire,' Bob joked about all his trophies. 'Usually all an award means is that it puts you out of work for eighteen months because no one thinks they can afford you.'

By mid-February, however, the bookies as well as the Academy of Motion Picture Arts and Sciences had made their choice. The punter's favourite, Bob Hoskins, was nominated for an Oscar as Best Actor. Michael Caine had also been nominated as Best Supporting Actor for *Hannah and Her Sisters*. Bob's BAFTA nomination a few days later must have seemed a bit anti-climactic.

'I'm amazed,' Bob said when he was interviewed on the news. (Apparently, Handmade Films wasn't. They were so certain Bob would be nominated that they had sent out invitations to a 11 February press luncheon – on 5 February, before the list was announced.) 'It's like being in the pub havin' a good booze-up every day and the brewery are givin' you the prize. Obviously, bein' nominated for an award – it's the Oscar – is extraordinary, sure, something you'd never think about, would ya?' Does any film actor *not* think about the Oscars? 'I think it's the best thing I've ever done, he continued, 'so if I was gonna get it for anything it's obviously *Mona Lisa*. It's a bit worrying, actually, 'cos like, *Mona Lisa* is the best thing I've ever done and I've been nominated for an Oscar for it – where do I go from here? You know what I mean?'

At the pre-scheduled press conference Bob said he was 'incredibly intimidated' to be compared with his fellow nominees – Paul Newman, Dexter Gordon, William Hurt, and James Woods. 'I'm doing what I love and I love what I'm doing,' he said. 'To be given a prize makes me feel fraudulent. Win or lose, you have got to be proud to be considered in that company. And if I don't win it's not the end of the world. Newman hasn't had an Oscar yet, and it hasn't stopped him from earning a living.'

With typical humour, he also said, 'If I win an Oscar, I am going to be the most boring man in the world. There will only be one topic of conversation in my house. . . . When I hit Hollywood, I'm going to be so gross you won't believe it. I'm going to stay in the best hotel I can find. I am going to drive to the awards in the longest limousine I can find and I am going to do everything in the worst taste I can possibly manage.' And if he were to win, he'd put his gleaming gold statuette to better use than Glenda Jackson's doorstop. 'I'd put it where everyone could see it, as soon as they came in the door! Gawd! You thought John Wayne was over the top! You ain't see nothing!'

Actually, all Oscar winners must sign an Academy document, agreeing not to sell or pawn their 8½-pound, 13-inch-high statuette without first offering it back whence it came.

On 22 March Bob won the BAFTA Award as Best Actor, and on 29 March he flew out with Linda on a private Steven Spielberg jet – he was the producer of the film Bob was shooting at the time – to Hollywood, prepared for the worst. 'Let's face it,' Bob said pragmatically, 'I'm going out there to go to the party. I am not going to spoil that by worrying about whether I've won an Oscar. From what I've heard it's a foregone conclusion that Paul Newman's going to get it.'

Oscar time is a showbiz institution as American as apple pie. It is about money, hype, and stardom. Every year in early spring teeming hordes of Hollywood leeches descend on the Dorothy Chandler Pavilion for an evening's entertainment, endless $315,000-per-minute commercials, and endless disagreements about who won or lost.

'To some, the Oscar is a one-armed bandit,' said the Hollywood gossip columnist Hedda Hopper. 'Actors, directors, and producers just have to pull that lever no matter what the cost.'

You can't actually 'buy' an Oscar, but you can come pretty close. Studios, cast, crew, loved ones – all buy advertisements for vast sums of money in the showbiz trade publications to celebrate the roles of the actors they wish to support. Usually to no avail. Peter

Brown, author of *The Real Oscar*, said, 'You can certainly buy a nomination and then help it along quite a bit. It is greed, envy, and hate. It is friend against friend, agent against client, sister against sister, and director against actor in a maniacal rush to take home a Golden toy.'

And merit – who are you kidding? Hollywood tends to be conservative, for one thing, not being overly fond of extremely successful films, science fiction, or comedies. It has a soft spot for socially worthwhile themes (like *Gandhi*), actors who have been or are ill, actors who 'die' during the film, or actors who should have won for a better performance but didn't (probably because of a socially conscious role or an illness). This guilt factor often leads to honorary Oscars. In 1986, six-times-nominated Paul Newman received an honorary Oscar 'for his many memorable and compelling performances' in fifty-two films. He was understandably less than overjoyed.

'It was premature,' the sixty-two-year-old said of the award usually given to those about to die. 'There's plenty of mustard in this guy yet. Still, you don't kick people in the butt who are trying to be nice to you.'

For 1987, Oscar-watchers quickly narrowed the field down to Newman and Hoskins, judging that Hurt had just won, Gordon was too black, and Woods was too much of a maverick. The buzz was, though, that Newman was a sure bet. They simply *couldn't* screw him a seventh time like they did Richard Burton – and now *he's* dead – especially since Newman was nominated for the reprise of Fast Eddie Felson, his Oscar-nominated character from *The Hustler*. Furthermore, Walt Disney's Touchstone Pictures had mounted a multi-million dollar campaign to support him, wife Joanne Woodward quietly lobbied for her husband, and the normally reticent Newman offered interviews to the press to talk about *The Color of Money*.

On Oscar night, Newman won. While taking a break in the Pavilion lounge, Hoskins, Woods, and Gordon had already toasted the victor – before he was announced.

Of course, the buzz then was that if Newman *had* already won an Oscar, Bob Hoskins *definitely* would have won for *Mona Lisa*. At least Bob's mate Michael Caine had won *his* Oscar.

Unfortunately, neither Newman nor Caine was able to attend the ceremony. Newman was busy in New York, editing *The Glass Menagerie*. Caine was stuck in New York, too, contractually obliged not to stray too far from Paradise Island in the Bahamas, where he was shooting *Jaws, The Revenge*.

184

Bob consoled himself with the obligatory party thrown by super-agent Swifty Lazar at Spago, the designer pizza/glitterati hangout on Sunset Boulevard, where the champagne was flowing. There would be other roles and hopefully other Oscar-calibre performances. But, of course, there would never be another *Mona Lisa*.

As Guys Phelps wrote in the *International Film Guide 1987*: 'In *Get Carter* (1971), Britain's first brutally realistic gangster film, Michael Caine played a small-time racketeer. . . . Ten years later, Bob Hoskins in *The Long Good Friday* incarnated the now traditional gangster-capitalist. . . . In *Mona Lisa*, Neil Jordan subtly completes the circle as George stumbles into an unfamiliar world of vice and corruption and finds behind it all, not the efficient faceless corporation or ruthless terrorist, but just another grubby gangster. . . . Jordan has taken a familiar genre and reworked it for the mid-eighties. Effectively using its London and Brighton locales, *Mona Lisa* is stylish without being conspicuously so . . . visually the film matches the lurid sleaze of [Paul] Shrader's *Hardcore* [or Scorsese's *Taxi Driver*] and is more ambitious in its comments on innocence and experience, fantasy and reality, male and female.'

'This part is the best fucking thing I have ever done,' Bob told Steve Grant in a comment not unlike what he'd said about Arthur Parker ten years before. 'I'm so proud of what I've achieved here I can't tell you. If I popped off tomorrow, I would feel that I'd left something behind that was worth it.'

Mona Lisa is still smiling, enigmatically.

20

Say a Little Prayer for Me

Bob's summer of 1986 was marked by two extremely costly events. One cost him an abiding fourteen-year friendship. The other cost the producers of *The Untouchables* £130,000.

Sally had been approached by Bob while he was appearing in *Veterans* in 1972. 'He'd been with two agents,' she explained, 'but they split up and he didn't feel he could go with either, so he came to see me. When I first met him I didn't like him at all. He was quite opinionated and very loud. But we got to swapping theatrical stories . . . and we had an understanding: I would or he would turn a picture around in the office if we wanted to end things. But it was nothing as charming as that.'

Sally was more than just an agent. She had acted more like a personal manager, paying his household bills, and sorting out his taxes: she had files chock-full of ongoing paperwork to organize his rather chaotic approach to paper responsibilities. She had also accompanied him to court during divorce proceedings and given statements, spending endless weeks with solicitors and bank managers. Moreover, she was a friend, like the sister Bob never had, and the office/house Sally shared with her mother Blanche and sisters Ann and Jane in Islington was his home away from home. Their split was as emotionally devastating to Sally as if it had been a husband who sauntered in after fourteen years of what you thought was a healthy and thriving relationship and announced he'd been in love with somebody else for ages, then departing with the caution: Don't bother ringing; my solicitor will be in touch.

'I have the greatest respect for Bob as an actor,' said Sally, who was far more gracious in discussing this break than Bob was in discussing her, 'and he was the closest thing to a brother for me. He had a key to my house and whenever he wasn't doing so well he'd come and stay.'

'In his private life he had been married to Jane,' said television director Mike Gibbon, who'd worked with Bob in *Thick as Thieves*, 'but Blanche and Sally Hope really looked after him. They had him staying there for months on end – and he'd really become one of the family. I think it's so sad that he left, a great tragedy. Forget the money part of it – he was like a brother. When Blanche died, we went to the funeral. There were an awful lot of Sally's clients there because Blanche had been so wonderful. If Sally or Ann weren't there, she'd make meals for the people who showed up and sort of hung about the house, and she'd babysit the clients when they needed help. The whole Hope family was so close, in a positive way. Bob came, and he was standing on one side of the grave with Sally and Ann, in tears, with this great grief . . . Sally had done so much for him. As a director, if I ring up Sally or Ann for something like *EastEnders* and say "I want a twenty-three-year-old with black hair and blue eyes, have you got anyone?' they'd say "Yes, no." Just like that. So many agents really waste your time and you get so fed up with it. With them you know you're not going to be messed about. It has always been rather odd to me that Bob left. I thought they were welded together.'

'It doesn't surprise me,' said Jane Hoskins. 'He owes her something he can't pay.'

'They were tremendously close,' said Nicholas Clay, 'and it's a great shame for Sally although she's big enough to handle that. It still must be a huge disappointment, I'm sure. They together did for Bob's career what it now looks like Bob did on his own.'

Bob had already made his decision and chosen another agent, the estimable Ann Hutton, before telling Sally; a point he originally denied. Nor did he 'turn a picture around' as a signal. There was an ugly, unwarranted, Bob-instigated scene in the office and he stomped out, never to return and refusing all phone calls, discussion, and without paying Sally a proper percentage of monies earned from deals she had set up, like *Mona Lisa* and the forthcoming *Prayer for the Dying*.

'Bob told me I hadn't served his best interests,' Sally says. 'Yet our work together was really nice, a real fifty-fifty partnership and it's sad when after all this time someone you care about and respect doesn't treat you properly. Whatever you may be feeling you don't try to do something against someone professionally. It was a deep blow and totally unexpected. After fourteen years of my output, my job – a job I did extremely well – a huge part of my creative abilities, I expected a certain respect. He hasn't behaved well since.'

Bob undoubtedly had his reasons. On a private level, well,

perhaps Linda felt threatened by Sally's familial relationship with her husband, a not unjustified feeling. And in a telling remark, Bob told Steve Grant, 'To tell you the truth, I wouldn't be a bit surprised if [Linda] doesn't start giving a few producers a run for their money one day soon.' An ambitious spouse would be likely to look at a tight-knit set-up with an agent as competition.

On a professional level, Bob may have felt the need for more freedom in his choice of roles. There had been a disagreement over a cameo role as Al Capone in Brian De Palma's *The Untouchables*. Sally had turned it down, because she felt it was too close to Owney Madden. Bob then took it. 'It was a very small part,' she said, 'and I was very surprised that Bob accepted it. I thought it was foolish for him to do a small role as a gangster; he should accept big roles as gangsters and small parts as aristocrats . . . a part where you're not too sure whether you can do it. I always wanted Bob to do "other roles". I think he was playing himself too often.' Actors, she believed, must keep, as Bob had done, stressing their versatility. 'Acting is a career that spans from age twenty-two to eighty. In between you're riding a crest, and you want to keep it going as long as possible. I don't think that all actors *are* versatile; they *don't* want to do everything – they'd rather play the same role over and over. That's the difference between a character actor and a leading man.'

Sally was also taking a 15 per cent commission, higher than the more customary 10 per cent, yet certainly not unheard of for someone who'd spent so much time with a client, at first taking 10 per cent of tiny fees and eventually working toward those plum Hollywood roles. That's simply the nature of the business.

That summer had been a major turning point in Bob's career. The pressures and sudden, major acclaim would cause anyone's head to spin, even an actor who'd been working towards that fame and accomplishment for nearly twenty years. It is the old Hollywood success cliché. Drop the ones who got you there once you get there. Considering that Bob was usually considered such a loyal friend, and that tales of his generosity and helpfulness to others in the profession abound, his behaviour seems more like that of a bad B-movie character than what you'd expect from a soft and sentimental person at heart.

'I got invited to a big party up at Spago for Bob when *Mona Lisa* was released,' said John Byrum. 'I didn't go but Stephen Davies [from *Inserts*] did, and I asked him what Bob was like. Davies said, "He was not there. His eyes were darting around, nervously." It must be so strange, the first real crack at Hollywood adulation – that's when you get bitter usually. You freak. You think why the fuck didn't this happen twenty years ago? I've seen this happen. They all dump their agent or manager. I think they think *you* can't think big enough, or will not be able to make the larger deals. You want to cover your ass with a big name.' Or maybe the person who knows you best, who is the reminder of your past struggles and foibles, is not the person you want to have marketing your new, as-yet-untarnished 'bankable star' image.

All Bob would say in public was, as Steve Grant related: 'When someone has controlled your life for so long and has enabled you to reach the point where you have to be and can be free, then it's hard, but it's one of those things.'

One of those things, however, that resulted was a malicious and reprehensible rumour that quickly spread around London saying that one of the reasons Bob Hoskins had left his agent was because she was taking 50 per cent. If, in fact, the source of this rumour was Bob, as must be thought likely, perhaps it was guilt talking; maybe deep down Bob, feeling so guilty about what he'd done to Sally, thought that if he made it seem that *she* had acted unprofessionally, then it was only right that he should leave her.

Bob had every right to leave his agent. That's showbiz. In the process, however, he had hurt a good friend very deeply. 'The fact of hurting someone I'm not very good at,' Bob once said. 'I just haven't got the heart.' A hard statement to reconcile in view of his actions.

'In one sense there is a huge sense of relief when that "ego" goes, that serving of such a big personality,' Sally said. 'I paid his maintenance and sorted out his taxes, and when you're handling the money, you don't know if you're doing it right. It becomes oppressive, as if you're handling all aspects of a person's life. As an agent, all your *creative* input is dedicated to trying to give actors respect, integrity and an intelligence the world doesn't think they have. You can accuse an agent of many things, but Bob's way of repaying all the hassle was to tell me to fuck off.' And as she had said about Bob: 'What's gone on before is of no relevance to now. If he upset someone, it's yesterday, it's gone.'

Meanwhile, Bob was preparing to accept a cameo role in *The Untouchables*.

Prohibition, 1931, when infamous father of organized crime Alfonso 'Scarface' Capone owned most of Chicago. The fearless four who took him on – and won – were led by the incorruptible Federal Agent Elliot Ness. They were the 'Untouchables', and their story became a thriller directed by Brian De Palma, with script by playwright David Mamet, and starring Kevin Costner and Sean Connery as a tough cop in an Oscar-calibre performance.

De Palma's first choice for Capone was Robert De Niro, who reportedly deliberated so long about accepting the role that De Palma went to his second choice, Bob Hoskins. '[De Palma] asked me if I would do him a favour and play the part in case De Niro couldn't,' Bob explained. He offered Bob $200,000 (about £130,000 at that time). Bob said yes and went off on a brief holiday while contracts were being drawn up and filming began in Chicago.

Then Robert De Niro, Bob's soulmate from *Brazil*, decided he might as well be Al. De Palma's producers acted honourably and paid Bob his fee in full. 'I hadn't signed a contract,' Bob said, 'and De Palma could certainly have got away with dropping me totally in favour of De Niro. But he at least insisted on paying me.'

Talk about pennies from heaven. De Niro earned at least $1.5 million and a percentage of the profits.

Bob, though, could still laugh all the way to the bank. His American agent, J. Michael Bloom, said, 'It won't hurt his career. I have seventeen film offers for him right now.' And this was said *before* the UK release of *Mona Lisa*!

One of those offers had an unexpected result. Film director Robert Altman wanted Bob to co-star with Tom Conti in a special dramatic presentation for ABC TV in America of Harold Pinter's *The Dumbwaiter*. Hoskins said no, and John Travolta ended up with the part, even though his Cockney accent was closer to Brooklyn than the Bells of St Mary-le-Bow.

But it was a journalist who ended up with the last laugh on the subject of Bob and *The Untouchables*. The *Daily Mirror*'s William Marshall interviewed Bob for a story entitled 'Tough Guy at the Top'. According to Marshall, Bob said about the pay-off: 'Makes you have a whole lot of new faith in human fuckin' nature, don't it, a thing like that.'

'He looked like Genghis Khan dressed by Oxfam,' Marshall went on. '"Ah, yes Bob, I murmured in jest, it would have been a greater act of faith in human nature if you'd given it back." His big throaty laugh gurgled away like bathwater down the plug hole and the cannonball head came down, suspicious brown eyes staring through menacing horn-rimmed specs.'

Scarface Al would have laughed.

'I'm no Irish Rambo,' Mickey Rourke announced. 'I was hoping to make a movie that would inform Americans, especially Irish-Americans' – of which he is one – 'about what is going on in

Northern Ireland. Goldwyn insisted upon turning it into another *Rambo*.'

A set of *A Prayer for the Dying* was not, by all accounts, a happy place to be. Based on the thriller written by best-selling author Jack Higgins, *A Prayer for the Dying* traces one Martin Fallon (whose name means 'stranger from outside the campfire' in Irish), doctor of music from Trinity College, who has become a disillusioned hitman for the IRA. Tired, filled with self-loathing, he wants out, and the only man who can help him is Dandy Jack Meehan (Alan Bates), a revolting lizard whose unsavoury criminal activities are fronted by a successful funeral parlour. Meehan has his terms for Fallon: kill a rival, and a passport to freedom will be his. Hunted by the IRA he has deserted, and the London police, Fallon reluctantly agrees, but his murderous act is inadvertently witnessed by ex-World War II commando Father da Costa (Bob Hoskins). Knowing that a confession is inviolate, Fallon seals the priest's lips, and the Father and the wayward Son battle for their lives while Holy Ghost Meehan tries to buy their silence. In the conflagrationary ending, when Fallon saves da Costa and his blind niece Anna, who had fallen in love with Fallon, a bomb blows the poor parish church to heaven and Fallon is killed by a large, ornamental crucifix. He can at last receive the prayer for the dying.

For the second time in Bob's career a crucifix would figure predominantly in a melodramatic ending. Only this wasn't the sardonic *Dog's Dinner*. It was a £6 million film directed by Mike (*Get Carter*) Hodges, and produced by Peter Snell for the Samuel Goldwyn Corp. And it was a problem from the word go, which was on 22 September 1986.

The casting had been a stroke of genius. The intense, cult-figure Rourke signed first.

'I set off after Rourke with the script,' producer Snell said. 'He is a character star. He is not an obvious romantic lead yet women find him enormously attractive. He has an incredible energy; he looks Irish. He read it and liked it very much and said, "Okay, I'll do it, but I won't do it unless you can find a director I'm comfortable with."'

'I became interested in the story and the screenplay sounded good,' Rourke told *Irish American* magazine. 'It suited me as an actor. Also, for a long time, I was looking for a part that would enlighten people about how and why Northern Ireland is the way it is.' And to make sure the film would not be seen as anti-IRA propaganda he asked for some control over script and director.

'It's a touchy subject,' Rourke said before shooting. 'It's about

191

the IRA but it's nothing to do with politics. It concerns a personal issue between an anti-IRA man and a priest. It will get me away from the stereotypical New Yorkers I've been playing. I'll have a Belfast accent and it'll be a stretch for me. It's about time I did that.'

Franc Roddam, famous for *Quadrophenia* and *The Bride,* was hired to direct, but, as Snell said, 'We agreed to part company only four weeks before the start of production when it became obvious that we were seeing the material from totally different standpoints. Franc's script made Fallon the merciless killer. If it moved, it got shot. If it was female, it got raped then shot. He saw the picture differently to Mickey and I [sic]. Mike Hodges was a gift from the gods. He liked the story, saw it as a very taut, fast-moving thriller. Roddam had wanted to make an Irish *Rambo.* Hodges's reaction was to take a lot of the violence out of it, develop the characters and the suspense. It was an approach that appealed immediately to Rourke and it was the picture I'd set out to make with Goldwyn's blessing.'

In the meantime, Bob and Alan Bates had been sent scripts. 'I'd originally been offered the part of Father da Costa,' Bates said, 'but I hadn't liked the original script and turned it down. Then they came back and offered me the heavy, and I jumped at it. As well as being a gangster, Meehan is the director of a funeral parlour, a great glittering palace of death in which he likes to do the embalming himself. He's quite mad, of course. Villains like that inhabit an entirely different reality to anyone else.'

Bob jumped at it too, then. 'I don't want people to think I'm just good at playing gangsters,' he said. 'What made the film appealing to me is that casting against type. No one will believe it.' And, he added, 'I'd met Mickey Rourke in America and wanted to work with him.'

'He needed to be strong to balance Rourke,' said Hodges, 'and he had to bring a sort of crude English power to the role to be credible as an East End priest who'd been a member of the SAS before he renounced violence and turned to the Church. After seeing Bob in *Mona Lisa* and *The Long Good Friday,* we were in no doubt that he was very much the "Cockney Cagney" the Americans are calling him. He has such energy and heart and a common touch, an infinite liking for an interest in his fellow man, a genuine compassion, which is his great forte. He's perfect for the part.'

Rourke had been working on his part for months. He studied with Brendan Gunn, a Northern Irish dialogue coach, which, as Rourke said, 'is very hard to do. I wanted, in this particular film, to maintain a certain concentration with the dialect.' He also visited

Belfast and conferred with playwright Martin Lynch about that city. Although he reportedly brought an entourage of his voice coach, trainer, agent, miner, personal assistant, and best friend to the set, Alan Bates defended Rourke's style: 'He plays an IRA hitman, so it's understandable to bring along a voice coach to get it right. In fact, I rather like the American method of questioning everything and analysing motivation in depth. Too often, English actors tend to rely on their great technical facility and play a role off the top of their heads.'

Bob prepared in his own inimitable way as well. As he jokingly said about the role: 'My old man is a Socialist, so I was brought up as an atheist, and here I am playing a Catholic priest. I suppose you could say it was a role made in heaven!

'I went to see a priest and said, "I'm playing one of you lot, give us a few tips." He said, "What you've got to remember is how a priest would stand. It's like this."' Back bowed, hands clasped protectively in front of the groin. 'Guarding temptation. That was the big pointer. I did the whole film walking around like that. I started to grow into it.

'I am getting more mellow and diplomatic as I get older and also I am beginning to see the other person's point of view. I'm less concerned with myself. Also, I've become very confident. Having the kind of praise I've had recently has given me the confidence, I suppose. I want to be liked, obviously, but I don't really worry about what people think of me. What concerns me more now is what I think of them.

'The fact that I do think of them means I think about their problems. I mean, people come up to me on the street, not realizing I'm an actor, I'm Bob Hoskins. They think I'm a priest when I'm wearing this frock [his long black cassock] and they come out with the most horrendous things. Then I look at the person and it puts the whole thing in perspective somehow. I couldn't tell them I'm just an actor so I have to listen and try to help.'

One distraught old lady approached this humble 'priest' and said, 'I'm so lonely, Father, and the pills don't work any more.' Bob softheartedly said, ' "Take your rosary, go and sit in a park, and have a look at the trees. Say every prayer on that rosary and think just what those words mean." It seemed to comfort her. I don't think I did wrong.'

'Bob was excruciated with embarrassment when he first put on the vestments,' Hodges recalled. 'I honestly think he would have run away if he could. I knew it was hard for him to play a priest – he told me he started having religious dreams and putting on random weight to look portly enough. Once he took it on, he got to the heart of the role and the character and started to work outwards.'

A Prayer for the Dying was shot on location primarily in the East End; in the derelict docklands; the old Cooperative Funeral Parlour (where a real mortician oversaw Bates's embalming scenes for veracity); the Woolwich ferry; Kennington Town Hall; and in the Anglican St Luke's Church (now up for sale), transformed into the Catholic Church of the Holy Name.

The problems on the set multiplied. A Goldwyn representative infuriated Rourke when he announced that he was unhappy with Mickey's authentic accent after the very first line of dialogue he uttered ('Could you lighten it up a little?' he apparently asked), though Snell had praised it. There were arguments, too, about the level of violence, about to what extent to reveal Fallon's depth of character and the complexity of his motivations, and about a nude scene where Fallon beds Anna which is not in the book.

Another problem was the closing scene, with Bob and Alan Bates on the roof of the crumbling church, which needed to be reshot. Both actors refused, stating that it was no longer safe, because it had been partly derigged. Tempers rose until a safety officer gave his okay. 'When we were up there, I had more than a passing thought about life and death,' Bates confessed. 'It was a hell of a long way up and just as far down. The fact is, when you reach the advanced age of fifty-two, your apprehensions multiply. I became painfully aware of all the things that could happen to my body if I fell. Bob Hoskins felt the same, but says it wasn't apprehension at all. Just wisdom.'

'The piece has taken quite a lot of different directions,' Snell said, cautiously. 'There's a certain amount of integrity I'm trying to keep with [Fallon] that I'm continuously having to fight for, instead of making it some kind of exploitation thriller. I don't want to make a movie like they do in the States where a guy picks up a fucking machine gun and kills 200 people.'

Nor did Mickey Rourke. 'I've worked on films where I've been "yessed" to death, then we've started shooting and I end up making a film I thought was not going to be made,' Rourke said, also cautiously, during the filming. 'I was only interested in making this film on the understanding that I could get across some of the things I found out first-hand . . . I don't want to glorify it, nor do I want to misinterpret reasonings or intentions. . . .'

He later said: 'It was becoming increasingly obvious that they wanted a lot of sex and a lot of killing in this movie. I kept thinking that maybe I could change it.' He couldn't. Goldwyn's fears were that too much introspection would mean commercial death in the cinemas.

All parties gratefully finished filming in November. At least Bob was philosophical about it: 'I know the film will be attacked,' he said. 'I got attacked for playing Mussolini as a human being. But drama is about humans. I think the film gives hope. [Fallon's] seen the futility of killing, the terrible pity of it all. He's been killing for what he saw as an honourable cause, he still thinks it's an honourable cause, but he's sickened by it and knows it has to stop . . . somewhere, sometime. Ultimately he dies saving my life. It's a thriller but it's also a kind of morality story, if you like. At any rate, I hope so. Michael Caine once said to me that there have only been three good gangster films to come out of Britain: one he did with our director on this one, Mike Hodges, a picture called *Get Carter*; one I did, *The Long Good Friday*; one we both did, *Mona Lisa*. I'd like to think *A Prayer for the Dying* will prove to be the fourth.'

No such luck. It seems the producer, director, and star each had a different conception and ended up working at cross purposes. At a press conference at the Cannes Film Festival in May 1987, where he was promoting *Barfly*, Rourke let rip with vitriolic, unprintable references to Goldwyn's interference. 'All Goldwyn wanted to do was make Seamus O'Rambo for money,' Rourke stated. 'I worked on my Belfast accent for six months. Goldwyn said he couldn't understand me. . . . They didn't care about my accent or the authenticity of the dialogue. The dispute between us became very draining. I had a mental breakdown and I'm only just coming out of it.'

He later told *American Film* that 'what [my breakdown] was really all about was a hatred for them, for hustling me to pimp, to make money for them by making *their* kind of movie. A doctor had to come and give me sedatives almost every day. . . . I *did* go to a shrink, I have to admit. But I *felt* like I needed a priest.' Not even Father Hoskins da Costa could help him out of this one.

Sam Goldwyn, displeased with what he thought was propaganda for the IRA and Rourke's supposed inclusion of self-penned speeches, had his own point of view: 'Mickey is a marvellous actor, but he should not have added those speeches. He got a million dollars for the film and also okayed the script.'

'Goldwyn is bad-mouthing me and saying I just wanted to make long speeches about the IRA,' Rourke retorted. 'I thought the movie was going to be a real opportunity to explain things.'

'Mickey Rourke doesn't know what he's talking about,' said Goldwyn.

195

In August, as the 11 September American release date loomed, director Hodges also publicly disowned the film. 'What was a fine film when I handed it over to you,' he wrote to Goldwyn, 'is now a piece of schlock.' He told the press: 'I don't like it; I don't like the music, it has no tension, and I don't want my name associated with it. The theme of the piece is anti-violence. I took out as much of [the violence] as possible and tried to focus on the character of Fallon. I don't know what they thought they were making, a caper film or what. It is not that. I reworked the script. I cast it and got the crew together and made the film on budget. They have a right to change it. I don't argue with that. But I have a right to have my name taken off of it if I am unhappy with it. And I am.'

The only person who was thoroughly pleased with the film was Jack Higgins. He said *A Prayer for the Dying* was 'the most faithful adaptation of a book since *The Manchurian Candidate*. Thriller fans want to know all the nuances of the characters, their reasons for doing the things they do. Very often a film will not do that, forcing them back to the book. With this movie there is no need to read the book. The story is there.

'When they told me Mickey Rourke was getting the part I was overjoyed,' Higgins also said. 'And I'm still overjoyed. He's great in it; done a very fine job, as far as I'm concerned. But Rourke's squawk – "I'm no Irish Rambo" – well, I think this is absolutely farcical. It's ludicrous. He doesn't know what he's talking about. As far as Northern Ireland goes, neither the book nor the film are about Northern Ireland. I've written a book about Northern Ireland. It was called *The Savage Day*.'

The American reviewers, however, didn't pull their punches.

'A hokey, lurid melodrama that cashes in on real-life political agonies for cheap thrills,' wrote *Time*'s David Ansen. 'Only Hoskins emerges from this pretentious mess unscathed.'

J. Hoberman wrote in *Village Voice*, 'Admirers of Bob Hoskins may legitimately worry whether the East End Cagney has been reduced to playing a Belfast Pat O'Brien. Not to worry. Turned-around collar or no, Hoskins does finally explode, clobbering three of Bates's punks with the cover of a metal garbage can. Needlessly underscored by half an orange neon sign spelling R-A-G-E, the demonstration gives this trash the requisite measure of flash.'

Mickey Rourke must have thought his prayers had been answered when the film died a quick death at the American box office. Months later, in the bitter *American Film* interview, he confessed: 'They've put it in the papers that they paid me my million dollars, which I was happy enough to get. Well, I've turned down two and three million dollars. *Everyone* in this town knows that I cannot be bought.'

However legitimate Rourke's gripes about his role and the way in which it was cut, the film's fundamental flaw was evident from the beginning – in the script he had approved. The book itself, while able to trace Fallon's desperation and moral dilemma in more detail, remains an extremely violent slice of IRA/East End life packaged into thriller form, with none of the poetry of *Mona Lisa* or cynical humour of *The Long Good Friday*. The story is filled with ugly sex, ugly killings, and ugly situations. No sympathetic portrayals, authentic accents, or months of preparation and psychological delving could change that.

Bob Hoskins, now revered by the critics, wisely said nothing while the controversy raged. His Father da Costa was an admirable attempt at playing against type, but any gangster-orientated film must have been a let down after the magical experience of *Mona Lisa*. And da Costa's rage, conveniently explained by his violent wartime background, is entirely one-dimensional. It would have been far more stretching for him to have played an entirely pacifist priest who doesn't know a Beretta from a barracuda.

'At last,' Bob said, 'a film my kids can go and see and be proud of later on. This is really children's fun.'

The film is *Who Framed Roger Rabbit?*, based on the novel by Gary Wolf; the executive producer is Hollywood golden boy, Steven Spielberg, for Walt Disney/Amblin Entertainment; the director is *Back to the Future*'s Robert Zemeckis; and the stars are Hoskins, Joanna Cassidy, Stubby Kaye, and a few animated friends. If Bob wanted to play against type, he couldn't have chosen a better project.

'It's the best script I've seen in years and I'm sure the film is going to be amazing. The special effects are extraordinary,' Bob said. It is certainly the most unusual part he's ever been offered, to say nothing of prestigious. The real actors, playing 1940s' characters, will be combined with animated ones – the first time cartoon characters from different studios like Disney, Warner Brothers (Bugs Bunny), and Max Fleischer (Betty Boop) will be on-screen together – as the cartoon Roger Rabbit, unjustly accused of murdering his director, hires a private eye, Eddie Valiant, to find out who framed him. Valiant has problems of his own, like being driven to drink after his brother/detective agency partner met an unfortunate end when a piano was dropped on him. Enter Dolores

197

(Joanna Cassidy), proprietress of the bar across the street. Where else!

'Bob and I got along great,' Cassidy said, 'and I felt perfectly at ease working with him. We had great fun wearing 1940s' clothes too. I'm responsible for helping Bob recover from the shock of his brother's death. At one point he says to me, "Why don't you go and find yourself a good man?" and I answer, "I don't have to – I already have a good man." We have a wonderful relationship.'

Far more crucial to the action, though, are the animated characters. Bob probably had no idea what he was in for when he flew off to Los Angeles for several weeks of filming at the end of November 1986. (He'd postponed the trip so that he could celebrate Linda's fortieth birthday with her, and was definitely not looking forward to the separation from his family which was inevitable because Rosa couldn't be taken out of school. 'They've travelled everywhere with me because I hate being on my own,' Bob said. 'I've got to do five weeks filming without them and I'll miss them terribly.')

'I have to act without the rabbit,' Bob explained. 'He'll be superimposed afterwards. You might think it sounds tricky, but my daughter Rosa is a big help there. She has imaginary friends that she plays with at home, so in the film I'll pretend I'm Rosa when I do certain scenes. I'm basing the part on her.

'It will be an honour to appear alongside such Disney classics as Donald Duck and Mickey Mouse. They are my absolute all-time heroes.'

Does this acting technique sound easy? As filming progressed, Bob returned to Elstree Studios outside London, and found out just how difficult it is to act to a four-foot rabbit as elusive as the one that Alice chased down the hole.

'It's verging on insanity,' Bob said. 'I'm in every scene. I spend all my time talking to characters who are not there. I look and respond to whoever my imagination conjures up for me. I spend my time fighting weasels and being thrown out of clubs by gorillas. . . . If the rabbit grabs my braces, they've got to snap in and out. But there's no rabbit yet. Like I say, very demanding.'

Not only was sustaining this imaginary life, 'acting to thin air', the challenge of Bob's acting career, it was also debilitating physically.

'Bob had to do so many mechanical, terribly technical things in this movie,' John Mackenzie said. 'Someone would read the rabbit's lines to him and he had to fight when this rabbit isn't there and they're pulling his clothes with wires. He had to do sequences time and time again and it was all to do with the wires showing. He would of course be very good at this part because he's so imaginative, so he *would* see a rabbit that wasn't there. But then if they start to tie him down and say, "Don't do that because it means showing the wire," then his wonderful imagination might suffer. Anybody's would! Bob should be able to cope, and if he gets through that, it means he's bloody fantastic because he's acting blind.'

Roger Rabbit is not the first use of this live/animation technique in a lavish Hollywood production. There was Leopold Stokowski greeting Mickey Mouse in *Fantasia*, Gene Kelly's 'Sinbad the Sailor' in *Invitation to the Dance, Mary Poppins*'s magic, Jessica Lange asking King Kong what his astrological sign was, and, funnily enough, at the 1987 Academy Awards ceremony, Bob and Linda watched presenter Tom Hanks hog the spotlight with Bugs Bunny, while giving the award for best achievement in animation, naturally. But *Roger Rabbit* would be the most complicated and expensive use of this concept in the history of film-making. There were over 2000 planned special effects. In comparison, Zemeckis' complicated *Back to the Future* only had thirty-nine. Nothing of this scale had ever been attempted before.

With a budget already in excess of the original $37 million, *Roger Rabbit* was costing well over $100,000 for each screen minute – just for the animation technique. 'That is really some pay cheque,' Bob said of the budget. 'There's no fooling about.' The man responsible for the dubbing-in of the cartoon characters was Richard Williams, considered by many to be the best animator in the world. He was Spielberg's only choice for the movie, despite his 'competition' with the animators at Disney.

Once the live sequences were finished the crew of animators took over in a race against the clock to finish by the unbreakable deadline of 4 July 1988 in America and later the same year in the UK.

For Bob, monster success (as opposed to monster failure à la *Howard the Duck*, George Lucas's mega-budget disaster) would be sensational, of course. His own contribution to *Roger Rabbit* will be his acting tour de force. The film is a comedy adventure unlike anything he's ever done before. It is a major Hollywood production not marred by scripts that changed on a daily basis. However exhausting, it must have been a relief that there were no temperamental star egos to placate. Rosa and her imaginary friends ought to like it, too.

In the spring of 1987, Handmade Films proudly announced that it had signed Bob Hoskins to a three-picture deal.

The first was *The Lonely Passion of Judith Hearne*, directed by Jack Clayton and based on the book, published in 1956, by Brian Moore, regarded by many as the best first novel since World War II. Filming, with co-star Maggie Smith as Judith, began at Shepperton Studios in early May, giving Bob only a short break from his exhausting bout with Disney perfectionism. Bob referred to his character, James Madden, as a 'bit of a phony'. He brings unexpected love to Maggie's middle-aged and frumpy spinster. Both Katharine Hepburn and Deborah Kerr had once bought the rights – the part is a mature actress's dream – but were unable to pull off the financing.

Despite its Dublin setting, only one week was spent on location there. One account in the *London Daily News* stated that it was thought that Bob might be an IRA target due to his portrayal of Harold Shand (at this point, the far more unsympathetic *Prayer for the Dying* hadn't even been released.) Reportedly, 'a spokeswoman denies they kept location work to a minimum amid security fears, but observers claim this sounds a bit ingenuous. The Dublin studios are among the best in the world and there are considerable financial advantages in producing films there.'

When Bob had been in Dublin for *The Woman Who Married Clark Gable* two years before, no such far-fetched claims were made. Undoubtedly the IRA is occupied with matters far more meaningful to them than the presence of an actor whose screen incarnation had got tangled up in messy business a few years before. And as one IRA member once said to Bob, after the release of *The Long Good Friday*, 'I wish we *were* that organized.' 'Why would they bother blowing the legs off some soppy actor who's done some silly film?' Bob also remarked in *NME* in September 1986. 'There's real issues at stake and I'm talking about a mere movie.'

For a man who's said he's 'not ambitious', *The Rawney*, Bob's second production for Handmade, should prove otherwise. Bob has co-written the script (with Nicole de Wilde), is directing abroad and also starring in this saga of gypsies during World War II. Co-stars include Dexter Fletcher, Zoe Nathenson, and Zoe Wanamaker.

'It's actually a tale my gypsy gran used to tell me,' Bob said, 'and because I'm close to this I'm going to direct it. I've no ambitions to be a director or to direct anything else, but this film has been so carefully cast that I reckon it will just about direct itself.'

'I'm gonna star and direct it as well to save dough – do it in Czechoslovakia,' Bob also told Steve Grant. 'It's cheap and the light is very special there, something about spaces that are very landlocked; the light is subtle.'

What Bob didn't say is that Handmade, knowing that Bob is 'box office' only as an actor – not as a director – insisted that he star in it before they would finance the project.

'I've always been a sort of old-fashioned itinerant jobbing actor and I've never had time to put into a project. . . . When I started out and acted less I had time to write and really got a taste for it,' Bob said about appearing on the Arnie Cole side of the lens. 'Now I've got a film script . . . it's a peaceful anti-war film, a subject I feel very strongly about. And I'm going to have a bloody good stab at setting it up and directing.'

Bob has always spoken out vociferously for human rights and against prejudice, and as he was pretty much a travelling vagabond before the Unity Theatre experience set him on the path to his true calling, he feels empathy for a culture that lives in caravans and takes to the road.

'Of course I'm shittin' myself,' Bob also said about directing, 'but I think it will be all right. The main thing about a film is getting a load of talented people together. Directing is just getting the best out of them with the least possible interference. . . . I'm working with some of the cleverest people in the business, and I'm hoping that once I tell them how I want it to turn out, the film will just make itself.

'Basically it's about people avoiding war and it's mixed up with an old gypsy legend. The Jews had a terrible time in the war but the gypsies had an even worse time. The camps were full of gypsies but the Jews have got a better publicity agent,' Bob said with outstanding tactlessness, especially for a man who'd played a Dunera Boy.

'I don't believe Germans are the enemy or the English or the Vietnamese or whatever,' Bob also said. 'I think war, the very conception of war, is the enemy. Historically it's the biggest insanity man can get into.'

'To be a director,' a friend of Bob's said, 'you have to be able to run a set. Bob is a chaos-maker: wherever he goes, chaos follows! I mean that in a positive sense, but it is one thing to think you can hire a bunch of your chums and have them magically fall into place, and quite another to be able to tell them exactly what to do. It will be interesting to see how well Bob does once he realizes he can't muck about and spend his evenings in the pub, because he's responsible for getting a film made.'

'I don't think directing really has to do with how good you are at telling people what to do,' said Ben Lewis, who like Bob is a writer and director, 'but how good you are at conceiving a film and understanding and using film *language*. Bob has such a vivid imagination that directing could end up being a terrific career change for him.'

When *The Rawney* is released in 1988, Bob's fans will be able to judge for themselves.

Bob's third film for Handmade is called *Travelling Man*, for which he will be reunited with Michael Caine when they both play hitmen. (Sean Connery originally intended to take Bob's part; it would have been the first time he had partnered Caine since *The Man Who Would Be King*.) It is, however, about time Caine and Hoskins appeared as equals, even if it is with guns blazing.

When asked what he looks for in a project, Bob replied, 'I don't want to do crap. You know, *crap*. I just look for a show that I'd like to see.' Bob could easily give up the small British independent productions, but he hasn't for the moment chosen the route that leads to Beverly Hills mansions, swimming pools, flash cars, and an avoidance of films that are real or have any substance. He's too loyal, too streetwise, too family-orientated, too much the yob from Finsbury Park – and proud of it.

'Of those born in Finsbury Park,' Don McCullin said, 'most of them failed at whatever they reached out for because they believed that they were not meant to have it, even though they dreamt about having it. At the last minute, if you gave them what they dreamt about, they wouldn't know how to handle it anyway. Yet in many ways, you saw more smiles there than you find anywhere today.

'And if you grew up in Finsbury Park it made you feel as if you had a grudge to settle . . . in respect. But when you're mature enough you have nothing but admiration for the accident that brought you into Finsbury Park, because what it does give you is an amazing grounding in life.'

And if you're Bob Hoskins, you take what you've been given, and you make yourself a star.

21

The Actor's Life

'I don't think I'm the sort of material movie stars are made of,' Bob Hoskins said. 'You've got to be a bit glamorous for that. I'm five-foot six inches and cubic. My own mum wouldn't call me pretty.

'Ever since *The Long Good Friday*,' he went on, 'people have said: "All right, your next film really ought to do it for you." And then the next. And the next. . . . There hasn't been a real turning point. I can't say I cracked it – that "I'm a star."'

But now, of course, he is a star. There have, actually, been several turning points in Bob's career: *Veterans*, which gave him confidence on stage that he could hold his own; *Pennies from Heaven*, which made him a television star: *The Long Good Friday*, which made him a film star; and *Mona Lisa*, which made him an internationally acclaimed film star. Hopefully *Roger Rabbit* will make Bob an internationally acclaimed film star of major repute; and *The Rawney* prove his talents in a directorial capacity. Whatever Bob's last project, however, that's the one he loves most – his 'best work'.

'Bob's not a critical sort,' said a friend who has also worked with him. 'He's definitely not the best judge of his own work. Everything he does is the "best thing he's ever done". In a way, though, that's a testimony to his own enthusiasm.'

Helen Mirren once said of acting that it's 'a series of compromises and disappointments and struggles interspersed with wonderful lucky breaks'. Bob Hoskins has had many lucky breaks. But he was able to back them all up with his astonishing talent. In one sense you're only lucky once. After that you must keep proving yourself – as they say in Hollywood, 'You're only as good as your last picture.' And as Jack Nicholson said, 'You can only be as good as you're willing to be bad.' No matter how good or bad *Bob's* last picture is, he is rarely anything but brilliant. And there is always the energy, that visceral understanding of the character and how to communicate himself to the audience. That magnetic pull of the Hoskins force field.

'He's a very raw, intuitive actor,' said director John Mackenzie, 'very instinctive. He acts straight from the gut and sometimes he, himself, doesn't know he's got the result. But that doesn't mean he doesn't have artistic control because he does, at the back of it all. It's wonderful for a director, because you're handling something volatile and very unique. And quite often you're not sure what's going to happen next.'

'I'm not a great study person,' Bob said. 'I try and pick up bits by radar, just by being around people and soaking up the surroundings. You gotta begin by finding the man's problems and analysing them, what he wants, what he hates. His pain, his humiliation, his pride. Then you let the part demand what it demands. You don't tamper, you don't get too intellectual. You let it grow, like gardening, like a flower. By the end you should be right in it, living it and not aware of your real self at all. But I've never played anybody else but me. I can't impersonate things.'

'Bob has a very clever method, a gift,' Alec McCowen says, 'because what a lot of actors confuse is their actual role, and what you *must* do it treat *everything* as if it matters. What matters is bringing a person to life – whether it's Restoration or any period, a comedy, a musical, a drama – the style should be left to the director and the author. Bob was as natural in *Pygmalion* as he was in *Pennies from Heaven* or *Mona Lisa*.'

'As an actor you are trying to portray life,' Bob said, 'and there was quite a bit of my life before I came into the acting profession that I can fall back on, that I can remember. I can see the other man's point of view because I have been there. It would be very difficult for a kid coming out of drama school or college to play King Lear; how could they handle that? My life before I became an actor equipped me very well.'

'I've never been trained as an actor,' Bob also told John Powers. 'But what I've seen of a lot of training, it's quite destructive. There are a lot of kids out there learning to talk like they *don't*, and walk like they *don't*, and be like they're *not*. And where the fuck are they? There's this empty thing that walks on the screen – there's nobody there!'

Bob is always up there, whether on stage or screen. Especially in film, he has a strong, obvious presence, like a magical current of electricity.

'Bob is almost like an American,' said director John Byrum, 'you *see* this volatility. Most British actors, like Michael Caine, are so in control of themselves. You got the feeling in *The Long Good Friday* about Bob that he *could* kill you. That's what great screen acting is. You don't know if De Niro's going to take out a gun and put it in his mouth and really blow his head off right in front of the movie camera in *Taxi Driver*. Scorsese knows that about him and milks it. Laurence Olivier doesn't leave you any openings. Nor is Bob afraid to play the darker and dumber side of all of us in *Mona Lisa*. One of the things you get trained to do in Hollywood is never to put in a scene where a guy looks dumb or stupid or inept because it's the nature of American movies that either you're an underdog or you're a winner; you beat the system. That's filtered down to the actors. Can you imagine any American actor playing George?'

Yet Bob does have to watch his tendency to get lazy, or to accept too many roles that are similar to ones he's already played. ' "I've got to be very careful what I do," he said, "because this could go on and on and I'm a very limited actor," ' producer Joan Brown related. 'This was in 1978 or 1979. "I know my limitations." In other words, his fear was that he would do his thing for a while, and then nobody would want him. He couldn't possibly have imagined this great American scene and opportunities, really, could he? He saw himself as a Cockney actor with a certain sort of look and style, and he must have thought, How many parts can there be for me? Without realizing that Harold Shand was around the corner.'

'Bob can be a very subtle actor,' director Thaddeus O'Sullivan said, 'but he's used to quite big and broad strokes, and that's how he feels it should be done. He's very lazy, though, and I think Bob's problem is that he's not as instinctive as he thinks. There's a really very mechanical thing. He knows he has that facility, which is to prove something quickly, simply, and well; you really have to take the part. And I don't mean intellectualize it, but you have to approach it in a fairly straightforward, step-by-step way rather than just fire away at it, because it has to fit into a whole. What the actor has to offer is really only part of a number of other elements.

'When Bob gets over his instinctiveness . . . when he actually sits down and concentrates and thinks, he's very good and sensitive and it's only then that I think you can get anything out of him. He can be very variable unless he gets to those moments on a consistent basis, where he can be relaxed and he knows that what he does is going to be okay. It's entirely due to nervousness – this bragging that "I can just walk out and do it." Probably in some parts it *is* the thing to do, but that doesn't show up his best qualities. It's just . . . he's lazy. I recognize it because I'm exactly the same. I know I have to avoid doing certain things because they're easy; I won't do them because I know I *can* do them. If Bob is made to sit down and think about something, if you can get him away from his distractions – he's a terrible one for "Well, we've finished that, now let's go on to champagne" – he's wonderful to work with.'

'Bob does burst on to the screen; he uses it and the camera likes him,' Sally Hope said. 'But if you keep doing the same roles the audience will move on to the younger version of Bob Hoskins. You must constantly keep in touch with your own talent.'

'Bob doesn't carry films yet the way Paul Newman does or Cary Grant did,' a friend said. 'Bob is one of the best, but he is still within a limited range as an actor. He can play heavies, and he is a great comedian. After all, Cary Grant came from a working-class family in Bristol, but you would never believe it! Hopefully Bob will some day be in the same class as a Paul Newman or a Harrison Ford . . . and then he will get fifty million Cockney gangster roles and fifty million more fans.'

'I'm typecast as a tough because I'm quite good at it,' Bob has said, 'because I don't actually *play* the tough. Since I already look like I could punch a hole in a brick wall I have instant credibility; so I go the other way and show affection and all the soft emotions, which are there in every man as well as woman. I play the tender side of tough.'

Nor is he afraid to display his vulnerability. 'For thousands of years, women have had to keep their mouths shut and play second role to the dominant male. Over these thousands of years, women have learned to express themselves without saying a word. . . . Acting is about expressing private moments, and men have spent all their time hiding behind this façade of masculinity. When you're in front of a camera, you've got to get rid of that. I think a really dignified person is someone who allows all that to show and is not afraid to be themselves.'

Bob has never been afraid to be himself while performing. What is slightly ironic is that he keeps insisting that he has no ambition, as if this dedication of twenty years is just a lark, and he may give it all up tomorrow so he can putter around in the garden or play with the kids or snap some pix with his Nikon F3, his latest hobby.

'I never go looking for anything. I just take the next job that appeals to me. I've no ambition, really. . . .'

'All I do is live from film to film. I have no plans, no career structure, and absolutely no ambition. If I like it, I just take what's given me.'

206

Whether it's film, television, stage, voice-over, or circus. But Bob is now in the position where he can afford to say things like that. A few years back, he would take nearly any role offered to him, not only because he liked it but because he had to. And being a workaholic, he gets twitchy if he's 'resting' – a polite way of saying you're unemployed. Luckily, that is almost never the case.

'I've never really been interested in money,' Bob has also said.

The other side of the story is told by a colleague. 'Bob is quite money obsessed. You don't somehow expect someone in a sophisticated business like acting to be like that. But you don't lose your roots; that's the very thing that makes you good. Michael Caine deals with it well; he's clever. He goes about it as a business, acquiring a restaurant, all the trimmings. He's a workaholic just like Bob.'

In fact Caine and Hoskins have talked about setting up their own film production company. That would at least assure them of 'control' over projects they wanted to pursue.

'Michael is the one who showed us how it could be done,' Bob once said of the actor who made Cockney acceptable on-screen. 'He has done some terrible films but he's never given a bad performance.'

Unlike Caine, though, Bob does not consider himself a jet-setter, more of a ''omey sort of bird' who'd rather be 'sittin' in me garden, playin' with me kids and growin' a few roses.'

Underneath the gor-blimey bluster, though, is a man following his heart, and determined to make a go of it for as long as he's able. He is not the sort to expect fawning adulation to follow him wherever he goes just because he got an Oscar nomination.

'I've been artistic since I was a kid,' Bob has also said, 'but I find writing and stuff like that very lonely. I like people too much. Acting is the social way of being artistic. I love the life and I love the work and I suppose that enthusiasm can be infectious.'

The real luck was in finding the metier. 'Up to that point,' Bob said of starting to act, 'I was a liar. I lived in my imagination. As soon as I walked on the stage, I realized I was home.' 'I'd find it hard to take seriously anybody who said they didn't like Bob Hoskins,' said producer Kenith Trodd.

'I've always had this incredible arrogance,' Bob said. 'If you don't like me, you've got bad taste. If I don't like you, there's something wrong with you.'

Most people like Bob Hoskins. He has now established himself as so much of a national institution that his charming mug shows up in all the newspapers on a regular basis. You know you're a legend in the punters' eyes when you appear in the *Sun* column: 'Twenty Things You Never Knew About . . .'; or when Reggie Kray asks you to work on a cookery book with him. You can see Bob smiling, next to Aldaniti the racehorse, raising funds for cancer research; or cuddling babies for the National Childbirth Trust ('He was so sweet with the mothers and asked them all about the babies so charmingly,' a spokeswoman said. 'You could see that he is an excellent father'); or sitting on the judging panel with Charlotte Cornwell and Barrie Keeffe for the Verity Bargate Award (established in honour of one of his biggest supporters) created for new playwrights; or watch him act surprised at his inclusion in *Who's Who*; or pull faces next to his wax incarnation in Madame Tussaud's. You can be amazed when the producers at Handmade Films announce that they have insured his life for £48 million; if he croaks, the money will go to *them*, not his family; or be really amazed when he appears in a feature in popular fashion magazine *Elle,* entitled 'I Wanna Be Bobby's Girl', where he posed happily for the camera as model Jeny Howorth towered nearly a foot over him in her Manolo Blahnik pumps; or be equally amazed when his face accompanies women's magazine articles like 'The Ugly Factor', about men who aren't conventionally handsome or sexy but are nonetheless now considered handsome and sexy. Bob Hoskins a sex symbol? With a rapidly expanding waistline and hair everywhere on his body but on the top of his head and a rather, as he put it, 'cubic height of five-foot six'? Must be the twinkle in his eye.

'People keep telling me that women are coming on to me all the time and that women everywhere fancy the way I look,' Bob confessed. 'If so, it always escapes my notice. I just don't tune in to those kinds of signals.'

'Linda, my wife, finds it hysterically funny. But I just find it confusing. The truth is that I'm not a good womaniser. I'm a homebody.' Bob Hoskins not a good womaniser? Perhaps not at the moment. 'If I saw an eccentric old bugger and a beautiful young girl sitting on a park bench,' Bob confided jokingly to a friend, 'chances are I'd talk to the old geezer.'

Cynics will always say that a man who has cheated on his wife is not ever to be trusted. Yet Bob seems to have settled, happily, with the woman who has become his heart's delight and true companion. 'She's my mate, my lady, my wife. I call her my Sugar Plum and we have a great, romantic life. . . . I love sending her champagne and roses. We're incredibly happy – I owe all my success to Linda. It may sound silly, but it's true. There's this terrible self-suppressing element to everybody – unless, that is, someone can come along and release it.'

Cynics, of course, will also say that men who speak so volubly in public about their devotion to their wives are usually the ones who have something to hide. Maybe it's just guilt for, as American president Jimmy Carter said, 'lust in their hearts'. Maybe not. Certainly those who helped Bob achieve his success along the way – colleagues, friends, agents – would feel a teensy bit hurt or surprised that their contribution to Bob's career is ignored in favour of that of a much-loved wife's, however lovely the force of the emotion on Bob's part.

'Before I met Linda,' Bob said, 'I used to have the most terrible black depressions . . . I haven't had one of them since. Going through that period helped with the confidence. I survived that, I came through it. It's like someone who died and came back. Life is very precious to them.'

Maybe, too, Bob has simply grown up a bit, secure in the comfort of a stable home life, definitely secure in the knowledge that he will not be limited to £50 per week as per his solicitor's orders.

'I was like a fighting cock. I've still got a quick temper,' Bob said, 'but I can see the signs now and avoid it. I'm more romantic too. I used to think it was soppy, but when my first marriage broke up I realized that's what was wrong with me – no romance.' Jane Hoskins might say that what was wrong with Bob was too *much* romance.

Bob Hoskins is also lucky that he has had a chance to start over again. It is always easier for the man who does not have custody of his children. Bob loves being a father, of course, as long as he doesn't have to change the nappies. 'I wouldn't miss it for the world,' Bob said of being a dad. 'The only time I find it hard is when I've got the kids on my own. I love it . . . but I can always say, "I've got to go to work now, love!"'

He can also hang out with his mates, like Hugh Cornwall of the rock band the Stranglers, with whom he had once put on a one-off play at the Almeida Theatre in Islington called *Charlie's Last Round*. Or maybe Bobby De Niro will ring up again and come round to dinner.

There will always be the new crop of avid fans who will love to hear Bob tell one of his usual tales. There are the staple legends: the Unity Theatre 'discovery'; the aborted *Richard III* in Hull where Bob humped off to buy the three theatre patrons a drink in the pub; Francis Ford Coppola ringing up, waking baby Rosa, and Bob slamming down the phone after calling the venerable director 'a cunt'; the twelve-minute car ride from Nice Airport to the Cannes Film Festival in a race for the Best Actor Award. There's also the time De Niro took Bob Christmas shopping in New York when Bob feared he'd be stranded there while *The Cotton Club* filming went on and on, and the story that he gained weight during that never-ending shoot so he could attain the same shape as Edward G. Robinson in order to fit into one of that actor's suits; and the time after Bob Dylan had met him at a charity bash – Richard Gere, Dylan, and Bob all appeared on stage – that the legendary singer went outside and chundered ('I don't think he was too well,' Bob said. 'Either that or I made one of my heroes sick.')

Bob has a lot of heroes. Dylan, Herman Munster, Bugs Bunny, Mickey Mouse. There are a few villains in his book too, one most noticeably in the hot seat at 10 Downing Street. 'England's in agony,' Bob once muttered in anger. 'That bloody woman has hurt the working-class people like poison. Like Hitler.' The working class of the East End seized upon Bob's outspoken views – well-known since *The Long Good Friday* – about the destruction of London life in the old neighbourhoods, and an organization of protestors against Yuppies in the Docklands, the Class War Group of Tower Hamlets, appropriated a photograph of Bob and plastered his likeness on posters and pamphlets while quoting him as saying, 'London is like an onion and the property speculators are ripping off the layers to get at the heart. They must be stopped.' Bob did not approve of this unplanned 'endorsement'. His comment: 'This will be passed to lawyers.'

When asked properly, though, Bob will always speak out for what he believes in. At the trial of actor/accused murdered/friend John Bindon in 1979, he testified that Bindon's nickname was 'Biffo the Bear', before apologizing to his friend in court. He was reprimanded by the judge. 'Well,' Bob said after apologizing, 'that is his character. He is comical and like a big teddy bear.' Nor had Bob ever seen him lose his temper.

And Bob supposedly has a formula so he doesn't lose his *own* temper: 'Keep me well fed, well loved, and I'm the most happy, easy-going of men.'

Perhaps Linda has tamed the beast in him too.

'Bob believes that he's charmed, that he leads a charmed life, and that there are forces there that will help him,' said Jane Hoskins. 'But when you have that kind of attitude – which is very confusing and frightening; this thinking that "I'm the best" – you are begging for a fall.'

Bob is in that dangerous position now where he has worked for twenty years to succeed as actor . . . and he has succeeded. It is an old and inescapable Hollywood maxim that as soon as you are built up, supported all the way by your fans, and have reached the pinacle of success, those same fans are waiting to push you off and relish every sordid, steamy, hideous detail of your plummet to the bottom. Bob is bravely risking censure by directing his first self-penned film, and starring in it too. 'There are two different types of critics,' said Sally Hope. 'The preview critics and the next-day review critics. It will be interesting to see how they'll be with his great departure.'

Many Hoskins fans also wonder if they will ever have the pleasure of seeing him on the stage once more. Film and television commitments over the next few years seem to preclude any such live appearances. Bob has often said that he relishes the opportunity to move from stage to film to television and back again: 'I believe by moving from film to stage and doing a little of everything, they all feed off each other, and as I find acting is great fun, I'll do anything that comes up.' Yet Bob has not appeared on stage since *Guys and Dolls*, and he is booked for the celluloid market for several years to come. There is nothing many Hoskins fans would rather see than their idol, there before them. At present their chances look dubious.

'There is no magic like the theatre when you know that you are making an audience feel something,' Bob once said, ten years ago. 'You are giving them a total experience. They say that the shock of giving a performance is like being involved in a minor road accident. But it's worth it.'

'It's wise to go from stage to film to stage,' Sally Hope said, 'to keep charging your batteries. The longer you avoid it the less you can do it. You must constantly be in touch with that fear.'

'The range of roles that Bob can do isn't very broad and the possibility of failing in the theatre is so high, for anybody, that actors very often don't risk it,' Adrian Noble said. 'Which is understandable, yet a shame, because it's wonderful that the general public suddenly discovered a flavour – and I don't mean to be rude by that – which theatre folk have known for years. "Oh, lovable Bob" . . . all those things Bob is . . . he doesn't even *have* to act; he *is* it, and it's delightful. This gives him great command and lets him do things he wants to do and get things done, which is fabulous. He is still very unspoiled.'

'You can run for four years in a play,' Gordon Jackson commented wryly, 'but more people see you in a film or television in one night. So if you're doing smashing films, well, why not?

Aside from the fact that films make lots of money, why must you go on proving yourself on stage every night? And Bob *has* proved himself. There's a real snobbery in England that unless you work in the theatre you can't act.'

When *Mona Lisa* opened in England in September 1986, Bob told Steve Grant, 'I have to decide what I want to do and whether I really want to price myself out of the world market which is what you do when you go to the States and take the big house with the big pool. I mean what is a million quid *for* – what's it for?! And do I really need to do another part, no matter how good, which is basically no different from what I've already done? The only reason I haven't done any stage work recently is because I haven't been offered anything decent, anything that is really any more than watered-down versions of past stuff. So really, where do I go from here?'

Obviously Bob meant what he was saying, but of the roles he has chosen – a feisty priest in *A Prayer for the Dying*, Al Capone in the part-that-wasn't in *The Untouchables*, lovable blimey-merchant in *The Lonely Passion of Judith Hearne*, the detective in *Who Framed Roger Rabbit?*, only *Roger Rabbit* is a true departure from any part he's ever played before. Given his stature and abilities on stage, surely there must be *some* old thing lying around, just waiting for Bob Hoskins to star in it.

Somehow, though, the image of Bob Hoskins getting inextricably sucked into the Hollywood vortex seems rather unimaginable. He's too in touch with his roots, too safe and comfortable in Islington, too used to nipping down to the pub and hanging out with his mates. Such a lifestyle does not exist in Los Angeles.

'Hollywood has become an institution with its own rules, for the last seventy years,' John Byrum said. 'It's fucking sick. It has nothing to do with films or talent or ideas. What happens is you judge your whole life by what table you get and who's at what other table. And you are what you drive. If you can't afford a really great car your whole life can be ruined at a stoplight.'

'Hollywood is the most abysmal place,' Jonathan Miller said, 'with its bullshit and sentimentality and the ghastly psychobabble. It's like spiritual contraception, or you can catch spiritual AIDS. The movie business is now a marketing enterprise, aimed at the centre of a simple, superb susceptibility. Making movies is like selling strawberry yogurt . . . bland, forgettable. It looks like health food but it rots your teeth.' Bob Hoskins is not about to get his teeth rotted after twenty years of bloody hard work in show business.

There are many roles Bob has said he wants to play. Some are pipe dreams; others may one day be reality. He *would* be a brilliant

Fungus the Bogeyman in a film based on Raymond Briggs's hilarious creation. He would also be a brilliant Archie Rice or Fred Karno (the Charlie Chaplin of England), or Winnie the Pooh, or Mole from *The Wind in the Willows*. (At least the shape is right.) In 1981, for instance, Bob was hot after the lead role as J. M. W. Turner in a film of the artist's life story. (Bob was a member of the Turner Society and helped present a plaque commemorating the artist's birthplace in Covent Garden. It would have been a good part, since Turner was a streetwise artist who knew how to reach the public.) And there are many other film and theatre deals that have fallen through, as always happens in show business, for one of many reasons such as money, availability, scheduling, or a better deal lurking just around the corner.

'Frankly,' said Nicholas Clay, 'Bob was never particularly attracted to the stage. It wasn't particularly his great forte either. You do it because you do it. Bob is somebody who's done things because he's done them, and I think that's why he's been successful, because he hasn't worked it out. He has played, if you like, and I use the word advisedly, the brilliant game of the fool. There's no one on this planet more powerful than a fool, because he doesn't work out what he's going to do, he just does it with joyous freedom – nothing touches him – and the fool is such a highly regarded entity because you can never guess what it's going to do. It cannot work itself out – it merely does it – and you just look at the result. With Bob, the results are incredible. And there's this wonderful sort of shrewd eye that Bob has, for a willingness to enter where angels fear to tread. That's one of Bob's greatest qualities.'

'I think the responsibility of the artist at the moment,' Bob said when *A Prayer for the Dying* was being filmed, 'is to give hope. I think a lot of plays are reflecting what we *have* got. It's very easy to state the shit; there is so much drama based on hatred and revenge. I feel that awful things happen in the name of love. I do believe there should be more plays and films to give back self-respect, to remind people that we are all right, don't worry, hold your head up, get on with it.'

He also said, 'Even if I hadn't had something of a success as an actor, I'd have been in a little theatre somewhere happy as a pig in clover. Put me on a stage in a good play with a good cast and a director who knows what he's doing and I'd be perfectly content.'

Bob Hoskins, jack-of-all-trades, finally master of one. Actor, writer, director, husband, father, gardener, homebody, mate, and well-beloved at that. Every woman's 'ideal of a bit of rough trade'.

Unlikely hero. Even more unlikely sex symbol. Box office draw. Potential superstar. Oscar nominee. The yob from Finsbury Park . . . who got out.

On his road to success Bob has made several detours, as we all do, into a few rough patches. He has been cruel, devious and unfaithful. He has been a bad husband and friend and nonexistent father; there are still colleagues he shuns and bonhomie he pretends. He is a trickster and a joker, but sometimes the tricks and jokes aren't so funny. Now, however, the stakes are much higher, and more people are listening and believing every syllable that falls from his lips. He is no longer the best-known secret to London theatregoers in the 1970s. He is a household word. Just popping out for a night on the town can get his face, and ever-increasing girth, splashed all over the tabloids. It's hard for any mortal to keep a sense of the street and 'roots' when a red carpet is rolled out wherever you stroll and metaphoric rose petals strewn in your path.

'I love being famous,' Bob said. 'Anybody tells you they don't like fame, fuck 'em. All that "pressure of stardom" is a load of bollocks.' Unless it's after the *Wogan* show and you're being mobbed by your fans.

Yet actors have always been the most insecure people in the world. Pirandello once said that every actor is always looking for a role for his house to feel like a home. Bob found his George. Will he find another one? Knowing Bob, the lovable (usually) mug with a heart of gold (only slightly tarnished), the answer must be yes. He will be like Dante, spiralling ever down the circles of hell, the lost and doomed and supplicating souls begging for a glimmer of hope or a silly little joke; and Bob Hoskins will natter on to them all, lords and ladies, yobs and wankers alike, in his quest for authenticity and his compassion for his fellow sinner.

Why, Bob Hoskins could even charm the pants off the Devil.